Given to Jean Grey[?]
   by Di Bates
after Winifred's death.

2.00

Well set-out but calls for tremendous
concentration. Easier to take as
expansion / consolidation of material
gained from other sources.

Adam and the
Kabbalistic Tree

Z'ev ben Shimon Halevi

Adam and the
Kabbalistic Tree

RIDER AND COMPANY · LONDON

Rider and Company
3 Fitzroy Square, London W1

An imprint of the Hutchinson Publishing Group

London Melbourne Sydney Auckland
Wellington Johannesburg Cape Town
and agencies throughout the world

First published 1974

© Z'ev ben Shimon Halevi

Printed in Great Britain by
Alden & Mowbray Ltd
at the Alden Press, Oxford

ISBN 0 09 119500 4 (cased)
ISBN 0 09 119501 2 (paper)

For the
Society of the Common Life

ספר זה מוקדש
לאגודת חיי הכלל

Contents

7

Editorial Note

The English transliteration of Hebrew differs widely. In this book the Encyclopedia Judaica's spelling of Kabbalistic terms is used, However, out of respect for the non-jewish student of Kabbalah, a table is set out to show the matching spellings used in the Western esoteric Tradition. Also included is a corresponding table of Alphabets.

The Sefirot		*English transliteration of Hebrew*
English translation	*Jewish tradition*	*Western esoteric tradition*
CROWN	KETER	KETHER
WISDOM	HOKHMAH	CHOCKHMAH
UNDERSTANDING	BINAH	BINAH
KNOWLEDGE	DAAT	DAATH
MERCY	HESED	CHESED
JUDGEMENT	GEVURAH	GEBURAH
BEAUTY	TIFERET	TIPHERETH
ETERNITY	NEZAH	NETZACH
REVERBERATION	HOD	HOD
FOUNDATION	YESOD	YESOD
KINGDOM	MALKHUT	MALKUTH

א	A	ALEPH	ALEPH
ב	B	BETH	BETH
ג	G	GIMEL	GIMEL
ד	D	DALETH	DALETH
ה	H	HEH	HE
ו	V	VAV	VAU
ז	Z	ZAYIN	ZAYIN
ח	Ch	CHET	CHETH
ט	T	TET	TETH
י	I	YOD	YOD
כ	K	KAPH	CAPH

9

ל	L	LAMED	LAMED
מ	M	MEM	MEM
נ	N	NUN	NUN
ס	S	SAMECH	SAMEKH
ע	O	AYIN	AYIN
פ	P	PEH	PE
צ	Tz	TSADE	TZADDI
ק	Q	KOOF	QOPH
ר	R	RESH	RESH
ש	Sh	SHIN	SHIN
ת	T	TOV	TAU

Plates

And God said:
'Let us make a man
in our own image,
after our own likeness.'

GENESIS 1:26

Preface

Kabbalah is an ancient but living Tradition. Preserved by esoteric Judaism in its orthodox form, its contemporary development has always been continuous, so as to meet the need of those in each generation, who seek spiritual illumination. This book, therefore, follows the latter Kabbalistic practice of speaking in current terms so that Knowledge does not become obscure, for while Kabbalah is often beyond comprehension it cannot exclude anyone in search of the Source of himself. Indeed to aid such people is defined by Israel's Covenant.

As there are two aspects of Kabbalah so there is a written and oral tradition to both. Of the oral teaching nothing can be said except face to face, and of the written the widely varied literature clearly demonstrates that the essence of Kabbalah cannot be contained in books. Therefore, this work must be regarded as one individual's understanding of what he has been taught, for though a Sephardish Levite I may claim no authority other than my own comprehension of Kabbalah.

One of the keys to Kabbalah is the diagram named the Tree of Life. This archetypal scheme is the divine model for the Universe and Man. Using its analogue we examine Adam, our study taking us up from the Earthly Kingdom of the body, through the Worlds of Soul and Spirit, to the Crown of Heaven. Using ancient concepts, modern observation, and the Tree, the interaction of the Micro and Macrososm is seen, reflecting in detail and total their source in the ultimate One.

LONDON WINTER 5732

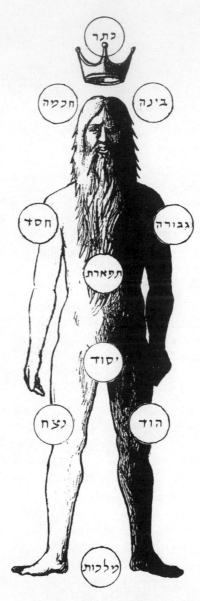

ADAM KADMON

Introduction

Adam and the Tree of Life are conceived in the same design. This idea originates in the statement in the first chapter of Genesis: God created man in His own image.

According to Kabbalist tradition God generates, out of the Void of Non Existence, wherein He is All and Nothing, the first state of Unmanifest Existence. From this World without End, crystalizes a realm of Limitless Light, in the midst of which, there emerges a point of no dimensions, called the First Crown. These three states of Unmanifest Existence become the negative background to the positive universe that streams through the primal point of the First Crown to evolve into the archetypal world of Emanations. This manifestation on its completion is known as Adam Kadmon, that is, the Primeval and Universal Man. Although composed of the ten aspects of the Creator, Adam is the symbol of a unified working whole, the first man being a living image of the relative universe.

The function of Adam Kadmon, it is said, is to act in the manifest world as the continuous counterbalance to the unmanifest side of existence. This process is at work now, in this instant, and every moment is a universal drama of adjusting change. Such is the scale of this balancing that every happening, from the most vast cosmic events to the minutest occurrence on the edge of emptiness, is involved. Herein is contained total existence, hovering between the poles of All and Nothing. However it should be remembered, while the relative world is in continual motion, the Absolute remains as the permeating silence, stillness and void, separate yet ever present, within and containing it.

Adam Kadmon is the Universe made after a likeness to God,

para. 2. of Mona Rolfe
"   3 of Jane Roberts / Seth

the allegorical figure abstracted by Kabbalists into the diagram called the Tree of Life. This metaphysical presentation is a comprehensive formulation of universal principles and processes. Based upon the divine aspects and their relationships, the Tree describes the archetypal design on which the Universe is modelled. The same template applies throughout all the lesser worlds, so that even the tiny species of mankind, indeed a single human being, is directly related to the original Adam by virtue of faithful replication.

As a miniature copy of the Universe man has within him not only the characteristics of Creation but also the attributes of the Creator. Through the inherent nature of his composition, an individual, therefore, has access to cosmic resources, and should he wish, the possibility, while still earthbound, of contact with the Divine within himself. Such a consciousness of the Presence of the Creator allows him to know and be known by God.

densification into matter in process of incarnating – for each + every life.

1. Kabbalah

The Hebrew word 'Kabbalah' means 'to receive'. Kabbalah is the inner teaching of Judaism. Its concern is knowledge, of God, the Universe and man, and their mutual relationship. Its origins are historically unknown and while it traditionally goes back to Abraham, it probably predates him by several millennia to the source of all human enlightenment—the first fully evolved man.

While principally Hebraic in form, because the Jewish esoteric line has virtually remained intact for over four thousand years, it is, in essence, universal. It could be nothing else.

'Hear O Israel. The Lord our God. The Lord is One.' This great prayer belongs to all men, in that Israel is mankind. It is also a reminder that while Adam is confined in an animal skin on Earth he must not forget his origin.

Adam and Eve are in exile, and people in every era have sensed deep in their memory a dim recollection of another kind of existence. This strange homesickness fades in most people as they become immersed in life, but there are some for whom the remembrance never disappears. Indeed the longing increases so that they seek to regain or at least find the gate to Eden. For this purpose myths, ideas and meditations have been scattered throughout history by teachings that possess knowledge of how to return. One such tradition is Kabbalah.

Historically Kabbalah is particularly interesting to us in the West because it underlies the Judaic-Greco-Christian ground of our civilization. Its basis is in the Bible although the system is never directly outlined except when illustrated by such example as the design of the seven-branched candlestick of Moses, King David's blessing on Solomon, the vision of Ezekiel, the Book of

Proverbs and later after the Biblical period had closed in the Dead
Sea Scrolls, the Talmud and the latter-day works of the Sefer
Yezirah and the Zohar. After the destruction of the Second Temple
by the Romans, Kabbalah took on many guises according to the
culture it was fostered in, for the Jews were widely dispersed.

These versions used Babylonian, Greek, and later even Islamic
terms, modified to suit the Kabbalah of that place and day. Sometimes the form was far removed from conventional Judaism and
Kabbalists had to hide their studies lest they be considered
heretics. Occasionally a school of Kabbalah emerged into the
open, long after its real work was done and only the outer form
remained. This often produced an unfortunate image for the
tradition both in and outside the main Judaic line. The mis-
association of magic with Kabbalah is an example. This leads onto
the fact, that the student of Kabbalah, be he Gentile or Jew, must
learn to recognize the essential teaching, for despite many corruptions, the content of Kabbalah remains the same, that is, the
relationship between man, the Universe, and God. Such objective
knowledge cannot be altered, although it may be described in
many ways.

As every age has its historical style, symbols and vernacular, so
Kabbalah has its own distinct tongues. It is said, according to
tradition, that there are four ways to comprehend reality. The
first is to understand only literally, the second, to view allegorically, the third, to perceive metaphysically, and the fourth to
experience mystically. These levels correspond to a man's nature
and depend on his stage of development, which is determined by
some of the factors to be discussed in this book.

Many Kabbalistic works are unintelligible for the above reasons. There are, however, quite a number of neo-kabbalists,
historical and modern, who mislead either in ignorance or
deliberately in order to remain exclusive or to retain a claim to
authority. Such people ignore the clear instruction in the Covenant of Israel to pass Kabbalah on. While the imparting of such
potent knowledge should be done with the utmost discretion, the
intentional distortion of the truth carries yet greater responsibility.
Certainly such information, in the hands of the evil, is dangerous

as science has shown us. However, Kabbalah, not being just of this world, has a built-in fail-safe device. As the word 'Kabbalah' implies, a man can only receive what he is capable of absorbing. If he misuses the knowledge he is automatically cut off from the flow of the tradition by his own act, and remains isolated in an imprisoning shell that thickens or dissolves according to his actions.

A tradition must remain essentially unadulterated. But in order to continue to be intelligible to each generation it must adapt to the time. This Kabbalah has always done despite the tendency of the conservative to preserve old forms. Further, Kabbalah cannot be passed on through books. It can only be received via direct contact with the living tradition. However, the function of books is to prepare a person, so that he may be able 'to receive'. Therefore we begin with a basic exposition of one of the tradition's chief tools—the Tree. When we have become familiar with its structure and dynamics we can use it, applying a combination of the attitudes of today and of eternal principles to examine Adam, that is you, who is your living embodiment of all mankind, Adam Kadmon and the One—the only authority in Kabbalistic tradition.

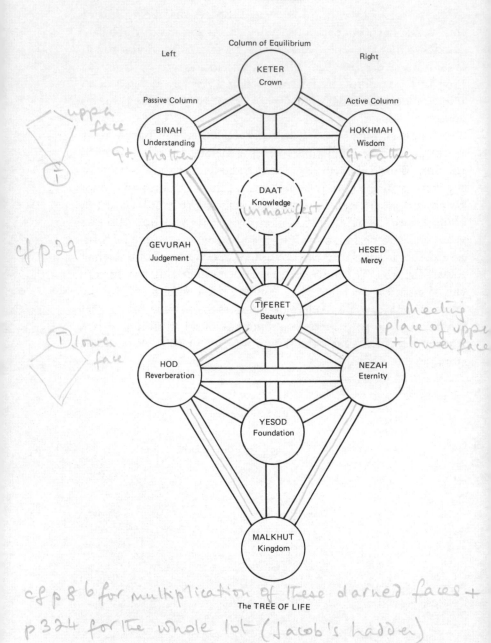

The TREE OF LIFE

upper face

ⓣ

cf p 29

ⓣ lower face

Meeting place of upper + lower face

cf p 86 for multiplication of these darned faces + p 324 for the whole lot (Jacob's ladder)

2. Tree of Life – Its dynamics

Adam Kadmon is the Universe. He contains the whole of manifest creation. Stretching between Heaven and Earth his head touches the ultimate crown of spirit, and his feet the densest of matters. Made in the image of God, Adam Kadmon expresses the ten prime attributes of the Creator and the four major laws which govern the Universe. The first of these laws is that All is One, the second: the action of the supernal trinity, the third: the law of sequence as defined by the Great Octave reaching from the head to the toe of the universal man, and the fourth: that between the top Do of the Crown and the bottom Do of the Kingdom are four worlds, each a realm containing a secondary Tree in its own right.

Beginning with the first and greatest Law, it must be remembered that All is One. That is, that everything in the Unmanifest and Manifest Universe is of a single piece, a garment without seams. Whatever happens anywhere effects the whole, and the whole has a direct bearing on even the most minute event. Nothing in lower or higher worlds occurs in isolation. Existence is universal with the Absolute present in every created thing. From this basis all parts of creation are connected, and while effects may be seen in this, or that time or place, their causes may be remote in relative terms. From the view of God this has no significance, because all is one.

At the first moment of manifestation the Will of the Absolute is signified by a dimensionless point. This crystallizes out of the three veils of Negative Existence. Such an unmanifest Universe does not have much meaning to the human mind. The best that can be said on the mundane level is that the Unmanifest is perhaps like the pregnant pause before a concert begins, or the moment just prior to the dawn when nothing can be seen or heard, yet everything is present and potential.

A Crown is the kabbalistic symbol used to describe the dimensionless point which is between the Manifest and Unmanifest. Such a Crown is hollow, and through its centre passes all that is to come into being. Everything that was, is, and shall be, enters through the circleted void of the First Crown.

From the Crown, called Keter in Hebrew, springs the supernal trinity. This is composed of the active principle defined by the attributes Hokhmah or Wisdom, and its passive compliment, Binah or Understanding. This triad forms the top part of the Tree, and creates, through the interaction of the Active, Passive and the Will of God, all the lower part of the Tree. In allegorical terms, the top of the right pillar of the Tree is called the Father, and the top left the Mother, with the central column as the balancing factor. Another way of describing them is to consider the right pillar as Force and the left as Form with the pillar of Equilibrium between. It is because so many descriptions have been used for each sefirah or container on the Tree that we will use the Hebrew names because for most of us, they have no pre-conceived and narrow associations. Thus Keter presides over Hokhmah and Binah, the great parents of Creation.

This all-important triad is the second great law that, by the Will of the Absolute, through Keter, creates events, which in turn leads on to the third law, that of the sequence developing out of the creative act of the supernal triad. This law can be described well in terms of a musical octave, the first four notes of which descend out of Keter across the active column and back to the passive column of the Tree. As it then transits the central column the sequence passes through an unmanifest sefirah called Daat or Knowledge. This invisible zone is sometimes known as the Abyss. It is a kind of access from, or into, the relative Universe defined by the Tree's structure. From the point of view of the Great Octave, it provides a vital impulse, should the Creator wish, to develop his Creation. In human experience, this same phenomenon is observed in any creative work which always has a critical point of difficulty near its beginning. Many a potential work of genius has died at conception because the will to go on was insufficient. Such a prompt is of high potency and Daat is the point at which it is administered. Without Knowledge, real Knowledge, no project, be it Creation, or a novel, or even making a cake, could be properly completed. If Keter is the first Do, Hokhmah is Re and Binah Mi, with Daat the natural interval before the Fa of Hesed or Mercy. This critical point is most important because though initial events may occur it does not mean they will necessarily develop. The Universe, indeed ordinary life, has had many incomplete octaves.

The Divine attribute Hesed or Mercy, situated on the active column, describes the function of expansion. When the Lightning Flash, as this zig-zag path of Creation is called, flows down the Tree and crosses to Gevurah this expansion is modified and controlled. Judgement, the English name for the Hesed-Balancing sefirah, acts as the passive complement to the dynamic of Hesed, as Binah does likewise to the power of Hokhmah. This demonstrates the functional roles of the two outer pillars which flank the central column of Consciousness running from the 'Do' of Keter to the 'Do' of Malkhut or the Kingdom.

Tiferet is the central point of the whole Tree of Life. Into it flow not only the Lightning Flash, but all the other sefirot except that of Malkhut. Its English name is Beauty, Tiferet locks the symmetry of the Tree into an essence. Here is the midway point between Heaven and Earth. All that has been is here, and all that will follow is ready to flow on down the zig-zag Lightning Flash. Into this central sefirah comes the confluence of all the various activities of the active and passive columns. So too does the Will of God striking directly down from Keter through Daat. It is a cosmic junction box and is called Solomon's Seat. Later on in human terms its significance will become evident.

The octave flows on to Nezah or Eternity on the column of energy. Eternity in this sense means that which continually repeats. When a function is recycled it cannot do anything else but be perpetuated. This is necessary at certain points in Creation or the whole relative Universe would be unstable and collapse. On the opposite side, on the column of resistance, is Hod, translated by some Kabbalists from the Hebrew root word, as Reverberation, which is more intelligible than the ambiguous but more religiously used term 'Splendour'. This name can be misleading, especially at this highly functional lower end of the two outer columns. Hod is the control on Nezah and they work together with the path descending from Tiferet into Yesod.

Yesod means Foundation. At first sight this has, like many of the other names of the sefirot (two or more sefirah are called sefirot) no sensible meaning. But as familiarity with the Tree progresses it will be seen to fit beautifully into a working pattern, as the basis, in the lower half of the Tree, of consciousness. In human experience, Yesod is the ego, upon which, through its education and internal and external influences, we base our view of the world. Such a critical point, at the second and last interval in the descending Octave of the Tree, is indeed the foundation of our Universe.

Malkhut or the Kingdom is the last, but not the lowest, sefirah. As the name implies it is a country, that is a domain, in which the Tree's roots are the elements or the body of Creation. Here compressed into one sefirah is all that has gone before. Contained in Malkhut are the tightly packed vibrations of an ever shortening monochord stretched from Keter over the frets of the other sefirot to Malkhut. In Malkhut is closely compressed matter, or constricted energy, depending on whether you consider the four elements as waves or particles. For us, as men, Malkhut is the physical world, the only visible part of the Tree of Life in our ordinary experience.

Here then the Great Octave of Creation and the great Trinity of active and passive forces mediated by the Will and Consciousness of God holds the Cosmic balance of the Universe in poise. For most men this phenomenon passes unnoticed even though it is continuous. Every day, every moment, we receive our daily bread via the Lightning Flash, but we do not notice, so oblivious are we, living as we do for the most part, in the bottom two sefirot.

The fourth great Law of the Universe is hinted at in Malkhut. Contained in this bottom sefirah are the elements of Earth, Water,

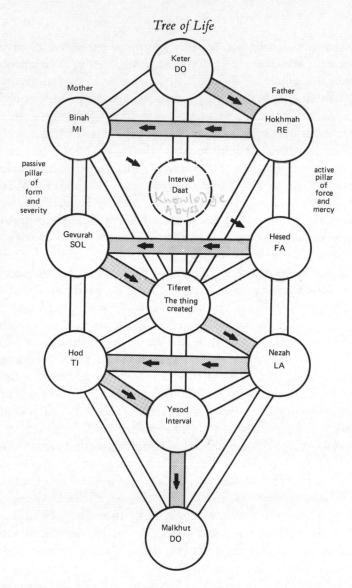

THE LIGHTNING FLASH

Here the impulse of the Will manifesting in Keter passes in an alternating pro-
gression from active to passive pillar as it descends through all the Sefirot and Worlds.
To quote the Sefer Yezirah: 'The ten Sefirot appear out of Nothing like a Lightning
Flash or scintillating flame, and they are without beginning or end. The Name of
God is with them as they go forth and when they return.'

Air and Fire. These are, broadly speaking, the elements of the Earth and the elements of Heaven. It is the latter we are concerned with at this point.

While the earthly elements describe the states of matter in solid, liquid, gaseous and radiant form, the Heavenly elements define the four distinct worlds between Keter and Malkhut. Like their earthly counterparts, fire or radiation penetrates air, which can permeate water, which in turn can saturate Earth. In the Heavenly context the World of Emanations is within the World of Creation which lies behind the World of Formations. This fluid realm moulds the bottom world of physical Elements and Action at the base of the Tree. On the Tree the four Worlds are set out as follows, remembering always that the upper affects the lower and vice versa. The physical or Asiyyatic World is broadly defined by the great lower triad formed by Malkhut, Hod and Nezah. The World of Yezirah or Formations is bounded at the upper edge by Gevurah and Hesed, with the lower side extending downward to Nezah and Hod. There is an additional zone described by the small triad formed between Hod, Nezah and Yesod. Yesod, at the pivot of energy and matter has access to both the Asiyyatic and Yeziratic Worlds. The Beriatic or World of Creations interfaces with the Yeziratic realm at Gevurah and Hesed, but like Yesod, the central sefirah of Tiferet acts as an extension of Beriah into Yezirah through the little triangle made by Gevurah, Hesed and Tiferet. Here the Azilutic world also meets, as the great upper triad formed by Binah and Hokhmah and Tiferet penetrates down through the Beriatic World of Creations from the World of Emanations, formed by the supernal triad of Binah, Hokhmah and Keter. Alternative systems by some Kabbalists use circles and diamond shapes centred on the central column to show how the Worlds co-exist.

In human experience these Worlds could be described in the example of a complete creative process. A sculptor receives, he usually does not know from where, an impulse, This at first manifests itself as an idea. Here is the effect of the supernal triad on a human scale. Binah takes the Flash of inspiration from Hokhmah and begins to consider it in terms of concepts. These are developed, should the invisible sefirah of Daat carry the impulse over, by Hesed, which in conjunction with Gevurah refines the idea ready to be passed on from the world of Creation, into its formulation stage in Yezirah. On reaching Tiferet, with the Aziluthic World still in touch through the Great Binah, Hokhmah and Tiferet triangle, the idea is worked on in the Watery realm into various models. These are passed back to be expanded and tested by Hesed and Gevurah but in their Yeziratic capacity as parts of the realm of Formations. Tiferet in the midst of the operation still carries the Beriatic World in the little triad made with Hesed and Gevurah so that all that has been is focussed in Tiferet, into what will follow. Nezah and Hod then take over in the process, making the well considered piece of sculpture a stable form, even though nothing has appeared to the outer world, perhaps not even consciously to the sculptor himself.

This 'cooking' process as some call it, may go on for months, even years as in the case of some books, whose authors said 'I could not begin until it was in fact already written in my head.' If it begins to appear in Yesod at the centre of the Asiyyatic World, the impulse to carry the octave over the final interval being strong enough, the sculptor starts actually to see the image of what it might look like. The composer Mozart once said, about a piece of music, that it was all there in his head, and was just so long. He held up his hands to indicate his measure. He went on to say, all he had to do was write it down. This last action is carried out in Malkhut, with tools and stones for the sculptor, and pen and paper for the writer. Unless this last step in the creative process is taken, the Octave is incomplete, and Heaven has not reached Earth, therefore there is no Creation. Here we see why Kabbalists consider contact with ordinary life as a vital prerequisite to their studies. God's Will can be aided, Creation assisted, in coming down, as well as reascending to Heaven after rounding the turning point of Malkhut.

Here then briefly are the four Worlds on the Tree of Life, each an integral part of the interaction of the sefirot, the Law of the Trinity, and the Single Wholeness of the One, manifested in Malkhut as well as Keter.

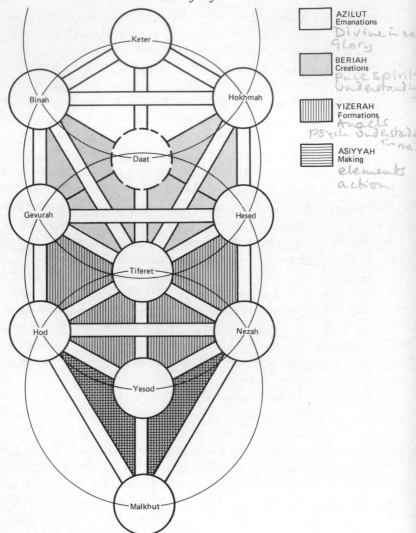

AZILUT
Emanations
Divine in no
Glory

BERIAH
Creations
Pure spirit
understandi

YIZERAH
Formations
Angels
Psych understand
in ma

ASIYYAH
Making
elements
action.

FOUR WORLDS

Any one of these views is valid because the Worlds co-exist and interpenetrate. This book, for the most part, adopts the system indicated by the texture key. Note how the higher Worlds underlay the lower.

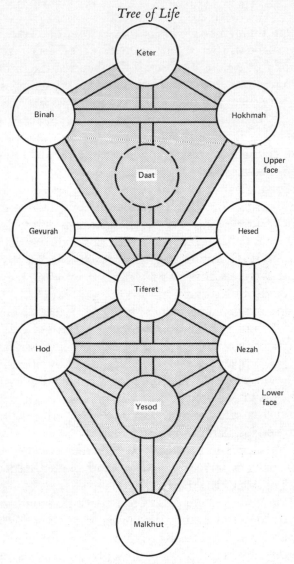

UPPER & LOWER FACES

When seen as the Tree of one World, the upper face coincides with the lower face of the World above, and the lower face with the upper face of the World below. This forms a continuous chain of the four World Trees that make up the Great Tree of the Universe.

There are minor Laws which work within the Tree, but we shall only mention four at this point, for they bear particularly on our study of Adam. The first is the fact that the principle of triads operates throughout the Tree, in that every sefirah is part of three or more triads and operates as an active, passive or connecting principle in any given situation. These minor triads may be also regarded as functional when related to the outer pillars and the centre column or conscious when the central column holds the balance between both sidepillars.

The second minor Law is that in each World is a complete sub-Tree. These, as the various Worlds interact, form a sequence of mutually interleaving Trees that make up a Jacob's ladder stretching from Earth to Heaven. Also, but not directly concerned in our study, is the notion that within each sefirah is a complete Tree. This accounts for the universal reciprocation operating throughout Adam Kadmon.

The third minor factor rather than law, is the phenomenon known as the upper and lower faces of the Tree of Life. While some Kabbalists have different views, this book subscribes to the idea that the upper bearded face is formed by Keter, Binah, Hokhmah and Tiferet, while the lower is bounded by Tiferet, Nezah, Hod and Malkhut. These two great faces are extremely important in our study of man because they describe the relationship between his natural and supernatural aspects. They also describe, by their interleaving with the trees of other Worlds, how everything is linked, penetrated and unified into the one great Tree of Adam Kadmon.

Finally the fourth series of Laws is concerned with the paths that connect the various sefirot to one another. These twenty-two paths are considered to be subjective, as against the objectivity of the Divine attributes embodied in the sefirot, for they adapt whatever is flowing through them. This is because of the alternative flows between each pair of sefirot, and the fact that every path is part of a total circulation. Because of this essential adaptability, it is possible for many different types of circulation patterns to occur. These are determined by what sefirah generates the initial flow, so that, for example, if Hod begins a motion towards Nezah it

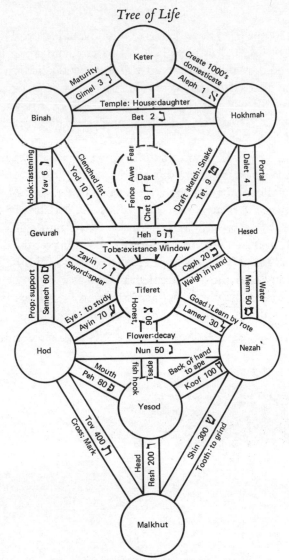

PATHS: HEBREW LETTERS AND ROOT MEANINGS

Here the Paths have the Hebrew alphabet placed on them according to the Lightning Flash sequence. The root meanings of each of the twenty-two letters give a clue to the nature of a Path, that is the relationship between two Sefirot.

must follow the triad flow down to Yesod and back to Hod. This causes the adjacent lower right triad to circulate along the path Nezah, Yesod, Malkhut and back to Nezah again. The circulation is likewise affected on the complimentary lower triad, and also above, and throughout the Tree. No Occurrence is without its repercussions. Thus the relative Universe is the necessary re-balancing in Existence of the act of Creation which disturbs the Equilibrium of Nothingness by the emergence of Creation out of three realms of the Unmanifest.

This for the moment is the basic theory of the Tree of Life and its dynamics.[1] It is suggested that unless one is already familiar with its vocabulary and workings not to continue until at least one can recognize the names and their positions on the Tree. To accomplish this it is further suggested that one draws the Tree up on a card and puts it in a convenient place where it can be referred to until the Yesodic mind has memorized it. It will be easier than thought because it is after all a self-portrait.

[1] For a detailed account see my book *Tree of Life*, Rider and Company, 1972.

3. Adam

'In the beginning', that is, when Adam Kadmon had been emanated into existence, God created heaven and earth, time, the
firmament and the elements. He also brought forth plants and
living creatures. On the sixth day of Creation God said 'Let us
make (a) man in our own image' and so a second Adam came into
existence who was the perfection of Beriah, and its steward.
Later, in Gen. 2:7, 'The Lord God formed man' and this third
Adam became the synthesis of the World of Formations. When
the yeziratic Adam fell with his Eve, he descended into Asiyyah,
the world we live in. These four Adams are an expression of the
four levels within the azilutic Tree of Adam Kadmon.

While the azilutic Adam Kadmon is the universal man the
beriatic is the possibilities of man. This stems from the fact that
creation begins to manifest only when the Lightning Flash passes
out of Azilut the eternal, and into Beriah the beginning of Time.
Like Adam Kadmon the beriatic Adam is androgynus (Male and
female created He them, Gen. 1 : 27) that is, still in a high enough
estate to be a single being (this was before Eve came on the scene)
containing both sexes, or in kabbalistic terms active and passive
pillars in constant union. This illustrates the abstract level of
Beriah which generates working concepts that are quite different
from the seed of the seed of an idea which emanates from Azilut.

The Adam of the World of Formations, is, as the name implies,
the various forms and varieties of men. Described sometimes as a
Watery world it adapts and modifies the archetype supplied by
the world above for the utilization of the world below. Whereas
one might think of the beriatic Adam as mankind, the yeziratic
World is its ever-changing manifestations, through the flow of

the generations, each with its particular adjustment to time and place. Thus the races of the earth are differentiated. The Hebrew is quite easily recognized in ancient Egyptian carvings as well as today in New York city, and the fat, thin, big or small Chinese, Negro or Scot is a form of variation of an archetype.

The asiyyatic Adam is you and I. The incarnated Adam. When our forefather and mother fell from Eden they were given coats of animal skins to cover themselves. These we wear today, until our death. This physical body is composed of the four earthly elements associated with asiyyah of the World of elements and action. Although tied to the Earth and divided into sexes, humans, while residing temporarily in Asiyyah, have all the other Adams present within. The task, it would appear, is still the stewardship of the Earth, but to regain Eden is our added brief. According to Kabbalistic tradition this requires that we not only rise up the Jacob's ladder of trees stretching between Heaven and Earth, but act as conscious participators in the higher worlds, thus helping the Shekhinah, or the Presence of God into manifestation below, so that Creation may return to the perfection which was present prior to the fall of Adam.

The Hebrew word 'Adam' means 'earth' and the body is indeed composed of this material substance. Included in the solid state are many minerals and traces of metals, enough iron for instance, to make a 2-inch nail, and sufficient carbon for 9000 pencils. A high percentage of the body is composed of water, about 10 gallons for a 10 stone man. This fluid is largely responsible for the circulatory systems of the body. Gases, or the state of air, are an absolute prerequisite for the living body and permeate all the liquid and solid structures and flow within the organism. The element Fire in the form of radiation and electrical impulse is also present and anyone who has been in the presence of death will recognize the departure of that curious generally unseen luminosity only the living possess. This radiance is totally absent in the corpse, as is the light of consciousness in the living eye.

Life is that breath which God breathes, we are told in Genesis, into the nostrils of Adam, to make him a living soul. (Neshamah in Hebrew.) This living being, like all other complete organisms, is based upon the design of the Tree of Life, and therefore follows its laws and dynamics. The organism of the physical body is no exception, and as with every other cosmic organization, it does not work in isolation but fits, interleaves, into the world above and the world below as an intermediary for the passage of Force, form and consciousness.

The living cellular human body contains, besides the working principles of the four elements, all other life forms present on the planet Earth. Based on the substance and interaction of the elemental worlds it exists in the vegetable kingdom inasmuch as it eats, drinks, grows, propagates and dies. A few moments' reflection on the body's anatomy quickly reveals that the lungs are a bronchial tree with all the characteristics of its vegetable counterpart. The hair, the skin, indeed the whole body except certain parts of the brain, are in a continuous process of growth and decay, by the constant replacement of cells. The various tubular systems have the same principle of osmosis as plants, and though our blood may be red, it is in fact sap. Even the most intimate physical activity of making love is an activity of the vegetable world. We may not need insects to carry the pollen from the male to the female part of the human race, but the process of fertilization does not belong to the Animal Kingdom.

Man is clothed in animal skins, his physical being having at its flesh and blood centre a vehicle by which it can transport itself about the space of the elemental world. Unlike vegetables, which are rooted to their habitat, animals can rove over a wide field and man also has this possibility through his animal body. Included in this animal aspect are all the social phenomena associated with family, tribe and people. These are expressed through relationships, be they enemy or friend. Group dynamics operate within human as well as animal communities and blend with the vegetable functions. Thus we have social gatherings, like the college dance, where men and women meet in tribal relationship, while also seeking suitable partners to help propagate the species. Nature is concerned with large numbers, and while the liaison between two lovers may be extraordinarily personal to them, it is in fact repeated a million times a day over the whole Earth. An evolving Man is not subject to the laws of vegetable and animal. This point is arrived at after passing through the mineral, vegetable and animal stages in the womb.

At birth the human evolution commences with the first breath. From this point, while incarcerated in flesh, the soul learns the lessons of the world of Asiyyah, simultaneously performing a cosmic task while also acquiring the experience necessary to grow as a soul. Life on earth is tough. Of that there is no doubt, but esoteric tradition says, that under these harsh conditions of maximum physical constraint, many things can be quickly acquired, that are not possible in the upper worlds. The pleasure and pain of the body are the vital teaching situation of the psyche. Illness, love, even war, may be important demonstrations to the non-sensual psyche, of laws it has to respect, both below and above its yeziratic situation. The incarnate soul is in a unique position in that it can examine the asiyyatic World through the body, and thereby see, in operational terms, the workings of the Tree. From this may be deduced, with experience on the psychological level, some idea of the spirit. However, as we must assume that we have only glimpses of the upper Trees we have to look at what we can see, experience in the tangible existence of our body. Here we follow the Kabbalistic instruction, 'If you wish to perceive the invisible observe the visible.' With this study of the physical Tree we will begin to climb Jacob's ladder.

The Body

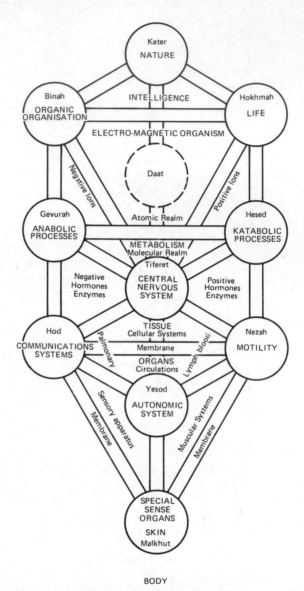

BODY

The body as a complete organism is based on the universal design of the Tree of Life. As such its principles and functions follow the dynamics of the original, but in organic manifestation. Seen as a balance between energy and matter the Tree explains how the various biological levels interconnect and operate.

4. The Four Worlds

The application of the Tree of Life to the examination of any complete entity is simple. First the essence of the creature is identified and placed on the slide plate of Tiferet in our cosmic micro- or macro-scope. This central point is recognizable by the fact that it is the nuclear focus of the being and performs what Tiferet does for the Tree in that it is the pivotal junction of most of the incoming and outgoing circulations, and is both created by, and acknowledged as, the centre balance of the whole organism. Thus, for example, parliament is the governing centre of a nation, but it only exists by virtue of the nation's consent.

This Tiferet point sits midway on the axis of consciousness while on either side the active and passive functions perform their vital tasks. A familiarity with the principles of the sefirot soon recognizes the different activities in any organization. Thus again in the parliamentary Tree the sefirah of Hokhmah describes the genius of a nation, while at the top of the other function column, the passive Binah defines the tribal law or constitution of that state. Hesed represents the powerful elders of the tribe, with the warriors of Gevurah fiercely debating new formulations of the law. Below Hod communicates between the people and government while Nezah carries out the eternal round of administration irrespective of which party is in power. On the central axis of consciousness, mass in this case, the people are Yesod, the foundation of the nation, and the head of state theoretically sits in Daat where the throne, in Britain for example, protects in the name of Keter—the Crown—the people who reside in that land, defined by Malkhut—the Kingdom.

In the case of the physical body the Tiferet of its Tree is the central nervous system. This includes the brain, the spinal cord and the myriad nerve cells throughout the body. Here is Solomon's Seat (in Kabbalistic language), of the physical organism. With this identification of the Tiferet of the body we can begin to set out the general principles that govern the organism in terms of the Tree, but first it is best to see the whole from the viewpoint of the Four Worlds, in the subtree of Asiyyah. This will give us a clear picture of distinct levels of operation.

Taking the asiyyatic world of the asiyyatic Tree, that is, the Great Triad formed by Malkhut, Hod and Nezah, we have the physical systems of the body. These are the actual structures composed of the element of earth, with the element water, percolating through the Hod, Nezah, Yesod triad, lubricating, and circulating, within the solid but permeable fabric of the body.

The architectural foundation of the body can be divided into three main cavities. These are the skull, the thorax and the abdomen, each of which holds the soft, structural, masses of the brain, heart and lungs and viscera. Such organs contain many processes belonging to the upper worlds, they are the vehicles for fine and complex operations. All these are hung on, and supported by, the framework of the skeleton.

In closer detail all living systems, be they muscular, vascular, lymphatic, pulmonary or digestive, have a physical structure, if only as a continuous tube from mouth to anus. These configurations may form great vessels, glandular ducts or minute perforations in the walls of tissue. All however, being permeable, facilitate the functions of flow, retention and drainage within the body, without which it physically could not operate. Chemical actions take place in the stomach but the treated food must be carried along past the various non-return sphincter muscles in the alimentary canal. The same is true for the blood system in which failure of a mechanical one-way valve might prove fatal. Such is the physical nature of the body that a clot or a bubble of air can disrupt circulation and balance in many processes. This gives some idea of the inter-linkages of the concrete anatomy of the body. At death all electrical, chemical and physical activities associated with a singular living process ceases. What is left is the quickly decaying elemental husk. This is Malkhut returning the body to its elemental state.

While Malkhut is the actual physical materiality of the body, Hod and Nezah, which compose the asiyyatic Triad, also play their part as functional principles. These sefirot we will deal with later as our main concern here is with the World of Asiyyah. This, it will be remembered, is the world of the elements and action and this interaction is what takes place in the asiyyatic triangle. Solids, liquids, gases and radiations ebb and flow within the confines of the anatomy. Heat, pressure and all the dynamics of physical law, including gravity, keep the situation from becoming static. Stasis is death. The energy and material configuration of the body, while appearing to remain the same, is in a state of constant change.

In Asiyyah this means that the most dense bones are being replaced as well as the finest traces of rare substances that the body needs for its balancing. Only some brain cells remain for the entire life span, the rest are completely replaced in a never-ending cycle of substance and activity, which builds up over the first thirty years to a self-trimming peak. After this the maintenance processes cannot repair the organism quite so efficiently, and the ratio of wear to replacement falls, as the organism's over-all vitality begins to fail. First the physical property of the skin's elasticity wanes, then joints stiffen, bones become brittle and the arteries become lined with fat. All these and many other accumulative inefficiencies create a gradual deterioration in the asiyyatic mechanism. This is the slowing up of the physical machine which is quite separate from the chemical and electrical activity of the body. Lungs coated with soot or nicotine stains may generate cellular, molecular and atomic mutations resulting in cancer, but the lungs still react purely physically in coughing, as the alveolar air sacs become clogged.

The great asiyyatic Triad is enclosed by paths which form the membranes throughout the body. While in the crudest manifestation this might be the skin, its dead elemental layer being the hide of Malkhut, membranes also include the finest and thinnest skins of capillary walls. In the small triad made by Hod, Nezah, and Yesod, the yeziratic World penetrates Asiyyah and it will be easily observed that while the organs may be the hardware of the asiyyatic body they interface with the Triad of tissue which belongs to the realm of Watery principle as well as Formation. As will be seen the organs participate both in the yeziratic and asiyyatic Worlds.

This sets out very clearly an important fact of the Tree, that is, that the side triads are functional while the horizontal middle pillar based triangles relate to distinct levels of operation. Thus while those on the left side of the Tree are passive in principle and those on the right active, the central configurations denote intelligence. To grasp this requires the acceptance of the concept of a hierarchy of consciousness even in inanimate materiality. This may be difficult for the strict physicist to believe, but in common life experience it is well known, especially in the arts, that certain materials do have a quality or life of their own. Jewel-makers use this knowledge in their craft and anyone with a certain degree of sensitivity can tell the difference between lively and dull stones and metals. Gold to the chemist may be a simple element, but it is more than just the fine sheen of its surface colour that has made it universally desired by primitive and civilized people throughout history. It has a living quality no laboratory instrument can define, as do certain gems which to pure science are no more than minerals.

Presuming we accept the concept of different levels of vitality or intelligence, we can see that the central triads of the Tree describe such a phenomenon, and where its place is, in a complete scheme. In the case of the organs, they raise the level of ordinary elements into biochemistry and pass them on into the yeziratic World of the body.

The yeziratic realm outlined by Gevurah, Hesed, Hod, Yesod, and Nezah, is the world of fluids and molecular activity. Here is the world, in Kabbalistic terms, of Formations. In the body this manifests in many ways. Here in the realm of bio-chemistry the elemental combinations taken in by the asiyyatic systems of the lungs and stomach are broken down and reformed into usable materials. At the level of cells this is vital because most incoming substances are unacceptable to the body at this level of asiyyatic arrangement. Thus for example in the process of digestion, complex foods have to be separated out into their simple components and divided into absorbable carbohydrates, fats, and proteins, unsympathetic substances eliminated, and waste products disposed of. All these processes take place in the Watery realm and the body is composed of well over half of this liquid. Most of the chemical actions inside the dead dry outer skin of the body operate in water, and the tissue which forms the substructure to the asiyyatic anatomy is maintained by virtue of the cell's watery nature. This is the Hod, Tiferet, Nezah triad. On another level but still within the yeziratic world the Gevurah, Hesed, Tiferet triad, deals directly with the body's metabolism, which, being of the molecular realm, and also partaking of the beriatic World, relates to the exchange of form and energy, but this will be dealt with in more detail in the chapter on the body sefirot.

The yeziratic World literally forms the body. That is to say it takes the incoming elements and transforms them into living energy and matter so that from the first breath of the babe to the last sigh of death the shape and character of the body is determined by the yeziratic activity of that person. Thus a man in his lifetime converts several tons of food into flesh. Each person not only replaces cells and repairs his organs, he also grows fat, or remains thin, or keeps within the optimum balance for his body-type. This is partly determined by the hereditary genes in the nuclei of his cells, which through his DNA molecular construction incline him to be tall or small, fat or thin, plus a few thousand other familial and racial characteristics. Just as important, however, is the kind of food he eats and how his body copes with over- or under-nourishment. This metabolic balance has a great effect on his bodily appearance or form.

Every man has the same basic asiyyatic anatomical layout but the variants due to sex, race, clan, diet and personal temperament are enormous. Western man has the possibility of balanced eating habits. His intake of foodstuff can include all vital ingredients for his bodily health because of the knowledge and wealth of his civilization. But, as observation records, while living longer than most other communities he is not necessarily more healthy. This may be due to another quality of the yeziratic World, which, in the upper Tree of his psychology, relates to the emotional realm of his life. In the ebb and flow of water, the upper and lower Trees interact more than is generally thought, so that the body's metabolism is affected by emotional responses. Indeed, the actual bodily form of a man describes his long-term emotional state. A woman may grow excessively fat because she lacks love and must eat to compensate, a man may grow thin on worry, his body burning up vast amounts of metabolic energy in its compensatory concern. Simple explanations of the delicate operations deep within the organs and cells which, unlike a pure machine, are intimately connected with a man's psyche. Here is the yeziratic World permeating and modelling the elements passing continually through the body, changing it over a life-time, from the 6-pound babe to a full-grown 14-stone man, to an old 6-stone shrivelled shell of a soul-vacated body.

The yeziratic World of the body is seen very well in the process of gestation. After conception has taken place, seen in Tree of Life terms as the meeting of the Mother and Father pillars in the invisible sefirah Daat, the world of Beriah or Creations begins to manifest in the sefirah Hesed, the dynamic expansive principle. In the womb of the pregnant mother the development of the embryo child literally takes place in water. Here is Yezirah. With the cell's multiplication at Hesed and its differentiation at Gevurah into specific tissues and organs we have the actual formation of the organism. Completing the yeziratic World are the sefirot of Nezah, which operate all the involuntary processes, Hod, the voluntary and communications systems, and Yesod, which on birth will be the image-making mind on the central column of consciousness. This is centred in the asiyyatic realm so that the body has a picture of itself, a read-out screen in computer terms, which the pivotal intelligence of the Tiferet central nervous system can operate in the asiyyatic World.

In our Kabbalistic scheme this asiyyatic Tiferet is simultaneously the Malkhut of the upper, or full yeziratic, or psychological Tree. For the gestating child it is the junction point connecting the life principle to the body. All these connections are formed in the yeziratic processes of the evolving organism in the womb. Out of the nourishment received by the mother, the yeziratic processes feed and build the babe's physical vehicle until its own organs are completely formed and ready to take over the asiyyatic functions for themselves. Every mother instinctively looks at her new-born child to see if it is malformed. Mother Nature, who operates throughout the physical Tree knows exactly how a body should be. In less sophisticated societies and in the wild, an ill-made-up creature is soon rejected and returned to the elements again for reformation. While this may sound abhorrent to Western medical practice it does indicate that there is an inherent recognition that all children do not always conform to the acceptable norm. Whereas minor lesions are acceptable, babes with major physical discrepancies are not encouraged to live. This is the power of the yeziratic World which exists in its own right, modelling, on the instructions of the beriatic World of Creation, the clay of the asiyyatic World, in the body scheme that is common to all humanity over tens of thousands of generations.

The beriatic World is the realm of Creation. In terms of the body it manifests the impulse of the descending Lightning Flash from Hokhmah into the physical world. In this context it is both atomic and subatomic in nature and is concerned with the making of electrical keys that will interlock in the lower worlds. As such they are the nuclei of seeds that will grow into view through Yezirah and into Asiyyah. Here is where creation takes place. At the point of Daat the Octave receives its crucial aid which allows the supernal active and passive pillars to continue an impulse begun at Keter. This manifests in the beriatic World so that out of apparent nothing energy and substance emerge.

Besides this miraculous event, witnessed through the macrocosm as well as the microcosm in the birth of substance, possibilities of the type of creation are determined. Thus through the formulation of Binah, with the dynamic of Hokhmah, the peculiar electromagnetic base of organic life is created before a single cell is made. This realm is both great and small and is reflected in galaxies as well as atoms, each being an aspect of the identical cosmic level. In the body, atoms and their negatively and positively charged components create the ground for the materiality and energy of the mineral, vegetable or animal body to be found in the yeziratic World. In Beriah the being willed by the Absolute through Keter is set out in creative principles so that the azilutic Triad can create, develop and manifest eventually in Malkhut. In Biblical terms the Lord called forth, created, formed and made the Universe (Isa. 43:7).

Such a world as Beriah is concerned with the operation of objective laws. Neither Divine nor Mundane, the work is cosmic in nature creating a universal matrix out of which all things familiar to us emerge. Science examines the elemental aspect in nuclear physics and plays about with its mechanics and mutations. Indeed disturbance at the atomic level during gestation will produce a deformed yeziratic and asiyyatic body, as Hiroshima demonstrated. Cancer belongs to this realm, and occurs when the instructions present in the genetic focus of the cell become scrambled, creating disharmony within the organism as a whole. Many pioneers of X-rays contracted this malady as the radiation, when absorbed, disturbed the basic structure pattern of their cells. Carcinogenic substances such as soot, may act chemically; this probably disconnects deep keys within the cell's information bank of genes. To get a sense of scale, consider that a minute speck a tenth the size of a full stop is a cell, and that it has a tiny nucleus within which forty-six chromosomes reside, and that each pair of chromosomes is composed of delicate filaments called genes. There are about 25 000 genes, each of which are in turn made up of dioxyribonucleic acid (DNA for short) connected with proteins. These DNA chains consist of a double spiral of molecules which store coded data. These data are vital to the well-being of the whole organism and are repeated faithfully throughout the thousands of millions of cells of a man.

At the cosmic moment of conception, when the single male and female sperm and egg meet, creation occurs. Beyond the dance of the chromosomes, deep within the molecular and atomic world, the genetic template is fused. Here all the possibilities become focused, and the generation and continual maintenance of the future body is tuned ready for the World of Formation. Out of a set of principles, myriads of characteristics are set in motion to be repeated in all the unformed cells, tissues; organs, limbs and body. The precision at this level is complex yet the principles involved are simple. In the realm of Beriah the miraculous is possible and occurs every day and everywhere. In man's body is his electromagnetic organism. It could also be called in its upper asiyyatic face position, simultaneously the lower face of the yeziratic Tree. This gives us another clue to its possible nature in that the realm of psychology is included in its influence. Here perhaps is an insight again into the root of cancer. More important it shows how a man's psyche can develop his body, use it as a vehicle to ride on the physical world into the emotional country of the soul.

Most people hover in the body, the dynamics of organic energy and form barely keeping them alive as vegetables. Whether this is a political or philosophical problem the reader can decide. It depends whether you view the Universe from within or from without. From the standpoint of our study it is stated that man descends to the earth out of the yeziratic World and while he may only be aware of his asiyyatic body he nevertheless possesses all the other worlds within him. To realize them is his choice, and this is possible under asiyyatic conditions by virtue of the fact that his Daat or knowledge is centred in the beriatic World of his body Tree. This organic consciousness gives him an individual ego focused in and on physical existence. Here he can look up, into the yeziratic Tree of his soul, or down, to know and control his body. At this point another conception and subsequent birth is possible, but of an upward motion.

Beriah is the World of Principles. Here are many possible configurations until they become formed in Yezirah. Out of the total knowledge contained in Daat, various combinations are created, to be formulated and physically implemented where they are needed. This sequence is observed in ordinary life, where an idea may be held in the mind for years, before it emerges into a particular work of art or invention. In the example of our study of the body it is the permutations possible in the unfertilized ovum. These in turn all stem from a great archetype, in the case of man—the azilutic Adam.

In the azilutic World are the purest aspects of the Creator. Here the Elohim exist for ever, while the archangels and angels work in the worlds below to make manifestation in the asiyyatic World. In Azilut are all the templates of Creation, the perfect, and to us eternal, realization of all things. The most complete of men reside in this realm, the original image of mankind throughout the Universe. From this world of Emanations the flawless model upon which we are based goes forth. While Beriah is concerned with principles, Azilut is the essence of essences unchanging, eternal, in its archetypal design. Should it be less, it would no longer be the Being it is. All creatures are replicas of its species archetype, each generation and individual being a variant of, suppose, the Great Reindeer or the Great Horse. No one has ever seen these mythical beasts but they undoubtedly exist. One might call them the genius of such creatures living eternally in an azilutic state before and after the animal exists in Beriah or in actual form in Yezirah, not to mention its brief sojourn of millions of years in the asiyyatic World, as did the dinosaur.

For our study of the body we reduce the scale but retain the principles of Azilut. In the asiyyatic supernal triad composed of Keter, Hokhmah and Binah resides the archetypal intelligence of Nature. Here, between the twin pillars of the life force and its organization in the form column, the classic template of the human body is held. Out of this, the Unmanifest but eternally repeated archetype emerges, on conception, into the electromagnetic world of creation in the asiyyatic Tree, the first tangible signs of a human being. Referring always to the prototype of Adam the babe is formed and born into the physical world to grow and mature into a full earthly man. What he does after Nature has set him up is his own concern. He may serve at any level. From Azilut he receives all the equipment he needs, though his is to choose how to use it. He contains perfection perhaps in spite of being completely unaware of it, because Azilut, like all the other worlds, permeates him, though he be a derelict tramp sleeping under a hedge, mind and body soaked in alcohol. The

Universe is ever-present and to quote the Poet Burns: 'a man's a man for a' that.'

The Azilut in the human body is all organic Life. Man contains all the vegetable and animal levels of natural existence. As Adam includes all these living creatures in Creation and has, as Genesis says, dominion over them, so man has responsibility for them. In its physical life mankind experiences these sub-realms. All men know hunger and mating, fighting and socializing. Men are also aware that at their heart they are neither animal nor vegetable, but something different, although looking towards the source of their body, most men see only the rulership of Nature. For a man who seeks further he must see life from above his body's view. Indeed he must separate from his Yesodic ego and recognize a watcher within himself, who seems to observe as if from another world. This watchman is the Keter of Asiyyah and simultaneously the Tiferet of the yeziratic World. As such it is the escape route back out of the wheel of tooth-and-claw existence.

Between the Tiferet of his body with its myriad intelligent but flight or fight motivations, and the Keter of Nature, is the Daat consciousness or Knowledge of his physical world. This lies on a path which ascends through the azilutic level of Asiyyah and gives rise to questions about the nature of man. These are not considerations about just men or even himself but Man and His destination and meaning. The body dies and even the most primitive of tribesmen suspects that something lives on, even if not in personal form. Here is a faint recognition of not only the yeziratic World of the soul and of all mankind (Beriah), but of Man as a single being. This azilutic Image occurs in many ancient stories that still carry their power today. History is full of the ideal Man image, although each age has cast it into a faint imitation of what a man should be.

In our own personal psychology we dream of our perfect man and woman, the idealized Male and Female descending from the androgenous azilutic World. Such is the potency of this realm that in our physical existence, with our asiyyatic bodies, we endlessly seek to find the other half of ourselves, so that the union that will result will be like the perfect love relationships written and sung about in folklore over the centuries. The universal recognition of this theme, despite time and place, is indicative and reflects a dim appreciation of the Archetypal World. However, before we can regain Paradise, enter the Kingdom of Heaven and make that most perfect of Unions, we must begin at the beginning, that is from Malkhut, on our level, the physical body.

5. *Lower Face*

On the Tree of Life the sefirot must always be regarded as principles. While the sefirot have names they may be also recognized as organizations. These merely express the function or level of consciousness operating through that sefirah. The triads likewise must be so regarded, in that on all Trees of Life the same phenomena occur but in different worlds and in different organisms. It is extremely important to remember, for instance, that the triad of Gevurah, Hesed and Tiferet in the body, the metabolism, expresses the same kind of awareness in its chemical way, as does the identical triad in the triad of government, and in the individual psyche. It is only the particular world, and the scale, that is different. These give rise to apparently widely differing phenomena, but in fact the nature and dynamics are identical when the principles involved are examined. Thus the triad Hod, Nezah, Yesod, known in Kabbalah as 'Flesh', is usually concerned with the life maintenance of that organization, be it trade and industry in an economic Tree, or the theory and practice of a profession. Without this interaction between Reverberation, Eternity, and Foundation, the lower face of the Tree, any Tree, would cease to function and that organism would collapse. This is exactly the case at physical death.

In our study of the body we begin with the bottom sefirah of Malkhut. The name Kingdom may also be understood as 'World'. In this context it can be seen as the outside world. A camera takes our portrait. Being a purely elemental machine it records a Malkhutian image on its film, unlike a human eye which has the foible of biochemistry, and even more important, a psyche to interfere with the picture. The photograph, unless impaired by human deviousness, is a simple optical response; that is, it has merely recorded the physical surface of our features noting, according to the fineness of film and lens, the textures, colours and forms of our face. What it sees is for the most part dead skin; only the eyes indicate an inner world and this by implication, as do the gestures of our limbs and the repose of our expressions. Even these are mere habitual arrangements of physical material, which are no more than fleshy surface ripples over a dark unseen interior. This outward appearance is Malkhut and is all we observe, in fact, of the body Tree. The rest is quite hidden from the physical eye. It is only by virtue of the Yesod of the yeziratic or psychological Tree that we can view inside this skin-veiled world without using the dissector's knife.

Malkhut is the outer part of the body, the skin or hide as it is clinically called. Its surface is made up of dead cells which both protect and segregate the body from the world outside. Being in direct contact with the external environment it has the crucial tasks to play of being both receptive and adjusting to, the state of the elements impinging on it. Besides being the organ of heat regulation through its various breathing and cooling apparatus, it also adapts to light, moisture, pressure and air. Put in Kabbalistic terms it responds directly to Fire, Water, Earth and Air in all their many manifestations. Interface between the outer and inner Malkhutian realms, the skin has to perform transit and filtering functions. Moreover, as the body's envelope, it has to relay vital information from without to within, so that the organism can not only survive, but live as comfortably as possible.

The body can be described as a complex self-regulating mechanism, continually adapting itself to an ever-changing environment, in order to maintain a consistent inner status of biochemical operation. To perform this miraculous balancing act, and men, unlike most animals can live almost anywhere on the globe, the human body has to gather data from a vast range of sources. These sense data enter via the hide or Malkhut. Some of them are consciously received but most of them are totally unnoticed by the ordinary ego consciousness that lives in this organic machine. These impressions, as they may be called, come from every

direction, and, for the body, through the vehicle of the four elements. For example, pilots say they fly by the seat of their pants.
Indeed one actually checked this out by having his backside
anaesthetized. The result was that he nearly crashed the light
plane he was flying because he could not assess the various shifts
in weight and pressure normally gathered by his backside. The
impression picture was incomplete and his judgement inaccurate.
In ordinary life we are in the same situation. As children we spend
much of our first years touching and throwing things, burning
and scratching ourselves, in order to build up a body picture of
our world. To ignore Malkhut in a modern as well as a primitive
environment is to court disaster. Among the higher organic life-
forms special organs have been developed to add scope and precision to physical perception. These organs are situated in the hide
and act as hypersensitive impression gatherers in each of the four
elements.

While the body acts as a total organ in its own right, sensitive
over every inch of skin to a background of impressions, certain
areas are more responsive. The hands, for instance, can differen-
tiate by touch more of a range than, say, the kneecap. While
we know this is because of the density of nerve endings just
beneath the epidermis, one may look on this form of sense organ
as concerned with the element Earth, that is the direct cognition
through tactile, solid contact. A child may see an object, but he
does not come to fully accept or know it, until he has touched
and handled it. Playing about with, pulling and pushing—even
for an adult learning how his complex new camera works—is an
important part of learning by the sense of touch. Eskimoes have
no mechanical culture, but during the Second World War,
relatively primitive hunters, having once stripped petrol engines
down and handled them, eventually became remarkably efficient
mechanics. This is the application of the generally considered
unimportant faculty of touch. For the body to be denied tactility
in any part is to be touch-blind in that area, a very dangerous
predicament in an elemental and often hostile world.

The element Water might be related to taste. This special sense
organ, however, works in cooperation with smell, the impression

organ of Air. Both of these senses are guardians and monitors of the air and water elements entering the body by its chief orifice. Whereas the ear, the other air special sense organ, collects data of a much finer order than most of the vibrations picked up by the body, the ear does not nourish the organism in quite the same way, although it does feed the body. Taste selects, checks and warns the organism about what it is ingesting. Without this watery alarm system we would quickly die. On the Air side bad meat, for instance, should not get past the sentry of the nose. If it does, the body informs itself via its taste organs of a dangerous intruder which is forcibly ejected by muscular action. This situation describes some of the functions of the lower triads on the Tree. Bad food, as in our example, is reported, via Hod or the body's communication system, to both the normal cyclic process in Nezah, and the autonomic system in Yesod. This generates a reaction in heightening the sensory triad (anyone who has been sick knows this phenomenon), which activates the appropriate muscle system to vomit out the offending material. The body's Yesodic or autonomic system does this without any need of stimulus from the person. It preserves, and is, the foundation of the body Tree.

The element Fire can be seen obviously related to the special sense organs of sight. Here, like all the other special sense organs, there is a chain of command through the autonomic system to the central nervous complex. In terms of the Tree the connection is not only up the central column but both side paths. Without this relationship between the active and passive columns of the Tree the organs could not properly function, that is respond and affect. It will be noted also that, though external, the senses are by nature part of the whole of the lower face, which contains cells, tissue, organs and all systems. The special sense organ of balance gives some notion of this overall relation to the lower face. Situated in the head, adjacent to the ear, this little bony formation filled with fluid, senses, interprets, and advises, the body as a whole as to its positional status. While the nervous or the autonomic nervous systems deal with the situation, the balancing organ, unless, and even when it is, beyond the earth's gravitational field, relates the whole organism to the outside world in normal Malkhutian orientation.

Together with the other special sense organs and the overall scan of the skin an impression picture is built up. Such information, however, is not just for coordination; it is also for food. While this may obviously be solid, liquid, gas or heat and light, there are many other nourishments entering the organism. These not only include fine traces of rare minerals and gases, but also the psychological input of the yeziratic Tree whose lower face interleaves with the upper face of the body Tree.

Man does not live by bread alone, nor does he exist only for his society. Manna descends from Heaven each day as the Lightning Flash comes down through the various Worlds before resolving in the Malkhut of this, the asiyyatic body. A man is what he eats and drinks, but he is also what he feels, thinks and believes in. As we look at our photoportrait the Malkhut image does perhaps contain everything. This may be true but it would take more than asiyyatic sense organs, however special, to perceive it.

The sefirah Hod represents all the communicators within the body. On the passive column of the Tree it is receptive and functional. While the whole of the asiyyatic Tree is concerned with the body, the side sefirot are manifest as working principles rather than hardware, although of course such physical electrochemical paths of communication as nerves, can be identified with Hod. Hod, however, is situated at the centre of five triads some of which are chemical, such as the hormones and enzymes; others, as circulation systems, like the arterial and venous which also act as fluid message carriers. All these functions are ruled by Hod which is concerned with Reverberating, as its name in English implies. This means, in its widest sense, to respond to, to pass on. Being at the base of the passive column, Hod receives data and sends it out to its respective departments. The ear and eye respond to their particular frequency of vibration, Hod in conjunction with the autonomic system of Yesod running a continuous conversion programme, passing across to the Motility of Nezah the basic life-maintenance data, and onto the central nervous system of Tiferet any information that might require a voluntary response from higher up the Tree.

Moment by moment millions of impulses pass through the body and many are completely automatic, ever repeating cycles driven by Nezah at the bottom of the active column. Here is the power. Situated directly beneath the energy releasing Hesed of biochemical katabolism, Nezah can draw on this dynamic resource to feed into the triads of cells, tissues, organs and muscles. If a leg has to be moved because a man wishes to walk, our body Tiferet informs Hod and Nezah. These, with the learnt and instinctive reflexes focussed in Yesod, operate the correct muscle triad, checking all the time with the sensory apparatus, that the body does not fall over or bang into something. If the movement is involuntary, as with fright, the autonomic system of Yesod takes over and the man finds himself instinctively avoiding a dangerous hole in the ground.

On the microscopic scale, even within the cell, Hod and Nezah operate. Hod is all the communications within the fabric of the unit. These can be mechanical circulations like osmosis or the chemical information carried in the genes. RNA molecules transmit, from a cell's nucleus to the ribosome assembly lines of the cell, the pattern of the DNA molecules, which form the genes, and subsequently the chromosomes of the cell. This message has to be absolutely precise, or the protein arrangement being made up for the daughter cell being born, will not be a replica of the parent. Such faithfulness is vital as mutations would cause not only the possibility of cancer, but the destruction of the whole order of the organism. Nezah on this level is the ability to repeat; the English translation is Eternity which is self-explanatory. Also included in Nezah is the dynamic which keeps the cell producing, circulating and breeding. The vitality and the reliability of the cell, its operation and function, need not be emphasized, as any malfunction would have a profound effect at all levels. This perhaps illustrates how the sefirot truly work, not so much in the mechanics, although they are present, but in the principles of communication and repetition. Hod and Nezah together with Malkhut form the asiyyatic triad of the asiyyatic Tree and therefore appear to be the most obvious functional sefirot at work on Malkhut.

The sefirah Yesod is not so obviously placed. Situated on the column of consciousness it is part created by the inflowing paths. The English name Foundation gives some idea of the sefirah's job. Here, suspended above the materiality of Malkhut, from which the organism is constructed cell by cell from the moment of conception, the Yesodic autonomic system is the body's consciousness of its own self-regulating processes. To do this, evolution has worked out a basic design for all organic creatures, and every animal, no matter how primitive, has this level of consciousness no matter how dim. All creatures wish to live, survive and propagate their species. It is a deep automatic instinct. Salmon swim thousands of miles to breed; mayfly live but a few hours to accomplish their mating; a young man's fancy turns each spring, however sophisticated or evolved his central nervous system may be.

Yesod is the viewing screen for the Tree, and in the body it not only monitors the autonomic processes, such as the pulse rate, temperature and breathing, it also wakes a mother who hears, despite her sleep, her child moaning. A large number of the nervous impulses are handled by Yesod and that part of the anatomy, clinically called the Autonomic Nervous system, is under its rule. In this, the flight or fight mechanism is triggered, through the precisely opposed para-sympathetic and sympathetic nervous systems. Here the sympathetic, in moments of drama, produces chemical and muscular changes ready for conflict, while its complement, the para-sympathetic system, can set the body regulation towards the conservation of energy and relaxation. These two systems operated from Yesod can have a profound effect on the body, changing it from a passive slow rhythm, into a tense, knot of muscle, heart beating, adrenaline surging, ready-for-action, status. This can occur quite outside of the command of the will of a person. Likewise a man can have little control over the workings of his organs. When he does try to exert an influence he usually throws the body out of balance.

The sefirah Hod is not only the communicator but the harmonizer of the body. Together with Nezah it relates to Yesod what is going on in the organs and what is happening in the chemical and cellular realms. Added to this is what is coming in from the outside world as perceived by the senses. On the other side, Nezah vitalizes the cells, tissues and organs as well as giving strength to the muscular systems. Both feed into Malkhut which includes the skeleton upon which the whole hangs. At the centre of this great asiyyatic triad is Yesod, the particular 'set' of that organic machine. Surrounding the whole is a membrane, separating, even though permeable, the asiyyatic, the mechanical processes, from the yeziratic or chemical processes, in terms of this body Tree. Here organs, circulations, muscles, limbs, all the large mechanical elements of the body, are separated out into distinct orders of operation, even though they are permeated by the processes higher up the Tree.

The yeziratic World of the body penetrates into the great asiyyatic triad of Hod-Malkhut-Nezah, via Hod, Nezah and Yesod. In clinical terms these are the side triads of the pulmonary and blood systems. As intermediaries between Hod, Yesod, Nezah and Tiferet they are important. The reason is that they are the point of change between different orders of activity. This and other changes of level in the organism are vital not only to make the body work, but to help us understand how the Tree operates.

In the body there are many systems even though all of them are interlinked into a single whole. These systems, or orders of work to be more precise, are classed as mechanical, chemical, electronic and intellectual. On the Tree they are defined not only by the four worlds but by the central triads. While the lower side triads of the sensory apparatus and the muscular systems describe the passive, receptive and the active power functions of the asiyyatic triad, the small Hod, Nezah, Yesod triangle involves the next two side triads of Hod, Tiferet, Yesod, and Tiferet, Nezah and Yesod, or the place where organs, tissues and cells meet, and work together, to join the physical and chemical worlds. It will be observed that only this path of membrane divides the tissue from the organ triad. Let us check this clinically.

Air enters the organism via the mouth. It is drawn in quite

mechanically by the sucking motion of the lungs. These are operated by the muscular system surrounding the flexible rib cage, containing the two spongy lung sacks situated on either side of the heart. The air passes down the wind pipe which divides into two bronchi, or tree-like formations, that again subdivide down into smaller and smaller branches, until finally, at the very end of each tiny branch, they resolve into minute airsacs with the thinnest of membrane walls, called alveoli. These alveoli are surrounded by an equally fine network of blood vessels which are their opposite numbers in the blood system.

Like the pulmonary tubes dividing down continuously, blood vessels change from large arteries and veins into delicate capillaries. The chief difference between the two systems is that the blood circulates throughout the whole body with a capillary network at the other extreme of the circulation cycle where the oxygen exhausted arterial blood begins to return as carbon dioxide in the venous blood. This is the crucial interchange. At the point of contact of returned blood, and air in the lungs, the oxygen, drawn into the lungs along the bronchi and up to the alveoli, passes through the dividing membrane of the airsacs and into the capillary blood stream. Simultaneously the waste gas of carbon dioxide in the venous blood passes out of the blood through the capillary wall and into the airsac, where it is sucked out mechanically by the lungs to be exhaled through the windpipe and from the mouth.

Meanwhile the oxygenated blood is drawn away by the pump of the heart to be sent pulsing round the body with its vital fuel. This whole operation takes place in the Hod, Tiferet, Nezah and Yesod complex. The air brought by the autonomic systems enters the organ triad. It then permeates the membrane path which, stretched between Hod and Nezah, acts as a continuously adjusting and controlling gas filter watched over by the central nervous system of Tiferet. This, together with Yesod, regulates the power cycles of Nezah, that are in turn monitored, and informed by Hod, of the body needs at that point. On passing into the tissue triad, the cells begin the chemical process of conversion, storage and use.

Using the digestion as another example, food enters the body mechanically. It is literally squeezed along the alimentary canal into the stomach where it is broken down mechanically and chemically into an acceptable form, fit to be passed through the membraneous walls of the alimentary tract. Through Hod and Nezah it is worked on by thousands of enzymes which act as catalysts. This is the process of conversion by the side triads before the operation of the Gevurah, Hesod, Tiferet triad of metabolism.

The cell is the key to all these processes. Building block of the body, the cell might be considered the principle of the whole of the lower face, the reflected image of the upper, which is crowned by Nature at Keter. In the cell are all the elements of the body. It contains all the levels of activity. Electronic and atomic in its elemental composition, it defines, by virtue of its molecular construction, the DNA pattern of its genes. These in turn determine the kind of chromosomes, and therefore the type of cell, and what species of creature it belongs to. In its anatomy it is the microscopic mirror of the whole body, eating and breathing, excreting, propagating and dying. It contains a rudimentary heart, nervous system, even a kind of muscle and stomach organization. It is the atom of Life. Divided further it dies and moves outside Mother Nature's domain and into the twilight zone of dead organic, and inorganic, matter.

On our Tree the cell occupies the whole lower face. At Malkhut, it is the continuous shedding of dead skin, as well as the sensitive fabric of the ear or eye. Indeed its role is wide and varied and some, like the elongated nervous cell, bear no apparent resemblance to a finger nail, or bone cell. And yet all are based on the identical organic principles, although specialization may play down, or point up, certain qualities. At Yesod, for instance, the cell carries on all the autonomic systems, it being by its very nature a self-regulating organism. The fact that it divides into epithelial, connective, muscle and nerve tissue, does not change this basic characteristic, so that throughout the body the autonomic process cannot help but operate. This is brought about by the sefirot of Hod and Nezah. Hod links the common principles while Nezah powers them. Together with Yesod the communication and repetition within the cells form organized tissue during gestation, and build organs.

The body, having been created by the beriatic World, and formed in Yezirah, now works through the cell, which is the bridge between the mechanical and chemical activities of the tissue and organs. The interchange, as seen on the Tree, is sideways, as well as up and down, and here we see the vegetable and animal principles interleaved, and the active and passive pillars of the Tree in action. The cell's simplest collective organization is the plant kingdom and the great asiyyatic triad can work for a man without him leaving his house, if he can be fed. In some tragic accidents, where brain damage has occurred, this situation actually happens. A man can exist in a coma; if he wants nothing but to breathe, eat, and excrete. This is the basal realm of the cells, the elementary vegetable life support system.

Taking the whole of the lower face of the Tree as a unit, we can see the organic machine at work. Contained in the great asiyyatic triangle, the sub-triad of the sensory apparatus penetrates the body, responding to external and internal situations; informing Hod, which via the autonomic of Yesod or the central nervous system of Tiferet brings about an effect. This may work, for instance, on the heart muscles of the Nezah, Yesod, Malkhut triad, making them push more blood through, for example, the organ of the liver, which in turn with its labyrinth of channels performs, on the cellular level, a metabolic action on the blood of adding and subtracting various substances. This bio-chemical interaction involves the Tiferet, Hod, Nezah triad of tissue systems, while the waste products are mechanically drained out into the bile ducts. Throughout the body the triads operate, even the most simple muscle served in its blood vessels, tissue and cells, by all aspects of the whole lower face. Everything is interdependent, no part may operate out of harmony without affecting the whole. Here is the first principle of the Tree of Life.

6. Tiferet

At the centre of the body Tree is the Tiferet of the central nervous system. As its position implies it is the focus of many paths. These paths, both on the Tree, and in the body, extend outward and inward. On the Tree the two-way flow relates to the various principles of the sefirot and the two conscious levels of Yesod and Daat. Yesod, in the body context, is the autonomic consciousness while Daat, the Yesod of the yeziratic or psychological Tree, is the knowledge or the knowing of the embodied ego.

The asiyyatic Tiferet, besides being the central nervous system is also the Malkhut of the yeziratic Tree and is one of the key connections between the physical and psychological bodies. As a physical manifestation the nervous system is the most complex feature of the body. Composed of billions of highly specialized cells called neurones, it is organized in an elaborate matrix throughout the organism. So sophisticated a development are the nerves, that some cells have evolved to nearly three feet in length. Covered with insulating fat and protein, they convey electrical signals along their length and form twin relay lines of sensors and effectors. These coupled paths permeate the body, in order to inform the central nervous system, and to effect a response. Both deep inside, and at the surface of the organism, this remarkable network not only operates in the eyes and ears to serve incoming light and sound waves, but also monitors the myriad critical functions within the muscles, organs and gut.

The most sensitive masses of nerve endings are spread all over the skin and these aid the body to gather data on temperature, moisture, and of course touch. They also watch for danger signals of excess heat, cold, pressure and any other physical threat. Such warnings are quickly relayed to the brain, the most evolved part of the nervous system, for conscious action, if an automatic reflex is inadequate. This giant clearing house in the skull deals with over a million or so signals a second, assigning some to reflex patterns posited in the brain by habit or education, and others to self-regulating instinctive processes.

Let us take, for example, when one sits down on a chair. While appearing like a simple voluntary motion, in fact several thousand events throughout the body have to be noted, analysed, and adjusted before you are comfortable in your chair.

Taking just one type of nerve involved in sitting down, the muscle spindle receptor lies along the fibres, deep inside one of our 149 muscles. This cell is very sensitive to tension or relaxation. The slightest movement stimulates the spindle, which conveys an impulse through a long nerve path to the spinal cord. Here it connects directly to the motor or effector nerve attached to that same muscle, so automatically balancing and counterbalancing the tension requirements of a person about to be seated. While this autoreflex action is in progress, signals from the spindle reach the base of the brain where they are related to the general muscle activity of the body. Here, with all the thousands of other sense data from the skin, joints, eye, balancing organs and of course the other muscles, it is gathered and merged into a general pattern of posture reflex. This is maintained by the three main automatic tendencies, the righting, the static and the coordinating principles which hold a chosen posture or maintain balance while the body is in motion so that one does not fall over when getting up from the chair. Visualize this incident happening at every moment. Moreover, our single example, of the muscle spindle receptor, involves the whole of the lower face. Multiply this ten thousand fold and one might get a notion of the work of Tiferet.

For obvious reasons such a complex system generates many combinations of action. Let us examine a series in the light of the Tree. A simple reflex like a finger pulling back from a stinging nettle is a straightforward case of sensory signals travelling from the stung skin to the spinal cord. Here the stimulus excites the motor neurones which cause the arm muscles to contract and pull the hand away. Here is Hod and Nezah at work. But being what is known as a reflex arc, that is an involuntary movement, not involving the brain and only passing through the spine, it does not directly connect with Tiferet. These reflex arcs are automatic and built into the body of a child during gestation ready for development. Here is Yesod or the Foundation prepared for by Mother Nature. Such basic reflexes are trained, and used in learning the skills of life, like hunting. In man quite a number can be educated into a highly sophisticated action or response, as any circus act or craftsman demonstrates. This is the work of Tiferet. As the simultaneous Malkhut of the yeziratic world, the sefira can operate through the physical Tiferet of the central nervous system. By applying the will of its psychological Yesod through the simultaneous Daat of the asiyyatic Tree, the ego can profoundly effect the organism. This is an important connection between the two interleaved Trees of body and psyche.

At the focus of the nervous system is the brain, the physical vehicle of ordinary consciousness. Situated at Tiferet it is in fact involved, via the paths, with the whole Tree. That is, it participates in the physical and psychological or upper and lower faces. Let us look at the lower face connections. The brain is an organ. While having no direct connection with the bottom side triads, hence no nerve sensors or muscles of its own, it does operate on the Hod, Yesod, Nezah and the Hod, Tiferet, Nezah triads. It has circulations of air, to mention the Hod, Tiferet, Yesod side triad and of blood, in the Tiferet, Nezah, Yesod triad. It is composed of tissue formed by special cells. These are a highly organized extension of the spinal cord, and perform more complicated tasks than the autonomic aspect of the nervous system.

The brain has three basic divisions: the fore-, mid- and hind-sections. The medulla or hind brain deals with the regulation of body processes. The cerebellum or mid-brain helps to maintain balance and co-ordinates the complicated movements such as discussed in our sitting down on a chair. The fore-brain, or cerebral hemispheres, are quite a different matter in a human being and relate to the upper face of the Tree, that is the psyche.

Huge in size, compared to the other parts of the brain, these folded half domes of tissue are receptors to all sensory impressions. However, what makes them quite unique in the body is that from them all voluntary impulses arise. If intellect is to be clinically located, it is suggested that it might be found in the layer of grey matter covering the upper surface of the cerebral hemispheres. Viewed from the Tree of Life one might suspect this is merely a point of interaction, the cerebral nerve cells being the physical manifestation of the Malkhut of the yeziratic Tree.

The cerebral hemispheres are composed of millions of nerve cells and these are organized into interconnecting groups of functions. Some, for instance, are responsible for sight, others hearing, both being the terminals for the nerves running from the eye and ear. This is equally true of all the various areas concerned with sense data. Also included in this part of the brain are the voluntary functions of speech and motor activities, which enable us to set in motion any physical action we may desire, if it is in our power to accomplish it. It is from this area we begin to learn acquired reflexes which require initial attention during the mastering of any movement. Thus we learn to walk and perform the complex movements of driving a car. When the reflexes have been sufficiently conditioned the voluntary part of the brain is relieved of the major burden, and only a simple stimulus is needed to activate a whole battery of actions. This is the whole of the lower face of the Tree centred on Yesod, but under the command of Tiferet.

Perhaps of particular interest to the Kabbalist are those regions of the cerebral hemispheres called 'the silent areas' situated at the fore part of the head. They appeared to the scientist who discovered them, while mapping out the various functional zones of the brain, to perform no obvious duties. Indeed it has been clinically observed that unlike a stroke which dishabilitates whatever function-zone it strikes, like that of speech, the destruction of the silent areas has no obvious effect in physical terms. It was observed, however, that the person with such damage did undergo a psychological change. In the case of an industrious and reliable workman it turned him into a laggard and cheat. While it is known that the decerebration of animals causes them little harm (they continue to fly or run as the mid- and lower brains can still perform) it is noted that all initiative is gone. This indicates that the will is affected. Moreover no new reflexes can be conditioned. In man the situation is similar. While the mid- and hind-brain and the various levels of the spinal cord can carry out automatic actions and already learnt reflexes, the ability to motivate has gone. This implies that the path between Tiferet and Daat in Asiyyah has been severed.

Also credited clinically to the brain is the emotional focus of the organism. Arising from the base of the brain are nuclei fibres which run into the silent areas of fore-brain. Here they merge with the intellectual activities and blend into consciousness. To be more correct and use Kabbalistic terms, this is probably the Hod and Hezah aspect of the tissue triad. Hod is traditionally related to the god Mercury who was not so much an intellectual as a very clever communicator. He learned at amazing speed and imparted it just as quickly. The traditional goddess assigned to Nezah is Venus who describes very clearly the attraction and repulsion principles in the body and all the cycles powered by her instinctive processes. Feeling is often mistaken for emotion, but as we shall see later the quality of emotion is not as obvious as desire, the driving force of Venus, and the motivation behind Nezah. This places the two streams of so-called intellect and feeling into proper perspective. A man may be very learned, but not possess a real intellect, and a woman may consider herself passionate, yet be quite emotionally cold.

While feeling and thinking, as we may call the Nezah and Hod faculties, are certainly present in the brain, it is the other paths reaching down from the upper part of the Tree that make a man a unique being. When the physical connections between the silent areas and the rest of the brain are surgically severed, this deprives a man of his drive. It also cuts him off from the possibility of psychological development, although it might relieve him of anxiety. Whereas it might be argued peace is attained, his asiyyatic and yeziratic Trees are no longer fully interleaved. This means that like a half-anchored balloon his psyche hovers, part in the asiyyatic World and part in Yezirah. One might ask of this treatment, indeed any other radical physical prescription, like shock therapy or drugs, whether it really does any more than put the patient in a limbo between two worlds. It is a Kabbalistic maxim that Heaven must be brought down to Earth. There can be no complete resolution until the azilutic Tree manifests and marries with all the other Trees in Asiyyah. Then all indeed will be one. For the psychologically sick person, unity is the one thing he craves for and to cut him off from the possibility in this life cycle is a great responsibility.

To sum up, the physical Tiferet might be considered as the Malkhut of the yeziratic body. It is not just the brain, or the central nervous system, but the sefirotal manifestation of the bodily essence of that person. While the whole Tree is involved, at this central point is all that has been before birth and will be until physical death, unless great changes occur in the Trees above, for it must be remembered that the body Keter is both the Tiferet of Yezirah and the Malkhut of the beriatic Tree of Creation. Bring about an effect from that world and you can raise your body from the dead.

7. Yeziratic Chemistry

That part of the body Tree defined by the sefirot Gevurah, Hesed, Nezah, Yesod and Hod, with Tiferet in its midst, can be loosely described as the yeziratic World of Asiyyah. In this zone of Formation the elements involved in life maintenance are re-arranged in a continuous series of biochemical processes. This constant transformation is important to the organism because it not only supports its vitality but sustains what is in fact a critically stable situation composed of widely varying substances and levels of physical, chemical and electrical energy.

Physically speaking, the body is a mixture of water, organic fat, carbon, phosphorus, iron, lime and minute quantities of various other elements. These components in pure element form are atomic in nature. However, in the chemical world they relate in thousands of combinations, some closely, others loosely, some in a simple marriage couple, others in complex families of millions of atoms. This level of action is known as molecular. Such molecular compounds are linked by attractions inherent in the structures of atoms. These bonds are called chemical and when the connection between two or more atoms is broken, energy is fed in, then released. The body uses this energy build-up, bond, and release phenomenon, as part of its biochemical activities.

Any living thing, be it plant or animal, is made up of H_2O, that is, a two-hydrogen to one-oxygen atom combination, known as the molecule of water. Anything living and cellular is also made up of three general types of chemical combinations. These are protein, fat and carbohydrates. There are other molecular substances in the body as well, such as gases that play a vital role, but it is well to remember again that three-quarters of the human organism is composed of water. This is an important medium for chemical change in tissue.

In the lower part of the yeziratic World of the body, the organs and cell tissues circulate and contain the fluids of blood, lymph and several hundred variations of watery solutions. It is here that many organic chemical actions occur, although some may happen in a large organ like the alimentary canal, others in the minute space of a cell. These biochemical interchanges are called metabolism. From the building-up of molecules and their breaking down, and subsequent release and bondage of energy, the body draws its strength and substance, that is, in Tree terms, the two side pillars of force and form.

Man cannot eat or make use of the molecular world directly for most of his sustenance. Therefore he has to have an intermediary. Plants are the bridge between the mineral kingdom and the realms of animals and men, and as such are consumed by the latter who can absorb them as organized cellular material. This enhanced state of mineral matter is accomplished by the interaction of earth, air, fire and water, that is the ground, air, sun and rain. Out of this combination the plant, that is, the living principle embodied in a particular species fixes energy in an organic form. Edible by beasts and man, its tissue is used as ready-made food stuff because the glucose or sugar content produced by plants is easily convertible into energy by the animal or human organism. Men also eat animals so that human beings receive in meat the end of a chain of concentrated consumables. What we are a link to, or who consumes us, will be touched on later.

Using the Tree we will follow the operation of eating to illustrate the workings of the yeziratic realm. When a man sits down to a meal, many things occur simultaneously, as well as in sequence, as the dinner is converted into usable energy and substance.

Food enters via the mouth. That is Malkhut. There it is masticated by the muscle triad of Nezah, Yesod and Malkhutian teeth. At the same time saliva containing the enzyme ptyalin, which acts as a chemical catalyst begins to break down any starch. Here the yeziratic World, which permeates the asiyyatic realm of physical action instantly makes itself felt. The mashed and slimy food is of course tasted and checked by the sensory apparatus of the Hod, Yesod, Malkhut triad—and enjoyed incidentally by the nervous system. The muscular triad, working under the autonomic action of Yesod, then pushes the thoroughly wet and already chemically disintegrating organic food, down the oesophagus, into the organ triad of the stomach. Here it is on the threshold of the yeziratic realm proper and is acted on by hydrochloric acid, mucin and the enzyme pepsin. Again it is pulverized by the stomach walls, as it is still just inside the great asiyyatic triad of membranes. After being well kneaded and mixed into a creamy paste to just the right temperature, it is passed on into the small intestine. All this is to accomplish the first phase of digestion of protein, the gastric juices of the stomach having been automatically brought into action by the nerve signals of sight and smell. This operation is controlled by Yesod which is the focus of the asiyyatic triad. The type of food entering the stomach is important, because the Hod and Nezah response has to be very precise in its balance. For every mouthful Hod will supply the information and Nezah the required reaction. Both of these connect with the biochemical side triads of enzymes and hormones which permeate the organism. As functional triads they indeed act as catalysts.

When the partially digested food enters the small intestine, bile and pancreatic juice drain into the duodenum, from the organs of the liver and pancreas, which have been stimulated by hormones in the bloodstream. Here various chemical actions aided by more enzymes take place. These help to digest the fats, proteins and starches of the food into fatty acids, glycerol, amino acid and glucose. This process is still within the triad of Hod, Nezah and Yesod or the alimentary tract, which still subjects the creamy paste to the laws of physical squeezing as it passes on down the tube of the gut.

When the useful portions of the food have been broken down enough by enzymes, the goodness is absorbed through the villi of the intestine by osmosis and thereby passes out of the asiyyatic triad, through the membrane between Hod and Nezah and into the triad of tissue. Here the carbohydrates, having been converted into simple sugars, are then transformed into glucose, the most common form of fuel used by the human organism in its metabolism.

Such an operation is carried out by the liver which works as part of the general physical circulation, the Hod, Yesod, Nezah triad and in the cellular triangle of Hod, Tiferet, Nezah.

As the food of our meal continues to be worked on by enzymes which will leave it lifeless, the gut pushes it towards the anus where it will be excreted at Malkhut. Meanwhile the extracted soluble substances are drawn into the tissue triad. Here they may be reabsorbed into the blood passing round the stomach or intestine, and then carried to the liver where, transferring back from the circulation triad, the goodness is stored or processed by the liver cells operating in conjunction with the two side triads of the enzymes.

The liver is a massive organ, the largest gland in the body and its job extends up the Tree from being part of the general circulation, through the conversion and storage of substance in the tissue, up via the functional triads to the biochemical triangle of Gevurah, Hesed, and Tiferet. Besides the proteins, enzymes and bile acids found in the liver are nutrients, minerals and vitamins, absorbed from the intestines. Here too are stored reserve supplies of glucose, fatty and amino acids ready for use. Also included in its functions is dealing with poisons and the residue of metabolism. All the waste products are recycled out via the bile ducts which make use of such concentrated stuff in aiding digestion. In this way the action passes down the Tree into the lower face again.

Other organs involved at this level include the ductless glands which are situated throughout the body. Unlike the heart, which is merely a physical pump, or the lungs which do a mechanical-chemical exchange, the endocrine glands secrete hormones, or chemical messengers, directly into the body chemistry. Situated in the Hod, Yesod, Nezah, Tiferet complex the glands control and coordinate many bodily functions. Some like the parathyroid produce a simple effect on the metabolism, others like its companion the thyroid, influence all cellular metabolism. The pituitary gland situated in the region of the brain coordinates the endocrine system as a whole. Its posterior part is composed of nervous tissue so that it has a direct connection with Tiferet. Moreover, it has a great say in the growth of an organism, controlling the number and size of cells in tissue and organs. Thus the pituitary under the rule of Tiferet has much concern with the whole lower face of the Tree.

Other ductless glands, such as the adrenal, control salt, protein and carbohydrate metabolism in their cortices, while the small adrenal medulla backs up the sympathetic nervous system, adding the necessary chemical stimulants when needed, The pancreas, besides producing enzymes, acts as a ductless gland for the hormone insulin, which keeps the level of glucose in the bloodstream constant. All these activities work off the information principle of Hod, the repetitive reliability of Nezah, the balancing automatic control of Yesod and the overall surveillance of Tiferet at the head of the lower face.

To develop an example of hormone action in detail we will examine a crisis. A man goes out into his garden, where he spots a cobra. Seen by his special sense organs, the central nervous system is stunned, but the sympathetic autonomic nervous system, instinctively activated, sends nerve signals to the adrenal medulla. This gland produces the powerful chemical hormone adrenaline, which quickly circulates through the bloodstream. The sympathetic nervous system is now on full alert, with the reinforcement of adrenaline throughout the body. Fear rises in the body and psyche. Hod and Nezah are awakened to capacity. Hod heightens all the senses while Nezah calls up all the alarm postures. The skin whitens as blood is withdrawn. The muscle triad tenses the limbs, while the heart hammers and raises the pulse and blood pressure. The gut muscles relax. In the organs and tissue triad, the body calls on the metabolism to increase, and sugar is thrown into the blood, as the liver rapidly breaks down stored glycogen. In the muscles glycogen is split into lactic acid, which is transported swiftly to the liver to be reformed into glycogen for reserve. The body is prepared to fight or run, its yeziratic and asiyyatic realms running high even though the man may be frozen to the spot.

How is the enormous power generated so swiftly and in so small a space? For the answer we must look at the nature of metabolism.

Observing first that the hormone and enzyme triads are attached to the left and right pillars as well as the central control of Tiferet, we are given a clue as to the active and passive roles of these chemical agents. Hormones, for instance, on the active triad can easily be seen as stimulating factors, while those on the passive are seen as retarding. Enzymes also follow this role in the biochemical process, by breaking substances down or linking them, that is as force or form catalysts. This helps us to begin to define the two sefirot principally involved with metabolic triads.

Gevurah, Kabbalistically speaking, is Judgement, the principle that brings to hard focus, discriminates, divides by precise selection and concentrates. It is sometimes called power and is the middle sefirah on the column of form working under the general law of the sefira Binah above. As with all the sefirot no one word is adequate, and the other traditional names for Gevurah like Fear, Severity and Rigor only give a hint of its quality.

In body terms Gevurah may be considered to be the set of principles that initially separate ingested foodstuffs into their three basic classes. Here the enzymes of the passive triad aid biochemical action in the many steps of assimilation of carbohydrates, fats and proteins into the body. Gevurah as the prime anabolic processor, is also responsible for the binding of molecules into larger concentrations, from which energy will later be drawn. Taking fat as an example, this class of substance is a compound like the carbohydrates of carbon, hydrogen and oxygen, but of a more complex nature. Each big molecule of fat is composed of small molecules of glycerol and fatty acid. These are separated into sub-components for absorption into the blood, either to be used for energy directly, or reconstituted as fat to be stored about the body as reserves. Such a breaking down, and building up process, with its fixing and releasing of the energy of chemical bonds is vital for the body, because the continuous exchange of substance and force preserves the critically stable organization of the cell, the basic building brick of the lower face of the Tree.

Hesed, as might be supposed, being an essentially active and expansive principle, governs the release of energy. It is a complement from the active column of force to the passive and resistant Gevurah on the column of form. These sefirot, with Tiferet form the triad of metabolism or the molecular realm of activity in the body.

On this active side of the Tree the enzymes concerned with energy release operate with great power although as catalysts they are never actually involved with the chemical action. Primarily accelerators, many enzymes work deep inside the cell completing highly complex operations with perhaps a dozen others, and all in perfect sequence. A few only work outside the cell that generated them because they are, in active form, too powerful to be contained. These particular enzymes, as for instance trypsinogen in pancreatic juice, are passive until they are activated and become potent trypsin, which digests protein in the intestine. There are thousands of enzymes in the body, some under Gevurah, some under Hesed. This chemical complementation between the principles of force and force gives the body its power and substance. At any one time the organism may use Hesed or Gevurah alternatively to reverse a process or change a structure. In fact both sefirot are always working simultaneously.

To illustrate this point proteins are large complex molecules constructed of delicate connections between thousands of amino acid molecules. These huge molecules may be broken down into simpler amino acids, which can be used for energy fuel, or combined, to form particular proteins for the structural material of the body. They may also direct chemical reactions taking place in cells. Here we glimpse the three different roles any participant in an event may play. Active or passive or conditioner, this triad principle operates throughout the universe and gives us some idea of the role of Tiferet in the metabolic triangle.

The triad Gevurah, Hesed, Tiferet in the Tree of man's psyche corresponds with self-consciousness. Working on the principle of parallels in all Trees, this triad, for the body, would be its own self awareness, and simple observation of one's own bodily state, reveals that metabolism is more than just chemical action. It also describes the body's emotional condition. A man may have a superb physique but this does not make him necessarily good or happy. Tension generated in the psyche will pass down the yeziratic Tree through its lower face, that is the upper face of the body Tree, and into the chemical and physical systems. Such psychosomatic maladies as migraine disturb the metabolism, constrict the nerves, and alter the calibre of arteries bringing about visual abberation, headache, vomiting and vertigo. Here the whole asiyyatic Tree is reflected right down to Malkhut with the central nervous and autonomic systems thrown out of balance by something in the psyche. Tiferet, as previously said, is the Malkhut of the yeziratic Tree and as the central nervous system is the physical link with the psyche. As part of the metabolic triad Tiferet can profoundly influence the chemical workings of the body, and vice versa, in cases where alien substances such as LSD produce psychadelic experience, for both the yeziratic and asiyyatic bodies. Modern clinical medicine states at this point in time, that schizophrenia may be the result of excess of certain substances. This is no doubt correct but what generates this chemical imbalance, the psyche or the body?

Tiferet, by virtue of its central position, has access to most of the body. In purely physical terms the body's temperature, which is created by the chemical action going on in the muscles, liver and tissue, is controlled by the nervous system. Such quite mechanical processes as sweating and the enlargement of blood vessels near the skin when the body is too hot, or shivering when too cold, are in the province of a delicate control regulator situated in the base of the brain. Equally true is the conditioning control over the subtle workings of the metabolism, although we interfere with the processes at our peril.

The deliberate abstaining from certain foods or practising a particular diet is the application of will on the metabolism. So is deliberate exercise or any regime designed to slim, fatten or strengthen the body. All of these can profoundly affect the metabolism. A man may give up sugar in his coffee or add an extra spoonful. This can cause a noticeable shift in the balance of his biochemistry as the body at first craves, then adjusts to, the lack or increase of the substance. Even a moderate smoker or drinker, who has attempted to break the habit, knows the bodily protest and psychological irritation of the first week, even finds himself or his body trying to find another stimulant to compensate for the chemical imbalance.

The metabolic triad is significant although no more important than any other on the Tree. Its significance is that it tells us something about the nature and speed of the molecular world. While the chemical realm is extraordinarily fast and complex, in comparison to the slow lumberings of the organs in the lower face, we can glimpse what chemical consciousness is. This might sound incongruous and unscientific, but with the universe viewed in terms of the Tree of Life it is obvious that nothing is dead or without consciousness. In our own everyday experience, we use the molecular realm to sense atmosphere, taste relationships, and check the phenomena of living, which is more than merely feeding the organism. The Hesed, Gevurah, Tiferet triad is the one which gives us a sense of well-being. The man, tired from a hard day's work, knows it well when he takes up his favourite hobby in the evening. Suddenly he has all the energy in the world, the lower face of his body Tree no longer being exhausted. Where does all this power come from? It is stored in molecular particles in his cells, tissues, organs and muscles. How is it released? Under the auspices of Gevurah and Hesed the whole of the yeziratic World of chemistry is at his Tiferet command.

When we are listless and run-down, we can actually feel the lack of chemical exchange in our bodies, even though all our organs may be in relatively good working order. There is a sluggishness in the organism which perhaps is the fore-signal of disease. As the name dis-ease implies, the Tree symmetry is distorted and a good physician will seek to correct the imbalance by physical or chemical remedies which may work on any one or more of the triads.

The yeziratic realm of chemistry is subtle and complex. It operates throughout the body. As the intermediary world between the electromagnetic level of the organism's Beriah and the asiyyatic cells at the lower face it has a very definite role to play.

Here is the material and power the body is built with and works on. Atoms in their pure elemental form cannot produce organic life. Present they must be, of course, because they are the basic building units in the physical Universe. Yezirah enables the electromagnetic world to manifest in flesh, be it green bark or human skin. Only through the yeziratic World can the energy and substance of atoms operate in living things. Without the realm of Formations nothing could assemble, grow, work its structure and then dissolve back into its elements. In Yezirah, chemistry performs all these functions and in the body such endless metabolic exchange between force and form is essential to its life.

8. Beriah: the electromagnetic organism

Beyond the world of molecules lies the world of atoms. While a molecule is a chemical compound like that of water a true atom is the smallest divisible unit of a pure substance. To divide an atom of gold or iron or any of the elements further will destroy the structure of the substance. Indeed it ceases to be that element. The dissolution of its atomic anatomy will also render it incapable of taking part in any molecular action. Move it out of the realm of chemistry into that yet smaller world of particles and waves where the physicist is not sure what is energy and what is matter. This is the beriatic world of Asiyyah.

Beriah is the World of Creations. In the area defined by Hokhmah, Binah, Hesed, Gevurah and Tiferet out of nothing comes something. At the invisible point of Daat is knowledge, that is, the archetypal world descending from Azilut above, manifesting in Creations. Out of Emanations principles emerge, which apply throughout the Universe. In our asiyyatic Tree this is the field of pure energy and matter as described by atomic and subatomic phenomena. Thus we get in the Macrocosm the same laws applying to galaxies and stars as to atoms and their components. Indeed from man's view, roughly half-way between this Heaven and Earth axis, the scales are commensurable, the particles of an atom arranged like a minute solar system, held, despite their enormous orbiting speeds by extremely powerful forces, from flying off and ripping the atom, and incidentally, the whole physical Universe, apart.

An atom, to get some idea of size, has been compared in relation to a golf ball, as that golf ball is to the planet Earth. An atom is composed of three types of particle; protons, neutrons and electrons. (Here the great law of three manifests in the most basic level of Malkhut.) These three factors are charged electrically, the proton as positive, the electron as negative and the neutron with no charge at all. Arranged it seems in a solar-system-like configuration, with the protons and neutrons locked by powerful relationships to form the dense nucleus of the atom, the electrons seem to orbit at tremendous speeds held in place by their charge's attraction for the central mass. Every element has this basic arrangement, the chief differences being the numbers of protons, neutrons and electrons and the latter's orbital path layering. Because of the dynamics involved, no atomic situation is absolutely stable in its positive and negative balance between the nucleus and its circling electrons. This enables many things to happen, one of which is chemical action as atoms, lacking, or having a surplus electron, seek a balancing bond, sharing with similar atoms of their own, or other elements. These bonds, depending on what elements are involved, may be made or broken and form the electrical basis of molecular-chemical action. In this way we see how the beriatic World enters the yeziratic in the metabolic triad of Gevurah, Hesed and Tiferet.

Such unstable atoms are caused by having their electron complement stolen from or added to, as there is an acceptable margin of tolerance. When an atom gains electrons, it becomes positively charged, and when it loses, negatively inclined. These imbalanced atoms are called ions. Such charged particles play a great part in the body's running and fit into their respective active and passive roles in the left and right functional triads of the Tree where they perform millions of tasks in every second of the organism's life.

Taking into consideration the sefirot involved we may gain some idea of the work of ions. The passive triad of Binah, Gevurah and Tiferet overseen by Binah is concerned with organic organization. It has a direct connection with the metabolic process of Gevurah and Tiferet. From this, one might speculate that this triad was intimately part of the building up of form, operating deep within the DNA molecules of cells. Here the spiral arrangement of the genes control, not only the chemical reaction within

the cell, but also transmit a store of coded information, for reproduction of the structural arrangements of proteins. The molecules
performing this exact task are ruled by the laws of the atomic
world which by the presence of Binah in this particular triad
causes their work to lean towards the principle of organic form.
On their own the ions would not do this, but inside this organic
Tree, on that triad, they are drawn into the processes of building
molecules, cells, and tissue, as well as assisting, on their atomic level,
in the resistant, or retarding action, of the passive triad of enzymes
and hormones.

On the other side, the triad topped by Hokhmah, or in this
instance the dynamic of Life, the ions assist the katabolic processes
to release chemical energy within the metabolic exchange. As
positive agents they may not be so apparent as the active hormones
or enzymes but never-the-less they do operate right down through
the Tree, being, by their atomic and elemental nature, the ground-
root Malkhut of the body's energy and matter.

Beside working directly through the metabolic triad, ions also
perform many other tasks, the body using their electronic
properties to its own advantage. One such example is at the
junction between nerve cells. While nerve message impulses are
primarily chemical, one cell stimulating the next, some critical
points of connection are aided by chloride and sodium ions which,
in mutual electron attraction, pass through the dividing cell
membrane and trigger the cells' firing mechanism. Such electro-
chemical contrivances are used by the body in many ways. To
excite or inhibit a chemical action is another example.

Examining Tiferet at the focus of the two ion triads we can
see how the body as a whole is aware of all its levels and functions.
By virtue of this central position the beriatic World, via the
incoming paths from Binah and Hokhmah, influences through
Tiferet the adjacent ion-metabolic triads. In this way the atomic
world participates in an orderly manner obeying the central
direction of Tiferet which, with the physical and chemical levels,
balances the organism as a whole. Remembering that Tiferet is
created by all that has gone before in the descending Lightning
Flash, and influences all that will happen on the way down to the

Do of Malkhut, we can see how the World of Creations works through the atom.

The controlling factor of the upper face, however, is crucial, and here we perceive that the over-all design which is focussed in Tiferet belongs, not just to the essential nature locked up in the DNA of the cell, but to the organism as a whole. While atoms and their substructure are vital in the building and dynamic of the body something larger in the nature of an over-all plan, generates the DNA coding and creates the kind of body you and I possess. This, since the upper face of the body is the lower face of the psyche, indicates that we create our own physical vehicle, the yeziratic World forming the clay of our bodies prior to birth and in continual modification, until death separates the lower face of the asiyyatic Tree from the upper face of Yezirah. This we will discuss later.

Tiferet then is more than the nervous system. It is also the essence of each of us, embodied in every one of our millions of cells. From this one may see how, in spite of many years' separation, one recognizes old friends, even though they may bear little resemblance to how we remember them at school or college. Tiferet, like all the other sefirot, is much larger and deeper than even many Kabbalists imagine. Just when one thinks one has got it contained, it opens up another cosmic vista. This goes on for a life time.

Returning to the body, it is apparent that any physical or chemical process is associated with atomic, and therefore electrical, activity as elements lock, and unlock their bonds, either in massive energy-matter exchanges, or in minute operations deep inside the genes. This electrical activity develops electric currents, and these have been known about for a long time. More recently the organs of heart and brain have been observed to generate electricity. So much so that modern medicine uses the phenomenon to measure abnormal functioning against normal patterns. The brain, for instance, has distinct rhythms of waves passing over its cerebral cortex and these can be clearly differentiated into large and slow, at the rate of one to four a second, to much smaller faster waves which run concurrently. These electrical charges originate in the cells of the brain and relate to the state of the person. Some frequencies amplify when the organism is asleep, while others, like the alpha waves of eight to thirteen a second, are never affected by slumber. Such waves, however, can be affected by activity in special areas of the brain, such as the visual zone which dampens them. These and many other rhythms are not only due to information arriving via the nervous system from the senses to their terminal cells, but to the periodic discharge of the cells themselves.

It has been observed that a normal brain operates electrically as an integrated unit, and no doubt this is true of the whole body if the analogy of the Tree is true. It has also been observed that to electrically stimulate a part of one of the motor regions of the brain makes the relevant limb move without conscious volition. All this suggests that besides the chemical connections there are electrical ones also. This brings us to the Kabbalistic fact which has already been stated, that each world has a complete Tree of its own. This principle is carried over, in that the asiyyatic Tree has its miniature Trees on each of its own sub-worlds. Thus the beriatic World of the physical body has all the sub-sefirot relevant to it.

In the kingdom of the atoms the left and right pillars are present, as is the column of equilibrium. One of the physicists' problems of the sub-atomic world is easily resolved. On the column of form, we have the particle theory, and on the column of force the wave conception. Between them is the axis of equilibrium which makes them both equally true, depending on which theory you apply. In our example of electric communication, the Hod of this minor beriatic Kingdom is the responsible sefira. Other sefirot can also be identified. For instance the constriction of Gevurah pulls the electrons inward while the dynamic expansion of the Hesed principle keeps them from collapsing into the nuclear mass. Nezah keeps them orbiting, while Hod, as varying velocity and distance, communicates to the atomic Tiferet internal and external data. Binah governs the universal form of atoms and Hokhmah their energy. The central column poses an interesting question, because here is a physical void, perhaps just a great idea holding the atom, even the whole Universe, together in equilibrium.

Electrical activity of any kind generates a magnetic field. This is easily observed in the case of the pattern made by iron filings round an electrically charged bar. The same is true of the living body, although this is not so easy to establish. Back as far as the eighteenth century Mesmer published a paper on animal magnetism but this, with his practice of hypnotism, fell into disrepute with orthodox medicine. Much later, work done by Kilner produced a screen of cyanine dye through which could be viewed the fields round the living body, and while the American military have no professional interest in such, till quite recently, suspect ideas they have produced instruments which can detect and visualize the infra-red field surrounding a hidden soldier in the jungle, or at night. While this is not magnetism, it demonstrates that what many people instinctively sense and use every day has, as yet, no reliable instruments to prove scientifically its existence. This brings forward the simple question, 'Did the radio Universe exist before the radio telescope?' We leave the conventional scientist to answer the questions that the answer raises.

Body magnetism has been known about for a long time. Most sensitive people are aware of it in their relationship with others. Some people disturb one by their very proximity while others harmonize by their presence. This phenomenon is not just physical appearance, nor is it perceptive by the ordinary sense organs. It is in the area around the person's body extending out in all directions, more intense when close, less so at greater distances. Many ancient traditions have diagrams of this body envelope of force. Some even draw the flow line, which appears not unlike the force lines round a bar magnet. It is said that this field is characteristic of the living and is not present in a corpse. It is observed by those who have studied it in detail, that the hand is a particular focus and also the head, with various centres accentuated by directed attention. In bad health this aura, as it is called by one school of thought, is dull like a failing magnet's field. From the Kabbalist's view, the magnetic field probably relates to the upper face of the body Tree and obviously permeates the

lower as all the higher worlds do down the Tree. Indeed, it is said
that many unclairvoyant people can sense the field up to two or
three inches from the skin.

More important than the proof in scientific fact is the implication of the phenomenon. Magnetic fields indicate power and
order. An iron bar will not develop such a field without its
internal structure either being aligned at the molecular level or
when an electric current passes through it. On the Tree we have
the formalization of Binah and the cosmic input of Hokhmah.
These two in conjunction with Tiferet generate the bio-electro-
magnetic field. As part of an organic body they in fact form and
vitalize a distinct organism. Being the lower face of the yeziratic
or psychological body it follows that this field has a particular
configuration in structure and power. In terms of the beriatic
World it actually creates an invisible body composed of particles
and energy, the two sefirotic poles, or pillars, generating atoms
which form the basis of our molecular biology—that is, the
DNA matrix of our cellular organism. This again brings about the
question of 'Which came first?'.

At conception, the male and female cells unite, the Father
Hokhmah with the Mother Binah. From this union springs the
division of cells. These are formed in the yeziratic World out of
the principles outlined in Beriah. While it is seen that the lower
face manifests the cellular body in Asiyyah, it is obvious that the
mother's body is merely supplying the material and energy during
gestation, until the child has completed its descent down the Tree,
into a complete coat of vegetable and animal skin.

One is led to suspect that the complete form is already in
existence in the yeziratic World and that one grows up and into
one's psychological body. Watching children and guessing what
they are going to be like as adults is a parent's favourite game, and
while many have wishful thoughts, it is apparent quite early on
what the character of the child is likely to be. This is the Essential
Nature showing through, that is, what one is born with, as
against that which is acquired by education and custom. This
Essential Nature is transmitted from the Tiferet of the psychological Tree, that is the Keter of the body, to the essence of every

new cell. The soul is sown in the body through the asiyyatic Tiferet, every cell generated expressing that person's particular being. At the centre of this great triad is the invisible sefirah of Daat. From a strictly bodily view it is the Knowledge inherent in the beriatic World both in the whole electro-magnetic organism and in the atoms of the DNA code chains. It is the focus of the unmanifest paths coming from Hokhmah and Binah and is the place where the living creature, whatever it is, has its body consciousness. This is the body's knowledge of itself. As the simultaneous Yesod of the yeziratic Tree it is the Foundation of the World of Formations, which hints at its function in the asiyyatic World. Here is the sense of ego, the awareness in the electromagnetic field, or in clinical terms, the activity of the brain and nervous systems of the body. Be it a cat, tiger or man, this is the everyday physical consciousness, the focal centre of knowing the world about them. Here a cat, a tiger or a man build a foundation for experience, implanting in the brain thousands of memories, which slowly construct a cat's view of his backyard, a tiger's territory in the jungle, or a man's vision of the world. This picture is worked on during one's childhood and later education. It is stored in the myriad little cell circuits in the skull, and for most people this is the universe they live in. For others, more adventurous souls, the inner world of Yezirah is also intriguing. There the upper Tree, like Jack and the beanstalk story, when climbed, opens out into another realm. But before we reach that strange and fascinating kingdom we have one more physical rung to climb.

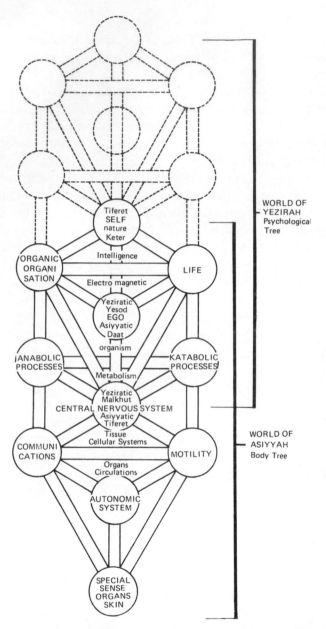

BODY AND PSYCHE

Each World has its own Tree. Here we see how the asiyyatic body and the yeziratic psyche are related by the interleaving of the upper and lower faces of their respective Trees. This makes a chain of connections until the Trees are separated by physical death.

9. *Azilut*

Binah, the Great Mother, Hokhmah the Great Father and Keter the Source of All, compose the supernal triad. In the Tree of the body this is the azilutic triangle of Asiyyah. Here is the archetype for what any Tree manifests in its lower worlds. In this case the triad relates the Heavenly Man to mankind, Adam Kadmon being the unmanifested seed of seeds out of which the beriatic World *pure spirit* creates the basic model of the human race. In terms of our body Tree we have the same module but in the relative physical organism. The source of this cellular structure is Nature who during our stay on Earth, supplies us with the necessary equipment. As such, Nature is the Keter of the Asiyyatic Tree.

From the point of view of physics, beyond the waves and particles of the atomic world, lies nothing tangible. Beneath the most minute speck of matter and flicker of energy—is void. Nothing fills it that science can detect although Divine presence is manifest in the Order of the Universe. Azilut is the realm of causes. From the supernal triad down is the world of effects. Science may track back to the margin of nothingness but it cannot even begin to explain Azilut. Even the metaphysician has much difficulty in spite of his longer range capacity and intuitive scope, and the mystic who has experience of Azilut can never describe his realization. So we have here a problem in that whenever we examine the Azilut World we can merely speculate, unless we are, by grace, granted direct cognition of that supernal kingdom, and this, alas, can never be accomplished by reading or writing books, a mostly Hod exercise. Accepting the following exploration as a Hod exercise, let us consider the supernal triad of the physical body.

The Azilutic Triad is composed on the active side by Hokhmah called Life, in this context. Life is the dynamic, the vital principle that activates the female seed egg in fertilization. In this fusion between it and Binah or Organic Organization, if it be the Will of God passing down through Keter (Nature in this Tree), the male and female pillars are brought into union. While before they stood in equilibrium on either side of the Tree, now in conception they are joined and must work out their creative interaction in the descent down the Lightning Flash to the Do of Malkhut where they will reach equilibrium again.

In our example of the physical body, Nature is the Crown and therefore all the aspects of living beings on Earth contained in Keter, must be present in the body that will develop out of the conception born of the union of the Great Triad, and all fathers and mothers. Mankind, in spite of its loaded name, is half female, not only in that every generation has roughly half of each sex, but in that every man contains his feminine side and every woman her masculine. This is clinically evident in the body in the un-developed opposite sexual characteristics. There are cases of course in which both sides are equally present not only psycho-logically but in physical fact. This leads to the speculation that the unfolding Tree of gestation, or the yeziratic Tree of the psyche, is in a state of imbalance, the female pillar being emphasized in the homosexual and vice versa in the lesbian. This is certainly borne out in the characteristic wit and bite of a strong Hod and Gevurah —Oscar Wilde and many other homosexuals, great and small, exhibit this side of their Trees, plus their meticulous concern with form.

From a clinical standpoint the fertilization of the female egg by the male sperm demonstrates the scale of Azilut. While the dance of the chromosomes determines the sex and carries over the characteristics of both parents, these are merely asiyyatic vehicles for a cosmic operation. It has been said that the conception of a child involves more energy than that evoked by an atomic explosion. The tiny event, apparently only too easily accomplished, can occur because of myriads of lives extending back to the first human beings, and, if we believe science, beyond through our primate ancestors to the lowly mammal who was born out of some mutant reptile. This creature lived amongst its cousins, who dominated the earth for millions of years, and they in their turn arose from remote fishy ancestry, which evolved out of the slime of the primeval organic soupy sea. All these creatures, including the first primitive cell, are present within us now, in that we contain the processes of all those kingdoms, indeed the salt sea itself in our saline blood. We may be able to walk about the dry land but we take the ocean with us inside our skins. Here is all Nature—Keter, the source of our organic existence.

From Nature comes the template of our body. All living creatures contain life and organic organization. These are manifested in the active processes of vitality and the passive organization of the form of a creature. The cell, the simplest living organic being, has its bio-metabolism and the structure to contain it. Should either energy exchange cease or the semi-solid form be disrupted impeding circulation, the cell dies. This is equally true of the sophisticated body of a man, whether in old age he dies of a too low vitality level, or is killed in his physical prime by a bullet destroying one of his major organs.

This relationship of force and force is archetypal in Hokhmah and Binah and operates throughout Nature. We see, for instance, the Binah form at work in the digestive canal, a common factor throughout the animal kingdom. Another Binah operation is that all living creatures have some form of nervous system and every species a method of reproduction. This is archetypal, that is, even beyond the species prototype of the great Goat or great Wolf, those invisible creatures upon which all goats and wolves are modelled.

Taking a Binah example in detail, we can see how the mammalian skeleton is a standard model. Certainly in each species the spine may be longer and the legs bent in a different way, but they are the same essential structure. The skull of a cat, a rat, a horse and even a man may appear to be vastly different, but it is only a question of elongation and distortion by Nature, who pulls the very plastic two-hundred piece bone kit into various shapes of rib cage, pelvis and skull, etc. The famous vestigal tail in man reveals how Nature, despite her changes of mind during evolution, still has to use the official mammalian outfit. In the horse the story is the same, its front knees are in fact its wrists, while its haunches are its ankle bones. Even the reptile kingdom is subject to the same standard model with the snake's withered leg bones still traceable in the skeleton. Binah is a principle, not a rigid blueprint.

Such a flexible template as the skeleton is, obviously, one of many organic organizations which head the column of form. These Binahric forms manifest down the Lightning Flash through Daat into Creation, which is given its dynamic by the secondary impulse of force coming directly from Life, at Hokhmah and meeting the Flash at Hesed as the ovum begins to multiply. Binah also influences vertically at Gevurah which differentiates cell growth and division under the laws inherent in organic organization. Likewise both Binah and Hokhmah feed into Tiferet the Father and Mother principles controlling the essence of the body Tree through the cellular fabric of the lower face. As recalled this operation lies beyond and within the electro-atomic world of the body's beriah, the Yesod image of Yezirah set out in the unmanifest sefira of the asiyyatic Daat or Knowledge. In this the body as a whole is conceived and known, both in the overseeing ego or Yesod of the psychological Tree, and in every individual atom, molecule and cell of that particular organism.

Hokhmah in the body is Life. This is a powerful principle which like Wisdom, the sefira's English name, is not easily understood. Wisdom comes directly from the Divine. It is so potent that one drop can change the course of a life—or in Asiyyah begin it. Hokhmah is also the potentiality. It contains the purest active principle before it is clothed in form. Before it is locked in the receptivity of Binah, it has every possibility within the context of its world. Life operates through a worm, or a man, as wisdom may come out of a babe as well as a sage. Its force is such that, even in the presence of destruction and death, it surges forward. During times of war it is well known that normal sexual mores break down, with a resultant spate of births and many a man, on the more individual level, on the death of someone close, has found solace for his grief in bed with a woman. This is Nature's way of replenishing the species, the dynamic of Life asserting itself. The post-war growth in the late forties of the birth rate of Britain illustrates this point.

Hokhmah sits directly above Hesed and in the body it is intimately connected with the katabolic processes of releasing energy. If inertia were too great in the body, even with the most rich store of resources, death would soon occur because the organism would quickly burn them up. Movement is vital to Life. After a good rest the body has to use up the potent charge built up overnight. Often one is ejected from bed not by the desire to get up, but by the inability to contain the pressure within the organism.

As an extremely complex mechanism the body has to maintain myriads of interlinking systems in working order. This ranges from the big general circulations down to the molecular operations in the cell. The heart has to pump, the nervous system keep up a flow of electrical and chemical action. The body heat has to be fed and trimmed within very precise limits. All these and many other functions require energy all of which flows from Hokhmah. While it can be argued that every living creature extracts energy from its surroundings, from air, light, water and solid matter, none of these can be converted into useful organic fuel, except by the principle of Life. One may attempt to feed a corpse. It has all the systems, and may have the necessary organic and inorganic materials, but unless it has the vital spark, nothing can ever happen. This spark is Hokhmah which derives its light from Nature.

Nature is Keter on our asiyyatic Tree. Part of the Earth, it is cosmic in scale. Vital to the planet and no doubt the solar system, the biosphere's ecology is a delicately balanced infrastructure and mutual energy exchange system at various levels of plant and animal. Even on a local scale the interdependence can be seen. Destroy or reduce one species and an imbalance occurs over a whole area if not the whole Earth. In Sumatra tigers preyed upon the wild boar, checking its numbers. White hunters came and slaughtered the tiger at one time, for reasons of their own, and as a result the wild boar multiplied. The increased herds needed more food and moved off their normal feeding grounds to attack the palm trees used for collecting the oil. The ravaged plantations died, and the industry dependent on their products closed, putting large numbers of peasants out of work. The people became exceedingly poor, and there followed all the usual social problems that occur when a community's economic structure is faulty. This adversely affected the trade and politics of that country whose instability then contributed to the world scene—all because it may have been fashionable for the local colons to shoot tiger for a season. This gives some idea of the interlinkage of man and Nature. But the bond is in fact even closer, Nature is an integrated whole and, as a part of the earth, adapts to the planet's needs as it evolves within the solar system. The solar system might also be considered as a complete but cosmic organism which is part of a yet larger cosmos of which we know little or nothing. Nature is the earth's sensitive skin for converting what energy and matter the planet draws in, like a living creature, from its surroundings. As a living membrane about ten miles thick the biosphere's constitution is as important to the planet as our skin and sense organs are to us. As each person is a complete Tree of Life, so Nature is in her own right, each order of flora and fauna operating according to the various sefirot and triads.

Man is unique, in that he contains them all, in principle, from the primates down to the smallest bacteria in his gut. Indeed mankind is the partner of Nature and over the long term affects her as a good or bad husbandman. Just as important, however, is the fact that man is the crowning species of evolution, the spearhead of intelligence and consciousness. This may not be true of the vast majority of humanity who live at the moment in the human equivalents of the vegetable and animal kingdom, but it is possible for those who wish, to evolve into the full Adam.

That a man stands on two legs, wears the latest gear and flies by jet everywhere does not make him evolved, or even civilized. His dominating appetite for good food and women makes him a fashionable vegetable, while the power seeking executive, or politician, or fame-searching scientist, or writer, only qualifies for the human jungle. All social activity is animal. Neither good nor bad, its prime concern is that mankind should get on, respect each other's territory and maintain the physical level of the species while the vegetable level feeds and propagates the whole. On these two counts mankind is part of Nature and the body Tree is a manifestation of this organic world. While man is a soul in essence he may, while incarnate in flesh, forget his real origins and indeed live out his whole existence in an animal or vegetable consciousness.

This is why the supernal triad is so important, for here a man may live under the rule of Nature at Keter, or make contact with the Tiferet of his yeziratic Tree. It is seen quite plainly when the body and the psychological Trees are interleaved that the yeziratic Yesod of the ego is the Daat of knowledge of the physical world. Here lives the Natural man. It can also be observed that this superimposed face, when observed by a man from his psyche's Tiferet, comes under his command. As the Keter of Asiyyah he can take himself out of Nature's rule. True, he still has to obey Nature's organic laws, but he has begun to awaken. This grants him the ability to slip out of her net of general law, into a life lived according to individual fate. A man who can place his own will on the Keter of the body Tree changes the title Nature to that of his own Essential Nature. Indeed it was from this sefira his body was born, but as a man, his original source was from the Keter of the yeziratic Tree.

When a person lives and has his consciousness in the yeziratic Tiferet, the body changes from a cage of flesh and passion, into the first of four ladders stretching from Earth to Heaven. This does not mean that the body is evil or even redundant. On the contrary, it becomes a powerful and important instrument. This is the point of physical life, that it is the teaching situation of the soul. Its trials, successes and failures are all material for learning, even suffering a lesson in acceptance or challenge. No life is meaningless. Every human being has the choice of being human, that is to reopen the gates of Eden and return from whence Adam came.

The Psyche

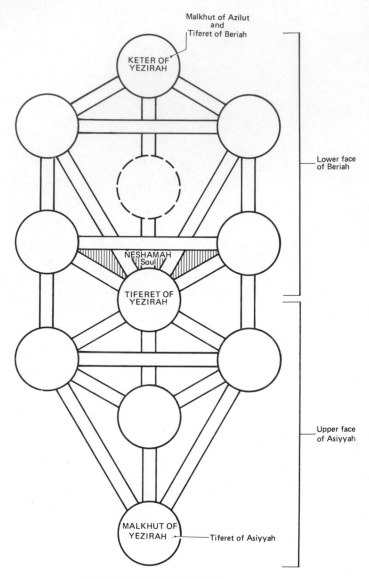

Malkhut of Azilut
and
Tiferet of Beriah

KETER OF
YEZIRAH

Lower face
of Beriah

NESHAMAH
Soul

TIFERET OF
YEZIRAH

Upper face
of Asiyyah

MALKHUT OF
YEZIRAH ── Tiferet of Asiyyah

YEZIRATIC TREE OF THE PSYCHE

Because of the interleaving of the faces and therefore the participation of the upper and lower Worlds, only the Neshama, the triad of the Soul, is truly yeziratic. Note also how the Keter of one World is the Tiferet of the World above, and simultaneously the Malkhut of the World higher still.

10. The Psyche

In man the yeziratic Tree is the psychological body. The psyche might be considered as the invisible part of a living person and that in a man which is his individuality. According to the Kabbalah, like many other ancient traditions, animals and plants have souls, but of a different order to man, who contains both these vitalizing principles in his organic body.

The unseen part of man has been recognized since the remotest of times, as early graves portray, in their often elaborate concern for the after-life of the departed. Mythology is full of tales of the other world, wherein the shades of the dead wander, unable to return to earthly home or people. The folklore of some peoples even considers sleep as the temporary separation of the soul from the body. Death is the final proof, even to the most dim mind, that something alive has left, the silent and still corpse empty as a vacated house.

During the last four thousand years among the more evolved communities much study was carried out on the psyche. This was usually performed by the wise men or priests, who either by long research or visionary glimpses pieced together an anatomy of the psyche. One such early study was Astrology, Alchemy another, both being extremely complex systems of psychology in the theoretical and practical fields. Kabbalah is another.

In later times the great religions included in their scope these ancient teachings on the nature of the inner man. In the West and Middle East Judaism, Christianity and Islam viewed the soul in much the same way, although each tradition modified its approach according to its needs. On the individual level each tradition,

moreover, had a method whereby every type of person was
taught in the language of his own particular nature, so that a man
of action grew to become acquainted with his psyche through
deeds, a man of the heart through devotions, and an intellectual
through the contemplation of ideas. These techniques brought the
committed disciple into conscious contact with his psychological
world, that is, his yeziratic body.

Some practices, for instance that of the Christian monk, were
designed expressly to eliminate the outer distractions of Asiyyah.
The heavy cowl of the monk's habit, was to shut off sensual
diversions, as was the simplicity of his sheltered life and environment. Indeed the same daily monastic routine was created to
induce the body into a natural rhythm which allowed the psyche
to be totally free for its concentrated effort to ascend from ego to
what is called in Christian Kabbalah the 'Christ centre', or Tiferet
of the yeziratic Tree. Many traditions also apply a multiple
technique which does not require withdrawal from the world.
This uses Asiyyah to advantage as a teaching situation. Both the
Islamic Sufis and the Jewish Hassidim have numerous stories in
which men in the full business of life give and receive insights into
the nature of the psyche and its development. One such example
was of the young man who on seeking out a great master discovered him surrounded by much wealth. Rejecting the sage as
corrupted by the world the young man then went to a teacher of
considerably lesser repute who lived in poverty. After stating why
he had not placed himself under the great man's tutelage, the lesser
master said this was the very reason why the teacher was great. He
was unaffected by wealth, whereas for himself, he had to live in
poverty because he had not yet acquired such detachment. This is
psychological thinking with quite precise criteria. Another quote
will illustrate the point. 'Knowledge is better than wealth. You
have to take care of wealth; whereas knowledge takes care of
you.' This statement is concerned with matters of the soul and
has a whole philosophy behind its loaded implication. In Kabbalah
the Tree of Life underlies many of its maxims and observations
and much of the Bible and its teaching on correct conduct is
related to its frame of references. But first we must set out the

psyche on the Tree so that we see the second stage of our examination of the whole of man.

What is the psyche in Tree of Life terms? It is composed of the upper face of the asiyyatic body and the lower face of the beriatic world, with the triad of the Neshamah, the individual soul, situated between and centred on the Tiferet of the yeziratic organism. The whole Tree is the intermediary, linking the World of Creation to the realm of physical action, with its Keter in the Malkhut of Azilut.

In ordinary life we cannot perceive the psyche directly although we may see it through the moving forms it expresses in the body. A man may hide behind his clothes and manner but he still reveals in these very ephemeral devices the nature of the person beneath. From a very early age we learn to recognize friend and foe by signs and feelings, as our rudimentary animal psyche responds to family and social situations. Later, as the middle part of the Tree awakens, relationships between individual people become more important than gang or tribal affinities and antagonisms. Here can begin the growth of the soul embedded in the psyche as self-insight evolves into a working connection with the upper part of the psychological organism.

Most of us live half in Asiyyah and half in Yezirah. This is because we are only conscious in our ego, which is situated in the lower face of the psyche, and the upper face of the body. We hover between two worlds, the inner and outer, and drift to and fro depending on which claims the attention. If it is a stomach ache it is the body; if a personal problem we retreat into a shadow image world beyond which lies a vast subliminal circus of thoughts and feelings. Behind the yeziratic Hod and Nezah is another realm of ever-moving imagery, from which day and night dreams, and sometimes unknown drives, urge us on to perform like puppets. Even beyond this psychological metabolism we sense, however dimly, a distant realm, wherein memories that are not our own, nor in our personal experience, reside. These objective pressures are influences that cannot be seen, invisible laws that overview our lives. Such powerful principles are sensed in the mind of a people and are reflected in the deep appeal of its lore and symbols. The return of the Jews to Israel after two thousand years is an illustration of such inherent folk memory.

Psychology is studied by modern science but much of this is confined to the Malkhut, Hod and Nezah triad of Yezirah which is concerned with instinctive mental mechanics based on sample observation of people in work and social situations. However, some schools do go deeper than the animal and vegetable sides of man. The Jungians, for example, acknowledge and explore the soul and spiritual aspects of man and have rediscovered in their study many of the conclusions come to by ancient researchers, for whom the old gods embodied the same significance as the theory of archetypes.

From the view of the Kabbalah our task is to outline the structure of the psyche. Taking the premise that the psychological body of man is based on the same design as his physical body we shall begin our study at the yeziratic Malkhut, and climb slowly up the second Tree within man.

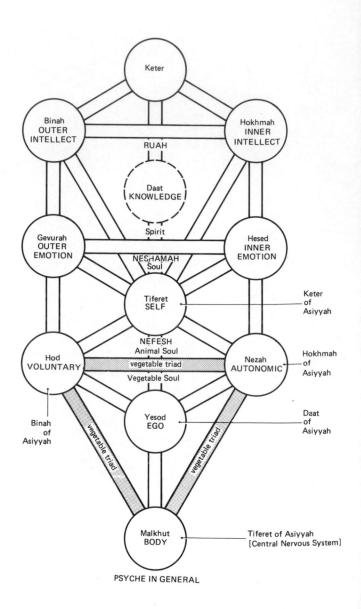

PSYCHE IN GENERAL

11. The lower great triad of Hod, Nezah and Malkhut

In the plates of the psyche interleaved with the body we see that the Malkhut of Yezirah is also the Tiferet of the asiyyatic organism. In clinical terms this sefirah is the central nervous system. As the Tiferet of the body the sefirah oversees all its functions and acts as the collection and distribution point of the upper and lower faces of the physical Tree. From the view that it is also the Malkhut of the psychological body it can be seen that the psyche is anchored to the physical organism with the yeziratic Hod and Nezah sharing the same Triad with the asiyyatic Binah and Hokhmah, so that the psycho-organic processes blend and focus on the shared Daat-Yesod sefirah in the centre of this complex (see plate opposite). Down the path from the asiyyatic Keter comes Will which may manifest in two ways. Directly from Keter, through Daat, if it operates as the physical upper face or through Yesod in the lower psychological face. In the case of a totally body-orientated man or animal, Nature's Will is Keter. In that of a man in touch with his yeziratic Tiferet or self, Yesod or the ego, acts as the intermediary between the two Trees. For most of us the situation is variable, our state of consciousness ever changing as we oscillate between the dominance of the body and the rulership of our psyche. Yesod for us is ego, the servant trying to play at master.

The Malkhut of the human Yezirah, for simplicity's sake, may be considered to be the brain. Composed of about ten billion neurone cells it might be thought of as the physical location of the mind. The mind, that is consciousness in the ordinary sense, is Knowledge of the body and Foundation of the psyche. The brain, an extraordinary organization at the centre of the nervous system, is the physical monitor, memory bank and viewing screen for both the body and the psyche. If we cut ourselves, the brain (via the nervous system) is informed and indicates the area of the injury, while simultaneously notifying our consciousness. Likewise if we are trying to solve a problèm, such as trying to unscrew a stiff bottle top without an opener, the brain will flash up suggestions from related topics stored in memory circuits composed of groups of cells set in electro-chemical patterns at a previous date.

We can imagine no images of what we have not seen. Even the most fantastic fiction has to be based on what we have known. Mythology is made up of fabulous beasts but they are all no more than a patchwork made from creatures we are familiar with. It must also be remembered that when we look at an object the optical image is converted into asiyyatic electro-chemical signals before being unscrambled in the brain as a readable yeziratic image for the mind. From this it can be seen how the Malkhut-Tiferet brain is an interchange junction participating in the physical and psychological worlds.

Whereas Descartes placed the seat of the soul in the pineal gland, it might be safer to assume that the psychological body permeates the whole of the physical body. Certainly it is true to say that even if a leg is cut off the brain still considers it there and has sensory reaction in a non-existent foot, but this is due rather to the mechanics of the nervous system than consciousness. Consciousness is of another order and while it is tied to the body and uses the brain, it is not subject to its laws in spite of the limits of cerebral imagery. All the images we use in our minds, may be based on the sensual world, but this does not mean that what they are, is the end of the event. We are at the foot of the yeziratic Tree, the World of Formations whose language is symbolism and allegory. At this point it is well to remember the Kabbalistic idea that reality may be comprehended literally, allegorically, metaphysically and mystically. In Yezirah the mind, or Yesod, uses the experience of the physical world as a vocabulary to explain what is happening in the body of the psyche. This is why Yesod is called the Foundation, and it is based on the knowledge gained in the world. With this in view the workings of the mind and the brain begin to take on another dimension.

An example of this is when we watch a western movie; the body knows that it is sitting in a dimmed cinema with light and dark shadows flickering on the screen before us. Yet simultaneously, as the eye not only reads the image as a flat plane, the mind accepts the notion of being in a sun-drenched Texas street in which two men are facing each other for a shoot-out. The physical situation is irrational but the body is cold, tense and fearful that the hero is going to be gunned down. As the villain falls dead the whole cinema sighs with relief; their adrenalin level begins to drop as the heart slows and the muscles relax. All this is illusion but the mind has accepted it sufficiently to profoundly disturb the body. The power of imagery, the language of Yezirah, is enormous and in this way operates through quite mundane situations to affect our actions. The significant gesture or expression of a man reveals what is going on inside him and we all know the impact of a loaded throw-away line. Comment is all the more potent when dressed in metaphor. This is the world of Yezirah using ordinary memory and associations stored in the brain to indicate a psychological state.

The yeziratic Malkhut then, is a clearing house, a translating unit and a depository of keyboards the psyche can play upon. It is the place where the physical essence of a person is manifest, both in the heart of the cell and in the body built out of essentially the same organic bricks. Here is the motor area that the Will can manipulate, and the zone wherein incoming experience can be conveyed from Asiyyah to Yezirah. Logical, organized beyond imagination, the fact remains that the brain can be led to believe in, and create, its own illusions. This ability to operate in the upper and lower realms is its strength and weakness, for, while a man may live an outwardly ordered life he may be inwardly confused, even dead. In reverse the opposite may be true of the mentally unhinged who live totally in yeziratic illusion without any connection with, or concern for, their asiyyatic bodies or outside world. As always balance is the correct formula, the brain and mind in working marriage, each attending to its different world, but both involved in the interleaving of the body and psyche.

Whereas Malkhut, the Kingdom of the brain, is a physical formation composed of earth, water, air and fire, or tissue, blood, air and electrical field, the Hod and Nezah of the yeziratic Tree are not, even though it is true to say that both sefirot are simultaneously the Binah and Hokhman of the body.

Taking Hod first let us see how the psychological Tree intermarries with the physical on the passive pillar. The bodily Binah as organic organization is concerned with the form aspect of the body. As the prime formulating factor it sets out the constraints and connections within a complete system, be it man, dog or ant. Moreover the asiyyatic Binah carries within its brief, not only the grand design of the creature, but every relevant principle, through the atomic, molecular, and cellular building blocks, that will form the organism. This gives us a lead into the simultaneous operation of Hod as the superimposed yeziratic sefirah. As the Hodian overlay on the Binahic design it has an inherent pattern of connections for communications. This not only operates through the obvious paths of the nervous system, and bloodstream, but also in chains of chemical reaction, and currents within electro-magnetic fields. This means that the body as a whole is brought into a total system of relationships. Thus, for instance, the sugar level in the blood is maintained, excess salt is rejected and a person standing too long in one position will shift his weight onto the other leg. By virtue of the communications between the various energies and types of material, the body is sustained as a biological machine until death, which terminates communication and circulation and so disrupts all the inter-dependent systems. This overall communication is the essence of Hod and vital for Life.

The most common name for Hod is Splendour, but it may also be translated from its Hebrew root as 'Reverberation'. In both Asiyyah and Yezirah this has many meanings. Hod also means to resonate, resound and echo. This suggests that an impulse is received and then reflected either back to source or elsewhere. The phenomenon may be recognized in sound and light, in the reverberation of the tympanic membrane of the ear, or in the arc of a rainbow, which reflects the sun's spectrum through millions of falling raindrops. Reverberation may also be found not only in atoms, molecules and cells but in places. Anyone who has been in an old theatre playhouse late at night, in a silent auditorium knows it is not at all silent, but reverberates from the waves set up by thousands of audiences and performances. To the insensitive person this phenomena may appear irrational but it is recognized by most of the human race in their respect for holy places which carry some kind of resonating charge. Indeed in any place where human activity has occurred with sufficient intensity, this yeziratic echo is easily detected by the sensitive Hod of our psyche. Such people as clairvoyants, that is genuine ones, have the faculty of Hod so well developed that they can sometimes see, or hear (clairaudient), the resonating patterns of events that happened long ago, but which are still present within the force field of a particular place. In this case they form with their yeziratic Yesod, a picture which describes what in fact is a slowly fading after-image of an event rather like when we shut our eyes and yet still see the outlines of a bright window we were looking through. This is reverberation.

Psychologically Hod is the communications aspect of the psyche. Operating through the asiyyatic Binah it serves the body as a sensor and responsor. However, being part of the psyche it can also inform the physical organism of the intentions of Yezirah. Out of this come the voluntary processes. The most obvious example is the manipulations of limbs and the delicate pressures of the fingers when controlling a tool. Hod selects the groups of brain cells to be called on when thinking out a problem. It is likewise responsible for the direction of our attention, be we driving a car, or listening to a story. Hod takes care of counting our money, and the stimulus of spending it, for it loves excitement and anything new. This relates to the learning process which files new data along the path towards Nezah where it is continually repeated in the brain until needed. Hod of course is the eye, but it also transmits as well as receives messages, as any glance between lovers shows. Reverberation occurs in touch and smell, but it also responds to abstract ideas that literally switch it on. Geometry, mathematics, any subject that is complex yet ordered and precise, affects Hod profoundly, although if it is not repeated by Nezah it fades away like an echo. This decaying reverberation is absolutely necessary for to sustain continually any sound or sight would not allow anything new to enter. We would be blinded and deaf for life by our first images and noises if this were the case. Hod echoes, then fades, although it may pass on to store useful reverberations in the body or the psyche.

The Hod of Yezirah works in the same way as in Asiyyah but with a different materiality. As formation is the vehicle of this world one can see how it might operate. Television is an illustration. Here the image of the screen continually changes form by virtue of a series of electrical reverberations which moment by moment slightly alter their configuration and convey a picture which reminds one perhaps of anger, or love, even the stillness of peace. These are yeziratic communications, every gesture, word and scene carefully designed by the director to set the viewers' Hod moving. This, however, is not enough, because pure sensation becomes dulled, and eventually boring. Even the most sense-stimulating show, if it is nothing else, is switched off unless there is a build-up of situation and meaning. This is supplied by Yesod, which retains an image of the whole story for the mind, and Nezah which reinforces the drama with its active power. No programme holds the attention for long if one of these three sefirot is missing, neither would our will to live remain, without the continuity link of Yesod and the drive and desire of Nezah.

Nezah means eternity or repetition. In the asiyyatic body the same sefirah is Hokhmah or the dynamic impulse of Life. This powerful principle on the physical level is the driving force behind the organism, the active input from the Keter of Nature. On the yeziratic Tree as Nezah it performs the task of repeating and sustaining both physical and psychological patterns. In the body it operates from the atomic level, through the molecular to the organic and physical cycles. In the psyche it is all the instinctive and involuntary process of both Trees. Placed opposite Hod and completing the great lower yeziratic face with the Malkhut–Tiferet sefirot it adds the active force to the flow of the paths in this asiyyat level of the yeziratic body. Because of the interleaving of the Trees at this point, Nezah plays an important part in the releasing of energy, both in the body, and psyche. As the last active sefirah in the upper Tree, and the first active in the lower, its vitality level is crucial to the whole man. A person with a malfunctioning Nezah has little stamina. His desires are weak, and he has no drive in his physical or psychological life. Every organism has to have a pressure of energy to work from, and call on in case of emergency. In time of danger the lowest of animals can muster great strength and speed, and even the delicate intellectual, when he needs extra effort to pass an examination, calls on Nezah. This is accomplished by the flow of energy across to Hod. Nezah can be broadly named the instinctive mind in Yezirah. Its qualities include attraction and repulsion. It is the sefirah of desire. When man meets woman there is a distinct reaction—sometimes of acceptance and at others rejection. It is rarely indifferent. As an observer on any bus or train will note, the game is continuous although it may not be any more than eye contact.

Such activities are instinctive and most positive. When a man who has been ill begins to notice his nurses it is a sign that he is on the way to recovery. This is Nezah, traditionally associated by non-Judaic Kabbalists with the goddess Venus. Many find this female symbol odd on the active pillar, but consider the atmosphere at a party; the presence of Venus is very positively apparent in the negotiations between the sexes and it is by no means passive, especially among the women, who dress and make up as part of a decidedly active campaign to attract men. Perhaps the phenomenon of spring will illustrate the point further. Each May in the northern hemisphere, as Nature adorns herself for the summer, literally millions of young men and girls become attached to each other. This occurs, and has occurred, for thousands of springs, ever repeating the eternal love situation. Here is Nezah embodied in the symbol of Venus, who recurs as the ideal in each youthful generation, be it in Botticelli's paintings or the top model girl in the glossy fashion magazines of today. All the images used in advertising are repetitions, the female legs and busts, and handsome male shoulders and hair styles, designed to arouse desire, calculated to set the yeziratic Nezah and the asiyyatic Hokhmah moving. Moreover, it works because most of mankind lives entirely in the vegetable triad of Hod, Nezah and Malkhut and so high boots, big hats, leather pants and miniskirts or whatever fashion moves people into action, are the tools of Nature; in Kabbalistic terms Hod, which loves novelty, is fed by Nezah which desires to be attractive, adorns Malkhut, the body. Neither good nor bad, it is interesting to observe that without the power of Nezah life could not continue and would be incredibly dull. As Nezah could be considered the repetitive input principle in the body so it is in the psyche. As the instinctive aspect of the mind it accepts what it likes and rejects what it finds unpleasant. It also circulates through the repetitions within the brain cell complexes, learned facts supplied by Hod. By practice and repetition Nezah can be made to accept a discipline—indeed, preliminary army training works on this principle, so that a soldier performs actions without consciously thinking. It is the same in education. No doubt in this book on the Kabbalah many ideas are strange and disagree with those that have been previously learned while in some cases they are actually repugnant. This is the power of Nezah. When a new pattern has been formed it circulates between Hod, Nezah and Yesod and any intruding idea that does not concur with the concept will be repulsed, while those close or akin to the outlook are attractive, and quickly assimilated. The element of desire is not exclusively body-orientated.

Another way of looking at Nezah is to examine what one continually thinks about and is drawn to. This will also indicate what one is repelled by. These motivations, for or against, are Nezahian and point out an inherent predisposition, coming from one's body-type. Man can be divided into roughly three physical types, the doer, the feeler and the thinker. These are quite distinct from ego-types which will be discussed later. The body-type is the physical approach one uses so that, for example, one man in a problematic situation will want to act, while another will try to think out a solution. Both these reactions are instinctive. The natural thinker may not in fact know anything about calculus or

Plato, but he will be curious to know how a thing works, or what would happen, before any action is considered. The instinctive feeler would possess insight and in a tight situation would generate an '*esprit de corps*' that would make connection between the thinker and doer possible. These types may well be created in the Hokhmah of the asiyyatic triad, which manifests in the Body psyche sefirah of Nezah. This would follow in the descent of the creative Lightning Flash down the Asiyyatic Tree during gestation. Such a physique would have the corresponding Nezah in its psyche.

Nezah then, is the instinctive part of the psychology. In essence our habits, it has likes and dislikes, but can be trained in conjunction with Hod, to instruct Malkhut directly, or through the paths that are focussed on Yesod. Its function is to bring power both into the body and mind, to maintain that vitality and sustain those mental mechanics, emotions, and real intellectual activity, that may be passed down from the upper Tree, into the ordinary consciousness of the ego in Yesod. As a direct participator in the body processes, it also takes care to preserve the physical vehicle, both by involuntary reflex in the psyche, and in the body, as any experience of a near car accident demonstrates. There, one's thinking is totally instinctive and overrides the trained reflexes of a normal situation. This brings us to the realization that the whole of this great bottom triad of Nezah, Hod and Malkhut is concerned with just living, that is operating as a self-preserving organism, with no particular need for deep thought or profound emotion. This is the lowest operational level of the psyche and might be considered the vegetable part of the yeziratic Tree. Indeed it has become manifestly literal, if one remembers that the bottom of the triad is completed by Malkhut which doubles as the asiyyatic brain and central nervous system, which do in fact grow and decay under the laws of vegetable matter.

Here we have in an undeveloped human the psyche of a person who searches like a plant only for sustenance and security. Such a man will be content to stay rooted in his village or work until he retires on his pension. He will not be interested in the animal need of ambition, of doing well, competing with or surpassing his peers. To breed a family will suffice. His contemporaries at the office, work bench, in his club or a pub will regard him as the salt of the earth, always the same, never passionate about any issue, accepting even war as a temporary disruption of his slow rhythm. The person who lives by this triad alone is vegetable man, with no particular desire for personal evolution, and there have been billions of them over the generations of mankind who plant and sow, make and serve humanity without complaint, maintaining farms, and shops, and now factories and services, with no particular interest beyond surviving in relatively congenial surroundings, just as a flower might in the desert or forest. All of us have this vegetable triad within us and it is our choice to be a plant or not. Neither good nor bad, everything has its place. Without such a kingdom the planet and mankind would die.

This great triad, however modest, is the first level of psychic intelligence. On death, when the psyche and the body separate, its field force, called by some the etheric body and by Kabbalists the Zelem or image remains for a while before it decays. In the case of immediately post-death apparitions it does happen that some sensitive people actually perceive this body field through their own great triad and visualize it with their Yesod. The same case may occur with ghosts, the vegetable husk of the psyche, perhaps earthbound by a long or highly charged state of love or hate remaining, but as a slowly dissolving psychic shell. The act of exorcism working from the beriatic World erases the configuration like a great wind blowing a dark puddle away. This gives us a glimpse of a fifth world known to the Kabbalist as the Kellippot of the World of Shells. Here is the traditional realm of demons, madness and evil, the refuse and misfits of Creation.

Returning to life, without this great triad we could not live. Our physical existence depends on the flow of its paths. From Nezah to Malkhut flows the active powerful, rhythmic force of life, from Hod to Malkhut the constant reception of data. Between Hod and Nezah the ebb and flow of impressions, both physical and psychological, flower and decay, so that the organism as a whole is in constant checking balance, be it perched on a dangerous rock face half-way up Mount Everest or at a smart

London cocktail party. Both these operations, and all our life situations, require the psycho-body in trim poise, otherwise we might fall asleep or run amok.

Ordinary consciousness is halfway between death and enlightenment and we live most of our lives in the twilight zone between the two. A moment's honest reflection reveals that we exist partly in a constant flickering realm of day-dreams and partly in eating, sleeping and surviving. It is only when we are aroused and enter the animal triad that we feel alive. Alertness and intensity does not belong to the great vegetable triad. Passion has no place in it for it is concerned with the optimum life-maintenance. However, we must never devalue this triad for at the centre of this vital complex is Yesod, the ego-centred Mind that we use as our foundation to view the outer and inner Worlds.

12. *Yesod: the Ego*

Yesod is created by the paths from Hod and Nezah converging on the central column. It is the sefirah of consciousness for the great vegetable triad of Yezirah. It is also Daat for the identical but great triad of Hokhmah, Binah and Tiferet of the upper face of the body Tree. As a dual sefirah it has access to both Asiyyah and Yezirah. Moreover, in the Lightning Flash sequence descending the Tree, this position is an interval in two separate octaves. The upper interval is the asiyyatic Daat, when the supernal triad begins to manifest in Beriah, and is the yeziratic Yesod interval before the Tree is completed in Malkhut.

Dealing first with the Daat of Asiyyah, we have seen how this normally unmanifest sefirah is the knowledge inherent in the chromosomes of the cell and in the body as a whole. Also, that after the fertilization of the ovum the body slowly fills out what appears to be the asiyyatic form of the yeziratic Tree. From this it may be supposed through Daat the developing organism is aware of itself as a single embodied entity, as well as having within it billions of DNA molecules. This sense of separate existence is demonstrated by even quite primitive forms of life. A plant manoeuvres for light, earth and water to survive. It is not interested in its neighbour. A worm does not worry about anything but its own skin. The Yesodic consciousness is body-orientated and forms an image of itself in man and worms.

Situated in the middle of the electro-magnetic field that enlivens the body, the Daat-Yesod consciousness perceives, both physically and psychologically. Physically, it interprets the electro-chemical action within the brain, as different complexes of cells are stimulated. The eye lens, for example, focusses on the retina, and the nerves transmit to the visual area of the brain a series of stimuli that are converted into an image, which is recognized by the Yesod–Daat dual sefirah. Likewise with touch, hearing and smelling—in fact all sensory data, internal or external. Indeed, when we cannot place a sound or smell, we are puzzled, and when a strange unknown ache occurs, which we cannot explain to ourselves, some of us are even distressed until we are told what it is and we can place it.

As part of the electro-magnetic organism this dual Yesod–Daat is measurable on instruments, and a person's psycho-mechanical state can be perceived in electrical charges and discharges of the body. The lie-detector, and the electro-encephalogram, operate on this phenomenon, although the interpretation will be subjective, inasmuch as the tensions revealed may be for many different reasons. A manic-depressive in high phase might well give off the same electrical signals as an artist in the full flood of creation. More important for our interest is the fact that the consciousness of the yeziratic Yesod has a physical aspect, and that it is not only present throughout the body but is focussed into an image-making mind which we call ego.

Yesod means Foundation. A foundation is that which one builds upon and which supports a structure. From the body's view this is quite precise, in that all the cells are based on the knowledge centred in the original combination of the parents' seed cells, which are reproduced throughout the organism. For the psyche the same is true, but in a different world. On birth, the psychological Yesod is in the same state as the body Yesod, that is, an automatic system at its initial stage. During gestation the asiyyatic image container of the body is slowly created out of tissue, then educated to perform its various tasks, to run and preserve the organism like an automatic pilot, while the central nervous system operates on a wider and more flexible scope. At birth, the Yesod of the psyche is in an un-educated state. As a simple consciousness it knows it exists and that it is the receiving screen for impressions of bodily sensations such as cold and hunger. Moreover, from the babe's first breath it begins to collect data about itself and the world outside. Of course, initially it is only concerned with survival, that is if it is committed to living, after the shock of birth. This powerful desire to survive is manifest in the babe's vital need of warmth and food, and its Yesod consciousness soon finds out how to obtain these quickly, by noting certain pleasant sensations and crying for their repetition. Even during the long periods a babe sleeps, Yesod is at work, no doubt becoming yet more acquainted with the body's internal activities. This is borne out by fact.

The moment the babe senses its stomach is empty, or its bowels are full, it shifts from the relatively dull consciousness of sleep, to the alert state of being awake. In Kabbalistic terms, while the whole of the asiyyatic Tree is functioning as an organic machine, the Hod and Nezah of Yezirah alternate in psychological emphasis; the Hod side when the child is awake, the Nezah when asleep, with both feeding in to the Yesod of the great lower triad, whose Malkhut root is in the asiyyatic Tiferet of the body. When sleep is present, Hod closes down on the number of external impressions being received, while Nezah, the instinctive sefirah, continues to maintain and build up the body. On awakening, Hod, via the paths to Malkhut and Nezah, informs Yesod that the body is hungry. The Yesodic consciousness grows brighter, and instructs the body Tiferet, to put the organism into a waking status. This alters the metabolism, already prepared by the cells and organs through the autonomic system which sent the original information on the hungry state of the body. As will be seen it is a complex operation which would need a complete study in itself, because all the paths on the body Tree are involved in the action of waking up.

The act of waking up is most significant because the consciousness of the child is turned outward, as well as inward to its gut and bowels. When awake the babe reaches out, touches, tastes, senses, and takes pleasure in contact with its mother. This is the formation of its first memories, that is, the beginning of the foundation of its psychological life.

From the moment of birth on, a man is gathering and assembling the material for his picture of the world. In the womb, during gestation, the embryonic Yesod is prepared, like a smooth cellular wax ready to be moulded. On birth consciousness is added and the Yesod is activated, the last interval of the octave completed as the consciousness emerges in Malkhut. From then on its attention is turned mostly outward to the world. At first it is only aware of its body. It cries and sucks, always seeking nourishment and comfort, its old supply via the umbilicus having been cut off. Later its awareness begins to widen. It hears external noises, sees moving lights and dark. It is disturbed by them because it has no framework to relate anything to. Slowly, however, its Yesod builds up day by day a primitive cosmology as it files information as to what is unpleasant, like cold, and what is pleasant, like sucking warm milk. Quite soon it begins to recognize the shape of the nipple as the source of its sustenance and slowly composes a tactile picture of the mother's breast. Gradually the alert, but as yet stumbling, consciousness perceives that the great warm, smooth, round being who feeds it, is also a protector from cold and other unpleasant sensations. Day by day the range extends and there begins the process of focussing the eyes, recognizing sounds, such as the mother's voice and smell, and later the immediate environment of the cot which means safety from the strange noises and sights outside.

Throughout babyhood this extending of consciousness continues, the psychological Yesodic foundation being slowly constructed by exploration and experimentation. The rattle thrown from the pram is the discovery of distance and gravity. Everything put in the mouth soon indicates what can and cannot be eaten. On a wider scale glimpses out of the window can be as awe-inspiring as viewing the Himalayas. The earliest memories of the great world always have this sense. My own first conscious memory of looking up into sun-drenched chestnut leaves made a deep impression. Such events all of us can recall and they form, with the minutiae of more ordinary childhood memories, the basis of our world picture.

The child from a poor family has his foundation, and the rich child his, both acting as a framework for their lives—no matter how much a later education might overlay these psychological conditionings. 'Give us a child until the age of seven' says a certain religious order, 'and we have him for life.' Indeed this is true of baby and childhood. The image of life, its quality and environment has a deep and lasting effect. The son of a farmer, and the son of an aristocrat, carry their foundations with them whether they rise or fall in life. All the memories, lessons learnt in family custom, or social mores, are set out in the Yesod of the growing child. Boys watch and copy their fathers. Girls study their mothers. Attitudes and techniques are observed by sons and daughters, in business and the kitchen. The relationship between parents is the model for the children, who often repeat their father or mother's problems as well as skills. Even grandparents give their legacy of background as the distant history of the clan is subliminally taken in by the child and becomes part of its own private folklore. A Scot by the name of Macdonald may not consciously think of himself as such but place him in the presence of a Campbell, the traditional enemy of his clan, and he will find his hackles may rise no matter how sophisticated he may be, or that the massacre of Glencoe took place over two centuries ago. This is the subtle and continuous work of Yesod as the basis of a frame of reference. During childhood we are instilled with the tales of our people's heroes such as King Arthur, George Washington, Sir Francis Drake and Lincoln. While as adults we may disregard them as mythology, men have fought wars over the ideals of such models.

A man brought up in a village has no other criteria. He sees everything in terms of his own experience. Until he breaks out and extends his framework he is contained and imprisoned by its limitation. The world traveller is under the same law. His Yesod may be wider but it is still confined to his personal outlook. He may have travelled the earth over and seen every sight. Yet for all his varied and exciting life he can only see what he wishes to recognize, as do we all. Even the philosopher, for all his cosmic view, can only relate in terms of his particular philosophy. Take him out of his foundation and he is lost.

It will be seen by now that the foundation built up in babies and young children is very important. Just as important is the realization that at birth a babe has no true ego, and that this is constructed day by day by the formation of the foundation, so that by the age of about seven, the end of childhood and the beginning of boy and girlhood, the ego is more or less crystalized. The word ego means 'I'. That is, the sense of 'I'. This is unknown to very young children who have little or no way of relating to the outer world. The sense of 'I' comes with the realization of separation. This occurs as more experience accretes in Yesod. Gradually 'this' and 'that' begins to manifest. Then 'I' and 'that' outside. From this follows the isolation of consciousness as the awareness of being aware dawns. In this the child, now more or less alerted to its body and its relationship to the world outside, sees itself no longer as a total experience including mother, relatives and environment, but as a fast-separating existence, in which a world of its own making, cuts it off from objective reality. A young child, for instance, begins to see toys as possessions. It demands complete attention for itself, sensing that it is not only cut off when the parent is not there, but that perhaps others are consuming its goodies. Whereas love was accepted as the norm as a babe, the boy and girl begin to demand it as a right, in their universe of which they are the centre. A baby is not consciously selfish but a child is, the more it establishes an identity in its Yesod. This is brought about, both by the child itself constructing an image of what it is, and by adults who require it to be all sorts of things, from an expert in social manners to a paragon in scholarship or athletics.

In more so-called primitive societies the same is true, although the ego may be required to concur with slightly differing family customs. This demand by adults brings about a secondary phenomenon which overlays the ego. This is quite precisely called the 'persona', latin for a mask, which is worn both to protect the ego, and carry out certain duties. The ego, as can be observed, is a very vulnerable identity. Constructed on the experience of Yesod, it is itself an artifact. Indeed, the ego is very unsure of its capability, which is why it often over-asserts itself. Direct assault on a man's ego can shatter him for life because his psychological foundations are shaken. Therefore the first line of defence is the mask of the persona, or 'personality' as it is commonly called.

A man acquires many such masks through life. Some, for instance, are acquired early on at school. The English ex-public schoolboy is easily recognized and if he has no confidence in himself he uses his public school manner for protection and attack in the hurly burly of life. Some masks are taken on later, for instance a profession such as medicine gives a man a distinct persona and he will behave in the manner expected of a doctor. Architects, actors and shopkeepers do the same. This persona is expressed in clothes, and jargon—so much so, that often one can recognize a person's job by his professional uniform and mannerisms. One can see this any morning, in the City of London or Glasgow's shipyards. To complicate things, in most people their work and home personalities are quite separate and different, and if the two are brought together socially the ego does not quite know which persona to use. A man may be quite aggressive at work but submissive to his wife. Such a situation is illuminating if it happens to ourselves because we see we are, in fact, made up of many identities. All of these are contained in the ego, which is the nucleus around which the many acquired aspects of a man congregate. These little senses of 'I' are facets of Yesod which, while forming the basis for them, cause them to rise to the surface of consciousness when they are needed. This is an important feature for it explains how a man may possess many masks, a whole repertoire in some cases. It also indicates how a person can be so varied or inconsistent and how he can deceive himself and others. Yesod, for all its structure, is a highly volatile sefirah.

While it is true that the psychological foundation of most people remains consistent throughout life (unless it is changed by a mental breakdown or spiritual advancement) it is for the vast majority, a hotchpotch of childhood observations, school and adolescent formulations, and work and marriage habits. This makes the ego uncoordinated, as is witnessed when the social mores holding a society are destroyed. When a community is under great tension, those with no real sense of ego collapse into a vegetable state, where they just exist to survive. Others with strong foundations, be it a deep belief or a strongly held conviction, remain stable. In German concentration camps, it was noted that normally stable middle-class personalities collapsed very quickly, because their egos were mostly outwardly supported by pleasant social customs and physical security, whereas religious and politically committed prisoners survived well, and with dignity, in spite of the inhuman conditions.

Ego not only has its frontal shield of the persona which is both a bridge and a barrier, it also has its hind part. Those experiences and aspects that a man does not like about himself accumulate on what one might call the dark side of the ego-moon of which the persona is the bright face presented to the world. This shadow lies between Yesod and the Tiferet or the Self of the yeziratic Tree. The path running between these sefirot is called by Kabbalists 'Honesty' and the name and the path reveal many implications. This will be dealt with in more detail later.

Ego then is the psychological Foundation of a man. It is created by his experience, and forms round his everyday consciousness an image of what he imagines he is like, partly created by what he has seen, and partly by how others have treated him. He naturally reveals to the world what he considers the most favourable aspects of his ego, while concealing, sometimes even to himself, the darker aspects. All these are contained in Yesod, which, besides being the background of his knowledge of himself, is also the day-by-day consciousness by which he lives.

All of us have this ego. We could not live without it. By it we negotiate our lives with each other and the outside world. In it all our thoughts and feelings, emotions and ideas are manifested. It is the viewing screen of our being, the place where we can make contact with our psychological world. No artist, business man, aircraft pilot, or politician can do without it. It has the power of the Tree above and the Tree below present in it and is the embodied sense of the personal. Here is the strength and weakness of man. Yesod is the last link coming down from Heaven and the first step up the Jacob's ladder from the Earth. Ego is precisely halfway between the Keter of the psyche and the Malkhut of the body. As such it is the consciousness of man at the first stage of development. Seen allegorically the Yesod is sometimes viewed as the moon reflecting the light of consciousness of the sun of Tiferet above. Here is the relationship between the ego and the self.

13. Vegetable Man

A vegetable man is a person who lives primarily in his body, that is, he is centred in his asiyyatic Tree with his consciousness focussed in the Daat of the upper asiyyatic face, which doubles as the Yesod of the lower face of the psychological Tree. This creates what we call the ego.

The ego-mind is organized to present to a man what he needs at a given moment. This need is met by yezirah's Hod which connects memories stored by Nezah's circuits in Malkhut, which is the central nervous system—the Tiferet of the body. As will be seen any bio-psyche operation is highly complex and must be carefully balanced, or the mind would be overloaded with too much data presented at one time on the screen of consciousness. Therefore, Yesod runs a limited central focus of awareness that can illuminate only that information which is required. To facilitate this, Hod groups memories into associations throughout the Tree using the sub- and sub-sub trees on every level in each world and sefirot. In this way we remember and can recall faces, names, places, smells, ideas and even things we have not known consciously which are lodged in the race or human memory.

All men have minds no matter what their type or level of development. However, this ego-mind may be biased not only by education but by the physical or vegetable type of a man. This physical type is determined by which particular sub-triangle is emphasized in the great asiyyatic triad of Hod, Nezah and Malkhut. When conception occurs in the asiyyatic Daat, the DNA formula is minted from which all the cells of the organisms will be built. This gestating body then fills out the form made by the yeziratic world and we grow into our body as if into a glove, so that at our physical prime we have expanded to the last niche of the yeziratic mould. This subtle mould is created in Beriah and only formulated in Yezirah.

All body-types fall into the three broad categories called the thinking, feeling and instinctive. They are known medically by the definitions, Ectomorph, Endomorph and Mesomorph, that is the man dominated by his nervous system, by his gut and by his muscles. These are distinct physical classifications and do not correspond to ego types which belong to the psyche rather than the body. The physical types may be defined as follows: the nervous type emphasis is principally in the triad Malkhut, Hod, Yesod, the muscular type Malkhut, Nezah, Yesod and the gut type in the asiyyatic triad Hod, Nezah, Yesod. All these types are formed in the lower face manifest in the flesh in the bottom face of the body Tree. As will be noted, all three physical types pivot on the asiyyatic Yesod. As the focus in this complex, it is the Foundation for all three, with each type possessed of the same degree of consciousness. To illustrate this point, consider the scholar having to survive on a desert island or a country boy in the city. Both are out of their depth, yet each is clever in his own place. Of course there are exceptions because no one is a pure type, but nevertheless the degree of awareness is much the same in the mean level of intelligence, the articulateness of one and the practicality of the other—a fair match when in their own environments.

Taking the instinctive triad first, we see how the muscle-orientated man is ruled. With the power of Nezah, the physical application of Malkhut and the autonomic mind of Yesod, an active, strong bodily type is generated. Such a man takes pleasure in action, preferring to do something rather than sit around. He likes his food, but as fuel for his ever-moving organism, rather than for its own sake. Initiation of events is his metier and the exhilaration of physical prowess. His mind may not be sophisticated, but he can handle himself with great skill whenever an instinctive knack or strength and tenacity are required. Such men have stamina, make excellent pioneers, soldiers, seamen and any profession that demands an aggressive approach. This does not mean violence so much as a positive attitude which is inherent

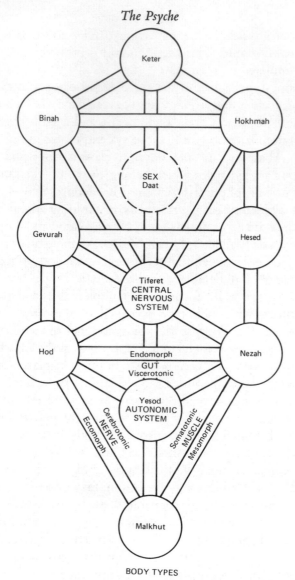

BODY TYPES

These types are in the great lower triangle of Asiyyah. Other clinical names used by science are included. They underlie and influence the ego types of the upper asiyyatic face, that is the lower psychological face of the Yeziratic Tree above.

from that side of the Tree. No explorer or enterprising business-man could do without it. Such an approach can be found in farmers as well as racing and truck drivers, footballers, dancers, painters and musicians, many of whom operate from instinct. Nor are the so-called intellectual professions without their instinctive practitioners: the surgeon, vet, engineer and many architects have action-orientated minds. The quality of these people is revealed in the dynamic of their work which is strongly flavoured by a power absent in the other bodily types. Further, one can listen to three kinds of music—the first may be cool and precise, the second full of mood and the last with a gripping beat. This last with its thudding pulse that makes one want to move is the work of an instinctive musician.

The second body-type is that of the gut ruled by the Hod, Nezah, Yesod triad. Such a person is placid in comparison with the muscle-orientated, but he is more sensitive. As a viscera type he responds with his stomach, sensing atmospheres and what is to be eaten or vomited psychologically. The gut person prefers a relatively quiet life, where he can maintain some sort of equilibrium, and yet sense and enjoy the subtleties of a situation. Such people are mutable, adapting themselves to circumstance and yet always surviving inasmuch as they are the reconcilers, the placators, often, between the cerebral nervous types and the men of action, both of whom will turn to a gut person for the sympathy only he can generate. Neither distinctly active or passive, the gut type's role can be either, and one often finds him in a profession where both qualities are required. As a go-between, they are found to be the more sensitive physicians, actors and teachers. The professions of urban society, especially the arts, are the visceral type's field. They enjoy good food for its own sake, and on the whole are more subtle than their two body brothers, although not quite so assertive, or apparently intelligent. The gut person who has Hod and Nezah as well as Yesod as his strong sefirot can draw on the power and sensibility of active and passive columns. As the centralized sub-triad, he also has a bodily inclination to the inner world, which is why many such types seem so impractical, having no direct contact with Malkhut except through Yesod.

Such a type, however, having the reciprocity of Hod and the creativity of Nazah, is often extremely gifted.

Physically the pure type is inclined to be plump and soft-skinned, quite in contrast to the muscled mesomorph. They are occasionally seen as entrepreneurs, like Serge Diaghilev, creator of the Ballet Russe, who had the drive of a dictator but the sensibility of a poet. Men of this and like calibre have a faculty to sense what the public wants and have the ability to arouse enthusiasm both in business and in the arts, in short, to be able to give the public its desire. Every big store wants a buyer with this talent and so does the newspaper editor and mass media producer. Advertising relies on such an ability to assess the mood of the consumer. This is the job of the gut person.

The nervous physical type is more easy to recognize. Like the instinctive man, the sefirah-Malkhut makes him outwardly apparent. Contained by Hod, Malkhut and Yesod, his features are sharper and his movements are indeed nervous in comparison to the other two. As a cerebral man, he is concerned with sense data but as facts. In difficult situations he will consider what he should do, rather than act on impulse or gut. He will examine and consider, speculate and prognosticate, do a great deal of work without having apparently produced anything. Nevertheless, he has his function. He is the observer, the commentator and analyser. His is the body-mind that will see the detail, the flaws, the endless possibilities to be taken or avoided. He will know the theory, the pros and cons, all of which are vital to modern Western civilization. The professions of such people are self-evident in science and technology, but they will also be in the law, in economics, history and philosophy. Indeed there is a place in the arts for the cerebral type, but his creations will be cool and without the feeling or power of the other two types.

The cerebral is essentially a receptive type as will be realized by observing which side of the Tree he rides on. Most of his observations are in response to, and his suggestions are usually based on, a respect for law (the form column). For this reason the academical world is full of such people, who in fact may not be particularly intelligent, which is a quality of consciousness, not learning. It will also be observed in human relationships that such clever men are often the passive partner to their women. Indeed one of the phenomena of college life is the brilliant, but totally ineffective, scholar when confronted with a full real-life situation outside the glasshouse atmosphere of a university. On the good side, the nervous triad gives Yesod a keen receptive edge, and the physical ability to sift through detail and discover principles. However, it must again be stated this is the faculty of the body-type—the bodily psychology.

Here then is a general description of the three body-types, all of which in the asiyyatic vegetable Triad converge on and use the Yesod's autonomic mind each in its own physical way.

However, there is another function of the asiyyatic Yesod and that is sexual. Through sex the yeziratic Tree is fused with the asiyyatic Tree. The union between the Worlds takes place in the Daat of Asiyyah and the Yesod of Yezirah where the lower part of Yezirah and the upper part of Asiyyah meet. From such a connection a child may be brought forth, if the Will of God descending down the central column intends it. While the physical manifestation must take place below, in the autonomic Yesod of the Body Tree, conception cannot occur unless it is allowed or willed from above. To explain: The sexual act not only brings the man and woman together but unites the male and female muscular and organ activity found in the great lower triangle of Asiyyah. Here the masculine Malkhut makes contact with the feminine Malkhut and inter-penetrates to the Yesod of each partner. If the union is complete, there is a distinctly experienced ascent, up the central column from the body Yesod of the autonomic system, through the consciousness of the asiyyatic Tiferet of the central nervous system, to the ego-mind, which often then experiences the detached observer of the self of the Tiferet of the psyche, before rising up to the Daat of Yezirah, where, as the Bible puts it, 'Adam knew Eve his wife and she conceived'. Here is where the beriatic and yeziratic Worlds interleave, and where the Knowledge of Formations and the Foundation or Yesod of Creations generate a child, if it is willed from above. Thus the real beginning of a new life to be incarnated, occurs at least two

Worlds above the fertilized ovum in the womb of the lowest face of Asiyyah.

In daily life the power of sex is very apparent. Unable to use the asiyyatic Yesod and Malkhut, except at the appropriate moments, sex works through the yeziratic Yesod projecting the energy and resistance, and imagination built up into the ego-mind and persona. Many people's personalities, for instance, are sex-based, and are designed to attract their opposites and repel any rivals. At the asiyyatic triad centred on the middle of the body-type triangle how else could sex express itself? Therefore it follows that the cerebral man will try to court his girl with a peacock fan of words, while the muscle man will display his faultless dancing or tennis. The feeling-gut type may say just the right word, or do the single perfect action, if his ability to assess the girl's mood is not too offset by being unduly unbalanced on Nezah or Hod. A man may indeed think he is thinking, feel he is feeling and act as if he were acting. In truth he is only responding to the needs of his vegetable body, if he has little or no connection with the rest of the yeziratic Tree above. He can write books, practice an art or be a great explorer, but he will only be doing it as the vegetable part of mankind requires of him. Millions of people each day repeat the same thoughts, feelings and actions and nothing really new happens as birth moves past growth into decay and death. As the Hebrew memorial prayer says, 'his days are as grass, as the flower of the field, so he flourisheth. For the wind passeth over it and it is gone; and the place thereof shall know it no more'.

However, if a man wishes to escape from the eternal cycle of vegetable existence he has to move out of the body triad and up into the animal kingdom where he will be one step nearer being a complete man. To do this he must contact his self and eventually live in his Tiferet, the central point of the Tree of his psyche. In this position he can survey all the natural kingdom and simultaneously, even while in a coat of skin, look up to Heaven.

14. *Tiferet — the Self*

Tiferet is the central focus of the Tree. It is at the head of the lower face and the foot of the upper face. It is the middle sefirah of the soul triad that it composes together with Gevurah and Hesed. Tiferet also lies at the midway point on the conscious axis between Keter and Malkhut, or Heaven and Earth. As the pivot of so many complexes it is particularly significant, although no more important than any other sefirah.

Beauty is the English translation of its name, and this quality is indicated by the nature of the symmetry convergent upon it. It also has this description because it is the essence of the whole Tree. Being partly in both upper and lower it can participate not only in the two faces, but also, in this case, in the asiyyatic and beriatic Worlds, above and below the yeziratic Tree.

If we recall how the Lightning Flash octave descends from Keter to Malkhut we will observe that all the centre column sefirot are in fact aspects of the same Will, whereas the outer sefirot are functional and sequential steps through the notes or six days of Creation, the first and last steps of Keter and Malkhut being the initial impulse note of Do of the Creator. Daat and Yesod, in this scheme, represent the crucial intervals in the creative progression when the process may slow down, even stop, after leaving the passive or resistant column of form. In each case the will of the middle pillar intervenes to carry over the flagging impulse to be revitalized on the active column. In the case of Daat and Yesod, the interval they fill relates to the octave of that Tree, whereas Tiferet is the top Do and the bottom Do of the Tree above and below. This again gives Tiferet a significance of its own, in that it is simultaneously Keter and Malkhut as well as being the mid-way point between the Do's on its own Tree Octave.

Into Tiferet flow eight paths or alternatively out of Tiferet flow eight paths. Moreover eleven triads focus upon this central sefirah so that it appears to have a number of wings, and indeed so they are called in the Kabbalah. These triads are both functional and conscious, and feed in and dispense out a multiple of activities on the active and passive sides of the Tree and in the upper and lower faces. Tiferet creates all these complexes and is created by them, being both the essence of their combined natures and nothing but an empty junction box at the same time. Last, but not least, as the pivotal sefirah on the central column, it can see into every sefirah directly, except Malkhut. Because of this almost total view Tiferet is called the Seat of Solomon.

In human terms what does all this mean? The comprehensiveness of Tiferet is plainly illustrated in the body Tree. As the central nervous system and the brain it has access to and information from the physical, cellular, metabolic and electronic triad, it is advised by the body Daat of ego and watches over the Yesodic autonomic system in the lower face. It is also the Malkhut of the Tree of the psyche and acts as the point of interaction between the soul triad and the body. How then does the yeziratic Tiferet relate to the psychological body?

It will be observed that the manifestation of consciousness in the lower great triad of the psyche is in Yesod—the ego. This can be considered to be the optimum consciousness required for life support. At such a level of intelligence a man can live a reasonable life, but only if his outer circumstances do not change radically. If they do, his foundation becomes redundant and he has to build another, and this is not so easy as is witnessed when a man retires after thirty years in the same job. Often he soon dies, because he has nothing in his yesodic Foundation to replace a lifetime's routine. The same usually happens when a marriage partner dies. Unless the survivor has built up a life of his own, or is prepared to construct a new Yesod with somebody else, psychological death ensues quite rapidly even if the body of the person lives on for a number of years.

If we follow up a crisis example we may get a hint of the difference between Yesod and Tiferet which is the essential self of a man. Most of us have been in a situation where events happen so fast that we know we can do nothing. Driving or sitting in a car which is involved in an accident is a common example. Suddenly someone steps out in front of the vehicle or perhaps it goes into a skid. Either way we try to take corrective action. The body moves with extra speed, dragging the wheel round or slamming on the brake. Our reflexes are excellent and yet it is as if everything were slowed down in speed like a slow-motion film. Yesod is doing everything it can to avert disaster. It pulls out all the stops of its standard alert programmes and yet, despite their obvious efficiency in actually getting one safely out of the crisis they appear sluggish and totally mechanical, which they are, when viewed from the different and obviously higher state of consciousness we have been shocked into. Moreover, such an acute state of awareness seems to be indifferent to the drama, indeed almost to the point of unconcern about one's own possible death. One views events as if from a high place. This is Tiferet looking down on the lower face with an impartial eye. It is not without emotion, that is certain, but Tiferet is not sentimental or concerned with what ought to be, as Yesod is always saying. It seems to be of quite a different order of awareness and for this reason Tiferet is sometimes called the 'Watchman in the Tower'.

This Watcher is by no means confined to violent events. It is quite commonly observed by those in love who see the world about them as extraordinarily beautiful—another reason for the name of the sefirah. Like the accident example the lovers are in a heightened state of awareness, at least before Yesodic dreams begin to overlay the alerting impact of two people actually penetrating beyond each other's egos. As described in the last chapter, moments of deep passion can bring a man and woman into Tiferet so that they meet and relate. Moreover, sex for its own sake is Yesodic ego and confined to the lower face. Should it be a real act of love the recognition and acceptance of another individual operates at the level of Gevurah and Hesed, the complementary components with Tiferet of the soul Triad. Here the

Watcher initiates the phenomena of self-consciousness, the beginning of spiritual growth.

The evocation of the Watcher is often witnessed in the practice of meditation. With it comes a sense of peace and integrity because the whole psychological Tree comes into balance and the person indeed does become for a moment integrated. Consistent practice increases contact with Tiferet so that a person, even during quite mundane situations, will suddenly come upon himself and see everything about him with the clarity experienced in meditation or crisis, but with a serenity ready to be imparted if needed. In some people the evocation of Tiferet through meditation, right action or contemplation has been so well accomplished that they become radiantly beautiful in nature and body, in spite of age and even physical disability. Such an achievement requires both knowledge and practice, but more, the recognition that such a state exists in us all the time, despite the fact we live mostly in the ego of Yesod.

As ego is the dweller in the lower or outer part of man, Tiferet is the dweller of the inner or upper room, as it is called in the Christian tradition. This gives more insight to the Christian Kabbalist name of Christ centre for Tiferet. According to several other traditions, including the modern Jungian school of psychology, Tiferet is named the Self. This brings us on to the relationship between Tiferet and Yesod.

The Yesod in the psyche may be considered to be the servant and Tiferet the master. In one Kabbalistic tradition (not Lurianic) Tiferet is sometimes called Jacob and Yesod Rachel, in a husband-wife combination. In this relationship the ego performs all the day-to-day tasks dealing with the domestic side of life, such as making a living and enjoying the normal social and personal activities of existence. Tiferet, on the other hand, is concerned with the whole of life, its long-term aims and fulfilment. If, as usually happens, a man lives primarily off his Yesod, his ego (a very vulnerable agent, subject to the prejudices of its foundation) runs his life. Such a man having no direct, strong, contact with the sefirot of Judgement or Mercy, or indeed with any upper part of the Tree, is advised by Yesod mainly on data coming only from

Hod, Nezah and Malkhut. These sefirot operate on excitement, routine and materiality, that is, the Way of the World. Such limited criteria generate fear and desire, so that the ego only does what is safe by the world's standards. What the family, the clan, and everybody else does is what matters and no individuality is possible. Certainly individuality is talked about by ego which believes that it does as it pleases, but actions belie this, and ego, seeking to justify its position, exalts itself, while simultaneously asking for approval from others. Here the ego acts as a barrier instead of a bridge, preventing a man from being exposed to his mistakes.

The function of Tiferet is to watch over Yesod, to guide it and increase its capacity to live. A Yesod under the leadership of Tiferet can call on the whole psychological Tree for advice and power. Indeed in dreams Tiferet often sets out in allegory, or even directly, the problems for Yesod to see. However, more often than not, the path between Yesod and Tiferet is blocked by the shadow side of ego and no communication takes place. This path is called Honesty, and as the names suggest, if it is afflicted trouble for the ego ensues.

Tiferet is the essential nature of a person. It is that which is peculiarly his. As the Self it is the individualized aspect of the Divine with which he was born. Situated at the foot of the upper face it is the result of that which has been. It is also the generating Sefirah of what will be manifest in the lower face, and eventually the body. Here is the area of contact between the Malkhut of Beriah and the Keter of Asiyyah, so that the yeziratic Tiferet is a major point of interchange involving the Worlds of Creation, Formation and Elemental Action. As the Tiferet of the psyche it is incarnated at birth and remains ever-present until death even though it may be totally ignored by Yesod. It is a seed buried in the earth of the body, ready to be fructified if a man wishes, so that it may grow downward, its flowers and leaves appearing on Earth, while its roots stretch back and up to Heaven for nourishment.

Another allegorical way of looking at Tiferet is to see it as the sun, with the ego as moon and Malkhut as the earth. As the sun is the pivotal point of the solar system, so is Tiferet central to

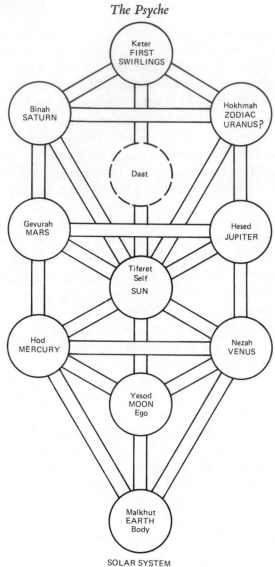

SOLAR SYSTEM

Following in the approach of the Kabbalistic classic the Sefer Yezirah, *kabbalists have placed the greco-roman planetary gods on the Tree to illustrate, in mythological terms, the nature of the sefirot. Using allegory and symbolism these yeziratic images speak directly to the psyche.*

the inner solar system of a man. Indeed traditionally, a planet and a Graeco-Roman god is ascribed to each sefirah in order to explain their natures in mythological terms. Such a practice of borrowing from another tradition was not unusual for Kabbalists, as the great Kabbalistic classic the Sefer Yezirah, illustrates. Symbolism is the vocabulary of Yezirah and each god and its stories described very precisely the psychological action and quality of its accredited sefirah. On the Tree, the outer pillar sefirot are related as follows: Mercury to Hod, Venus to Nezah, Mars to Gevurah, Jupiter to Hesed, Saturn to Binah, and more recently, Uranus to Hokhmah, but this is a speculation. The older Kabbalistic traditions place the Zodiac in the Hokhmah position, with the Primum Mobile at Keter.

In our allegorical picture Tiferet is likened to Apollo, the sun-god of truth in mythology. So bright was his awesome beauty that few could look him directly in the face and meet his penetrating eye. In terms of our psychological Tree this means facing oneself and seeing what one really is. Such a profound insight often means the blasting of our Yesodic ego image and not many people are prepared to do that.

The ego of Yesod in our allegory is indeed like the moon, only the reflected light or consciousness to our psychological sun. As such we often mistake the reflected glow as the source of light and pay homage to a reflection of reality. When the Yesodic-moon totally eclipses the Tiferet sun any illuminating truth is blocked and a psychological coma ensues. Many people prefer to live in a partial eclipse situation, because the ego has built up an acceptable, and relatively comfortable, foundation. Only a few wish to really make changes in themselves, or their lives. When a man with the power and light of Socrates walked the earth it was unbearable for those who lived by convention and ego to come under his scrutiny. They said he had to be eliminated before he destroyed the public Yesod of the State and corrupted the private Yesod of the young. This antagonism has occurred throughout history, every great teacher provoking powerful enemies especially amongst those officially representing the Truth. Baal Shem Tov, the founder of the Hasidic movement, was excommunicated by the orthodox rabbinate and St Francis of Asissi was an embarrassment to Papal authority. Even in ordinary life people who are too honest are unpopular. In strictly psychological terms, although the ego tries to obscure the truth, it cannot totally succeed because, above the realm of the moon, the sun still shines and what is more all the planets continue to turn about the focus of the sun. So it is within man, the upper part of the Tree always operating at full capacity within the psyche, despite Yesodic clouds, materialistic logic and belief that the only real world is that of the Malkhutian senses.

Tiferet is the inner consciousness, as Yesod is the outer consciousness. Both have their respective jobs to do, Yesod to be the manifest moment-by-moment awareness, and Tiferet to be the overall perceiver of the being. However, there is more to this Tiferet than the one in Asiyyah. As the simultaneous Malkhut of Beriah and Keter of Asiyyah it contains all that a man can be as an earthly Adam.

As an entity, what a man's Tiferet is, is dependent on the whole Universe for its existence. In a strange paradox, Tiferet is everything and nothing at the same time, so that if a man comes to the self and becomes an individual, he simultaneously ceases to exist as a separate entity because he *is* existence. In such a moment of realization of his own nothingness a man may perceive the Malkhut of Beriah, the heavenly Chariot and Throne of Creation, and perhaps glimpse as Ezekiel did 'the likeness of the appearance of a man above' (Ezek. 2:26) the distant view of Adam Kadmon in Azilut.

The Tiferet of the self is the point where the upper Worlds of Azilut and Beriah connect, in man, with Yezirah and Asiyyah. Here is where the Divine Will and creative impulse express, in yeziratic form, the psyche of a man, and manifest his being, in his body.

Tiferet is the heart of hearts. It is the self of a man, that likeness of Adam Kadmon who is the image of his maker. To become fully conscious in Tiferet is to become the Watcher, who knowingly looks at himself and is known by Himself. In traditional Kabbalah Tiferet is called the Holy One, blessed be He.

15. *Nefesh: The Vital Soul*

The lower face of the yeziratic Tree might be termed the psychology of natural man. This is because it interleaves with the body Tree and is partially subject to the laws of the physical realm. As discussed in the chapter on the vegetable triad, a person who lives mostly in this great triangle of Hod, Nezah and Malkhut is ruled by his body type and has a fairly mechanical set of thoughts, feelings and actions.

With the little triad of Hod, Nezah and Tiferet just above the great triangle, a new dimension is added to life. This triad is called the Nefesh or animal soul. In the strictly body Tree it can be called intelligence. This is because in relation to the little lower central triad of Hod, Nezah and Yesod, called 'Flesh', the Nefesh is a higher state of awareness. While the vegetable aspect of the body is remarkable in its ability to cope with different conditions, its activities are primarily confined to routine matters. The Nefesh is of quite a different order. As the animal part of the Tree it is more alert and flexible by virtue of the contact with Tiferet.

The plant kingdom is more or less always at the same level of consciousness, and in the vegetable aspect of man the heart pumps, the glands secrete, the organs perform their various duties to a greater or lesser degree depending on the demand. An animal is quite different, its range of consciousness is wider than a plant's and can vary from deep sleep to the passive alertness in Hod, like a cat watching a mouse, or the passionate activities of mating or hunting in Nezah. This triad is vital by nature, being paralleled in the asiyyatic body Tree by the triad formed by the organic organization of Binah, the Life Principle at Hokhmah and the crowning sefirah of Nature at Keter. This supernal combination in the Tree of Asiyyah gives the animal a consciousness, perhaps not of itself, but of its species—hence a dog always recognizes other dogs and has a special relationship to them. This triad in the case of man makes him feel an animal affinity with other men. The Nefesh is present in every man and woman. Composed in its lower part of Hod, which gives it facility and versatility, and Nezah, which supplies power and desire, it attracts to and enables people to communicate within a herd or community situation. This is seen in clans, clubs, pubs and football games. Negatively it also creates conflict, in that, in all herds of animals and people there is always a struggle for leadership or social status. On a larger scale massive herds of humans form animal identities which fight over territory and we witness this tendency in nations. Conversely we see the positive on the Nefesh level in the grouping of allies, trading partners and cultural exchanges. In Nefesh desire and fear are generated, so is excitement, and cunning, diplomacy and cruelty. Here is the history of natural man.

In individual man the Nefesh is a twilight world of consciousness that oscillates between dim vegetable awareness to that acute state just before becoming aware of oneself. In animals this consciousness of being conscious does not appear to happen, because its Tiferet is the Will of Nature, not the individual animal. In man a moment of extreme physical danger or deep sexual ecstasy can bring him into the presence of himself so that he seems to be living in a world not of the asiyyatic earth. This is so, in that, at such moments he is in contact through Tiferet with the upper part of the Tree, because in the situation of possible extinction, he may be ready to die, and in the instant of profound passion, he may be ready to live. This is why the themes of love and death are so often linked in mythology. They are close because they both involve the Tiferet of the Nefesh triad as the experiencer of the body Tree is crowned, by passing into the asiyyatic Keter and beyond, into the discarnate realm of the soul, formed by the triad Tiferet, Gevurah and Hesed.

On the more mundane level, the Nefesh is that which literally animates us. It is the vital principle that moves us about as a voluntary organism. We can walk, talk, fight or run, and have the choice of a myriad other options, which we share with the animal kingdom. Most of us avail ourselves of these animal traits, and enjoy the pleasures of its realm, as well as suffer the tooth and claw of its darker side. This negative aspect we acknowledge but do not always curb. Those efforts, from individual pacifism to the United Nations, are all attempts to offset the violent side of man's animal nature. Until men behave like men, that is work from above Tiferet, the ideal can only be a salvage operation as one community, like a troop of baboons, tries to steal, or rule another group's territory, or natural resources.

Both the north Atlantic treaty organization and Warsaw pact are natural laws of the animal kingdom. Each animal has its space, every sparrow its territory which it must defend or die. Men may form alliances over millions of square miles but the principle is the same. Countries like Carthaginia and Babylonia are gone, leaving only a few bones and feathers, buildings and artifacts, as trace of their once-proud hold on that space. The eagles have moved in, and nations, unconsciously accepting their animal natures, use symbols of predatory beasts as emblems to frighten other animal nations. The lion is a favourite one, and what man on the personal human level does not secretly consider himself a magnificent animal. Indeed many without the physique, dress to make up the discrepancy, increasing the chest, the shoulders and the suppleness of the limbs. The Zulu warrior or Red Indian brave are no primitive exceptions; the sophisticated Western man has his animal gear. It may be a fashionable casual outfit to enhance his masculinity to women, or it can be a well-cut and expensive business suit to show his professional peers that he is successful, and therefore a formidable man to be respected. Whether on the beach, at the corner of the block, in the alley, or the boardroom, the Nefesh asserts itself. In women the same is true. The whole of fashion and the home-making industry, is focussed on the female need to be a desirable, fertile and companionable animal. All this is neither good nor bad, despite one's personal view on freedom for men and women. The true state is that neither is free as long as the psychological Tiferet in each person represents only the species of natural man, whose God is Nature in the Keter of Asiyyah.

From the point of view of evolution, it will be seen that the Nefesh triad is a distinct upward step, both in Nature, and in individual man. This triangle, the first predominantly yeziratic triad, is called Awakening Consciousness. It is a quantum jump in level quite as wide as that between stones and plants. This consciousness is a completely new dimension as is witnessed in the phenomenon of love, when everything takes on not only the quality of lucidity but a totally new significance. Sounds that were never heard suddenly become apparent and harmonious. Sights, once familiar as drab background, seem to become like enhanced landscapes of extraordinary beauty. People who appeared before to be just shadows, become like enlarged, enriched, characters in an infatuating drama which, somehow, seems to have expanded life out of the normal confines of routine living. Indeed, the whole of nature becomes of particular interest, as a kind of connection with all living things is made apparent in the heightened consciousness of the experience. Here is the triad of Nefesh at work, sometimes operating off Nezah, when active, and sometimes off Hod when receptive. And yet it is occasionally more than the passionate interest in the beloved. When the Tiferet of the Nefesh is touched the really miraculous occurs. Suddenly the gates of Eden open giving a glimpse of what is possible for the soul.

The Nefesh triad is connected with the inner part of man. It is the next threshold of consciousness after that of the great lower triad on the yeziratic Tree. Its orientation is psychological although it is still part of the natural or earth-bound man. In the Zohar, one of the traditional Kabbalistic commentaries, the rabbis discuss how the Nefesh tarries near the grave of a dead person as the vegetable body decomposes. This connection is maintained until the body has returned to its original mineral elements. They go on to say that while the Nefesh is earthbound, it hovers above the living concerned for their welfare, even interceding with the departed soul and spirit on matters that require supernatural attention. Whether we subscribe to this or not is our personal business, but from the view of direct experience many people sense the atmosphere of decay about a cemetery in current use, whereas very old graveyards have not got this slightly rancid feeling about them. Quite the contrary, there is a distinct sense of peace. From this it might be concluded that the Nefesh, if it is strong enough, does survive the immediate vegetable death of the body. Indeed it is a not uncommon phenomenon, in a house where someone has just died, for a pungent and untraceable smell to occur. This is, no doubt, the breakdown of the invisible part of the vegetable body, and the beginning of the decay in the Nefesh. In the case of those who have a very well developed Nefesh the process of dissolution may be pleasant or unpleasant. While the vegetable man just vanishes into the pool of Life known as Nature, the Nefesh we are told survives on the momentum of its desires. These may be to rise up or remain earthbound, as in the case of a man who has spent a lifetime acquiring wealth, or a woman who gave herself to anyone.

Both these extreme cases would be bound by their Nefesh to spend some time, as most traditions imply, in a period of limbo before they became entirely free of their desires. It must also be said that such people with strong animal natures, also have great possibilities inasmuch as they have the dynamic to attain a subtler level of psychology. Many saints began as intense sinners and Christ was more interested in the erring than the righteous who needed no help. Mary Magdalene was a prostitute, a woman of a strong animal nature, and Buddha had known all the pleasures of sensual delight. So let us be quite objective. There is no morality except that which takes you towards or away from self-realization.

The Nefesh, in conjunction with the great vegetable triad, completes the lower bearded face of Yezirah. This configuration, called the Natural Man, contains both the ego and the self. As the top of the Asiyyatic Tree and the bottom of Yezirah, it not only reflects the physical types, but includes another set of sub-triads called the ego types which are composed into a fourfold figure by paths focusing on Yesod. Like the body types we have all the ego types within us, although we may predominate in one at any time.

16. The Four Ego-Types

The four ego-types are quite different from the three body-types. While it is true to say that both of these orders in effect share the same yesodic ego, their perception is not of the same level. The body-types we have observed are generated in the vegetable triad of the asiyyatic Hod, Nezah and Malkhut. This triad is concerned mainly with routine reaction, principally to the external world, with the gut type having an intermediary, but nevertheless mechanical, role between the inner and outer worlds of a man. This 'Flesh' triad is different from the other two body-types in that, being more physically internal, it can be dimly aware of the psychological state of the man and of others. This is the reason for the particular sensitivity of the gut person. However, none of these body-types must be mistaken for the four ego-types which are primarily psychological by nature.

The four ego-types make up a four-leaved figure within the lower yeziratic face. They all pivot on Yesod and are in fact aspects of the ordinary working psyche. This psyche is that part of a man that deals with the everyday world, sometimes externally, at others internally. Being situated on either side of the central column all the triads are functional, those on the left receptive and those on the right active. However, there is a secondary sub-system in which the lower triads are outward looking while the other two are introverted by nature. These four triads may be called by the following names, although these are inadequate when their full subtlety is considered. The Hod–Yesod–Malkhut —the Logical. The Nezah–Yesod–Malkhut—the Sensual. The Hod–Tiferet–Yesod—the Intuitional. And the Nezah–Tiferet–Yesod—the Responsive. This four-fold complex has parallels in

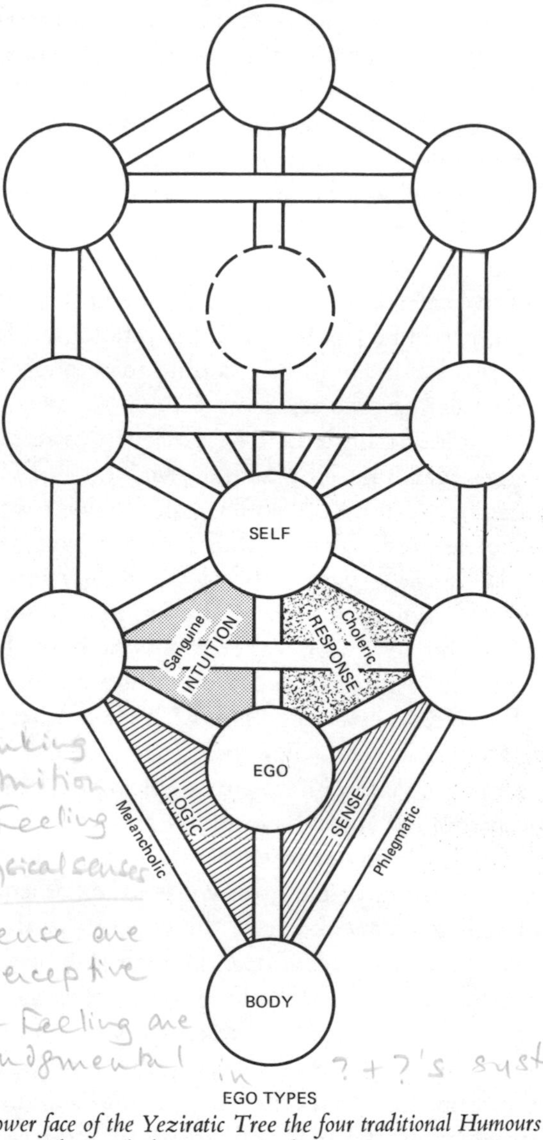
SELF
Sanguine
INTUITION
Choleric
RESPONSE
EGO
LOGIC
Melancholic
SENSE
Phlegmatic
BODY

EGO TYPES

Within the lower face of the Yeziratic Tree the four traditional Humours and modern Jungian types may be matched. As a system they are in everyone. Many combinations are possible, depending on the circulation flow of the paths that form them, and in the pairing of opposites and complements. All are connected by the ego which is their foundation.

ung:
gic = Thinking
ition = Intuition
ponse = Feeling
se = physical senses
ition + Sense are perceptive
inking + Feeling are judgmental in ? + ?'s system following Jung

the modern Jungian school and probably in the original meaning
of the Four Humours in ancient medicine, which considered the
balancing of the phlegmatic, melancholic, sanguine and choleric
elements in a man as crucial to his health. In the light of the slow
acceptance by modern psychiatry that many diseases are psychosomatic, this doctrine, though usually understood physically, may
have more to it than twentieth-century science credits.

Considering the whole of the lower face as an ego-centred
consciousness we can see how each of the functions contributes to
Yesod, which, it will be recalled, is the psychological foundation
of a person. But before we can examine these contributions in
detail, we must define each triad.

Taking the logical triangle first we observe that it is composed
of Hod–Yesod–Malkhut. The sefirah Malkhut will give it a
powerful practical flavour concerned with the outer world of the
elements, whereas Hod, with its ability to scan and collect data,
will accumulate a wide variety of facts strongly influenced by
Malkhut, which it will formulate to the ego in a detailed sequential format. It could not be any other way because the foundation
of anyone who lives in this triad would have to be ordered in
a schema of empirical evidence. This at its most extreme is the
computer intelligence which files everything in classes and relates
only through proven experiments. It is not interested in woolly-
minded speculation. It must have tested and reliable cases. We
all have this aspect within our psyche and could not work without
it. All the accumulation of facts, drawn from experience, especially when learning a new skill, are the concern of this triad. In
terms of temperament we recognize the highly skilled technician
and people concerned with the running of machines and organizations, which must have a reliable sequential pattern to exist. Here
is the scientific method, the precise argument of logical philosophy. In the courts, advocates, however emotive in their defence
or attack, must apply the practical reason of the triad to every
case. One also finds this triad at work in economics and invention.
In personal relations two men might not get on, but when working on a piece of machinery they can communicate, because of
the common law of logic that both must respect, when taking

the thing apart and putting it together again. In the time-honoured conflict between men and women over logic, one or other of the parties is working off a different triad and the illogical is not always confined to women. Logical thinking has its place, but it is inadequate to handle deep psychological questions. A man may be a mathematical genius or a walking textbook on psychology, but that does not mean he knows anything about human relationships, or even himself. The triangle of Hod–Yesod–Malkhut is primarily for examining the outer world. It is lucid and ordered in its approach. It can have the scale of astronomy, yet it is by nature a lover of detail and the minutiae of working parts. As an information bank the triad is excellent, but not for major decisions of policy because it lacks a real sense of scale.

Lying diagonally opposite on the upper part of the lower face is the triad of the responsive type. This is created by the vision of Tiferet, the imagery of Yesod and the power of Nezah. The combination has a touch of emotion in it. While it has not the cool method of the logic triad it has an inherent balance because it is connected with Tiferet. Thus while a man may not be able to fault a rigid argument, he will feel it is wrong and try to correct it by the introduction of the larger view supplied by Tiferet plus the dynamism of Nezah. An example of this is the diplomat who negotiates a difficult situation by first pointing out the larger issues than those being presented by pragmatic conclusion, and then reinforcing his case with a Yesodic image of what could happen, with the Nezah power to persuade. Talleyrand, the great diplomat of the Napoleonic era, besides winning many diplomatic victories had numerous conquests amongst women. This is not surprising when it is seen which sefirot he worked with. The talent of this triad is the ability to react and assess the point of equilibrium. This is because the triad can pinpoint a deviation by reaction and attempt to put it into balance because it has the Nezahian capacity to initiate action. The Responsive triangle is an inner complement to the Logical which can only analyse. Related, because of its Tiferet connection, more to the essence of things, the triad's disadvantage is that it is less articulate. A person who works off it tends to be unable to say precisely, as logic would like, why he feels that a thing is good or bad. This is not judgement with its well-defined determinants, but a reaction. Such a phenomenon is usually associated with women who, much to their menfolk's annoyance, are often more accurate in their feelings about a situation, in spite of not having all the facts. A similar case is found in the arts, where out of apparent studio confusion there emerges work of balance and power. The Responsive triad is well demonstrated in the analogue of a pair of scales in which any action instantly generates a reaction to correct the balance. The judge in court has to develop this psychological function. He listens to both counsels and on the jury's verdict must come to a conclusion based on the case as a whole. The sentence he gives takes into account the man's previous record and his particular difficulties. This requires not just knowledge of law but a wide insight gained over many years at the bar. All of us use this faculty in our ordinary lives when sizing up people and situations.

The sensual ego triad is the function of psycho-physical appreciation. Like the logical triangle it is concerned mostly with the world outside. Using the qualities of Nezah, it—like the logical triad—overlays a body type. Whereas logic relates to the cerebral intellectual, the sensual corresponds, in psychological terms, to the muscular or instinctive type of man. As such it sees things outwardly in the form of action. Such a person may well be intelligent, but he will express himself in activities involving what he calls real life. He has no time to sit and think and would rather be experiencing than reading about it. Rock climbing will appeal to a person with this triad predominating. So will acting, and dancing, because it helps the psyche to express itself, and this is most important on this force column triad. Many painters work primarily from here. The Flemish domestic pictures with the smell of fish and fruit almost coming from the canvas illustrate this point well. Women are seen as women, not goddesses or nymphs. The flesh trembles and flushes, and there is mud on the ground. To a person operating off this triad things are as plain as the nose on your face. He is only interested in ideas if they produce results. Miracles? He will believe it when he sees it.

Embodied in all of us, the sensual triad has some very important tasks to do. For instance, while the logical triad absorbs theory the sensual triad practices it. To learn to drive a car without the sensual triad means that one theoretically knows where the gear change is, but not the actual experience of touch and different pressures. One may read how to correct a skid, but it is this triad that gets one out of it, when it happens. Practical and instructive, the sensual triad will take care of you in spite of a logical conviction which may well kill you. An instinctive reaction to stepping on to theoretically sound ice is a good example. An honest to goodness 'let's get the hell out of here' in a dangerous situation can save one from the thinking triad that reasons that one should be able to cope. Many people who have listened to this instinctive mind owe their lives to the good sense—as the word implies—of the sensual triad.

The intuitional triad composed of Hod–Tiferet–Yesod is one of the inner pair and as such complements the active responsive one. As Hod would imply, its job is to gather data and relate them to the clear eye of Tiferet and the image display of Yesod. At this point it is well to remember that both the inner triads share the Tiferet–Yesod path of Honesty and therefore are concerned with the proper relationship of the ego to the self. If only the logical and sensual triads were at work, Yesod would be easily fooled into the notion that the outer world was the whole picture of the universe. Indeed this is the case of people who ignore their inner psychological triads. It is for this reason that the function of intuition is slandered by the purely logical and sensual, who regard it as irrational, each according to their own outward-looking criteria. But as any person with insight knows, without this faculty many important scientific discoveries would never have occurred. The Intuitional triad has the remarkable ability to scan at high speed. It can pick up on its sensors, connections normally unseen by the slower outer psychological triads. Its job is to inform both the self and the ego—a very special responsibility only matched by the responsive triad on the active other side of the Tree. As a kind of psychological radar it can screen unseen a person or a situation, although someone else's same triad can of course pick this up. At this level dialogue is possible in complete physical silence and may take place successfully over considerable distances.

Intuition is the perceiving of what lies behind the face of things. Such a function is very useful to many people, such as the psychologist who deals with the invisible world. To the trained intuition, the psyche, as we are discovering, has an anatomy like the body, indeed it is as real as the city of New York. This appreciation can only be reached by intuition. While the logical triad may try to reason about psychology, it generally reduces everything to a colourless system more related to white rats and behaviourists' dogs, and the sensual triad that does not recognize such a world says, 'It's all cuckoo land.' The responsive triad on the other hand acts as the dynamic to this inner world and works with intuition, providing that the rest of the lower face does not block, or interfere with, these inner processes.

What does all this mean in everyday terms? Let us take the charged circumstance of a lovers' quarrel. The man and his girl are temporarily estranged. He talks to her through his logical triad, trying to analyse and explain what has gone wrong. It is quite useless. The girl sits opposite him, pale-faced and weeping. His sensual triad wants to comfort her, but his responsive triad prevents him, because he knows the moment he puts his arm round her she will push him away. Meanwhile his intuitive triad is continuously searching for something he has said or done to precipitate this crisis. His ego is hurt and concerned for its own wellbeing and it clings to the rationale of the logical triad to justify itself while the sensual triad becomes more frustrated. 'What's wrong?' he asks. The responsive triad passionately desires to make things good again. Suddenly the intuitional triad, because of its connection with Tiferet, sees that his ego is imposing impossible Yesodic demands on the girl. The logical and sensuous triads cannot see this because they are only ego-centred. 'You only want your way,' the girl says. Initially the man increases his logical triad's justification, and reacts in his responsive triad against the rejection of his desire, generated in the sensual triangle. Through all this his Tiferet watches quite impartially operating through the two inner triads down the path of honesty waiting to flash the truth which rescues ego from its false position. 'All right' says the man, 'I am egocentric. I'm sorry.' The girl looks up. Their eyes meet and two Tiferets connect. The upper emotional triad of Gevurah and Hesed may come in as the moment is enhanced by self-consciousness. The man places his arm round the girl. The two outer triads are now happy, the sensual because it has the initiative again and the logical because of the ending the quarrel.

Here then are the two extrovert and two introvert triads at work. It will be seen that many combinations are possible, some temporary, some permanent. However, it must be pointed out that one may transcend these triads as one does the body-type and make contact with Tiferet. This is everyone's birthright.

17. The Lower Face as a Whole

We have now seen how the lower face is composed. This is the realm of one's personal consciousness. Centred in the ego, formed on our foundation, we view the world created by the body sefirot and triads, and the psychological ego types. Here is the realm which we normally exist in and may indeed die, without any idea of the psyche that lies higher up the Tree of Yezirah.

Taking the ages of a man's life, it is possible to see how this can come about. At birth the body Tree is formed out of the image of the yeziratic World. Nature designs and supplies the hardware but the resident soul can do with it as it pleases once it has taken possession. At the beginning of the leasehold, the soul immediately starts to return from whence it came, by climbing up the Lightning Flash to Yesod. Here in babyhood it constructs a private world which is aided and abetted by the three body triads of gut, muscle and nervous system. These in time, in conjunction with the operations of the body and the psychological Tree take the forming ego-consciousness up to the next step of childhood in the focus on Hod. At this point facts, figures and all manner of curiosities are activated; encyclopaedias, museums and endless questions feed the Hodian faculties and are filed in the brain of Malkhut, the mind and memory of Yesod, along the paths surrounding the thinking triad. At this point intellectual games are played with great seriousness. These range from card tricks to calculus and include the school game of examinations and academic studies. In leisure the same Hodian flavour will be expressed in the love of mechanical and ingenious toys, chemistry sets and amateur magic. Books will occupy a great deal of time and so will conversation, trickery, petty thieving and cruelty of a rather cold kind. Excitement is always present, the more reverberation the better the game or activity. Speed and thrills, cunning, and admiration for the deft, the shrewd and the clever, is the criterion. Many people never grow out of this stage, and while their bodies may mature, the psyche never progresses beyond the Hodian stage. Some grown men still play with train sets, participate in intellectual games quite seriously, and indulge in pursuits long considered the amusements of children. Neither good nor bad, because flying kites can be quite relaxing, as can messing about in boats. Such pleasures or obsessions belong to Hod. Without Hod there would indeed be no excitement in life. Existence lacking curiosity is boring, and no inventions would be forthcoming, neither could there be any progress. This applies not only to the material world but to the psychological.

When the shift along the Lightning Flash moves across to Nezah we see a profound change in a boy or girl. On touching the active column puberty occurs. The dynamic period completes the asiyyatic vegetable triad and the person is ready to fulfil their biological functions. As an expression of this change preoccupation with scholastic activities gives way to interest in physical appearance. Girls suddenly become deeply concerned with clothes and make-up, the boys, with asserting their masculinity. This may be seen in the gear worn or the powerful motor bikes they ride. Sex is present in everything they do. Sometimes it is violent and sometimes gentle. One crowd will dance, another fight and another hold an orgy depending on the practice and custom of their society. All will have the strong active sefirah of Nezah running through their activities. Here the instinctive function is explored and experimented with. A succession of passionate relationships is passed through, each one a cycle of elation and exhaustion, attraction and repulsion. This stage is totally sensual, though again it can vary from the virile beat of pop music to the gentle and subtle love lyrics of modern folk songs. As such, it lasts until the next stage, Tiferet, when the person reaches his prime.

Usually most people prefer the enjoyments of Nezah and the excitement of Hod to being fully responsible for themselves. This is the quantum jump from the vegetable to the animal kingdom, and the possibility of becoming a complete man or woman. Such a task requires courage and maturity, and few wish to relinquish the known pleasures and pains for the unknown. Certainly, everyone has glimpsed, or will glimpse the upper world, but to the natural man the supernatural world is too ephemeral, while the physical one is lasting—at least for a period. This conclusion becomes embedded in Yesod and people live on in a dream of everlasting youth, offsetting the day when they are no longer as physically beautiful or attractive as they were. Time passes and with it excitement and vitality begin to wane and it is often at this point that a man or a woman begins to question the meaning of existence. The honest relinquish the mask of outgrown youth gracefully, and begin life again, while those who cannot believe in anything else but the body, and materiality, continue to exist in a world where devotion to Nezah or Hod is out of place. Such lives eventually become totally repetitive, oscillating within the vegetable triad until death breaks the slowly flagging rhythms. A harsh picture one might say, but the Kabbalist is not concerned with a sentimental image or interested in continuing the illusions in many people's lives. Most great religions discuss this problem and offer a solution. The early life of Buddha clearly illustrates his conclusions about the ephemeral character of vegetable living, and the strange reversal of view when a man sees the so-called fleeting moment of truth as in fact eternal.

Returning to the lower face of the Tree of the psyche we can now see how mechanical laws operate if a man is ruled by his body. When he establishes contact with his Tiferet, a completely new situation is created. Usually the ego is the active principle but with a man's consciousness centred in the self the rulership comes from above. This means that the influences flowing through the various paths and triads operate in a different way, so that a man has real judgement and real mercy. In more mundane terms, instead of being dependent on what he has been taught and has stored in his Yesod he can discriminate and love without fear. Whereas before, his Hod called on collected facts as the basis of decision, now his Gevurah takes over with its discernment and discipline, in the illumination of Tiferet, and the formulation of Binah. Here is a very different order of judgement. Likewise, with access to Hesed, the instinctive reactions and considerations of Nezah are over-ruled. No longer can jealousy intrude or personal attraction and repulsion influence a man's ordinary but often unwary consciousness. Tiferet is for ever watchful and will direct operations providing the path of honesty between it and Yesod is not blocked.

The lower face as a whole is the psychology of a fully developed natural man. Such a person does indeed contain the baby, the child and youth, but they are incorporated, via their experience and sefirotic significance, into his ordinary working psyche. Such a person can enjoy playing exciting games, eating well, and making love. None of these highly pleasurable activities are precluded in a normal man or woman. Indeed in Kabbalistic tradition a person must be normal in everyday terms. Living life, doing business and having a family are part of Kabbalistic practice. If a man cannot cope with earthly problems how can he deal with Heavenly situations? The Kabbalist is no moralist. The Almighty designs each life so that the person can learn the maximum amount in the least time. Even disasters are provided for this function. Too much success creates an inflated ego and our failures draw attention to a neglected aspect of our nature. A man or a woman is as big as his or her consciousness and this has to be deeper and wider than the surface events they are living through. It is here that the work of the lower face ends. As a psychological tool it is superb. Subtle and complex, it is capable of dealing with all of ordinary life situations, just as the body can cope with a wide range of physical conditions. However, as will be concluded, it is, in fact, the lower aspect of the psyche's anatomy, and is principally concerned with the application of the invisible world's influence in ordinary life. This is paramount, because in the Kabbalistic tradition Heaven must be brought down to Earth, so completing contact between Keter and Malkhut and one is no longer an incomplete Tree. Whereas in some traditions the object is to become detached from the world, Kabbalah states that while we are in exile we do the work given to Adam, that is to till the ground, and await the coming of the Messiah. This will occur when we are fit to receive him, and he may arrive at any moment for each of us. So our position is plain. We are where we are needed. No one else can fill our place. Each one of us has a particular job in the universe, and we have the capability of fulfilling that destiny. But before we can perform it with the maximum efficiency, we have to know what we are and what is our capacity. For this purpose the Kabbalah is studied.

So far we have been acquainted with the body and the lower psyche. The second part of the book is concerned with the upper realm of the supernatural man. Here is the far country we have heard about, even glimpsed at a distance. But first of all we must prepare or we will just be playing games with maps.

18. Practice

Up to this moment only the theory of the Tree and its application to the body and lower psyche have been dealt with. Now we must apply what we have learned via the receptivity of Hod, and switch across the Tree to the repetitive activity of Nezah. In this way both pillars of ourselves are brought into relationship and can manifest in at first Yesod, with the construction of a new foundation, and then perhaps, with diligent practice, raise the consciousness to Tiferet.

Stand the asiyyatic body upright and raise the hands above the head to form a V. Sense the active pillar in the right arm and the passive in the left. Centre on Tiferet just below the heart and let the middle column flow from the Crown above your head through the vertical axis passing through throat and crutch to the feet. Stand like this for a long moment and when a sense of equilibrium is obtained sit down with the hands on the knees.

Holding the same balanced position in body and psyche allow the sense of the Yesodic ego to fade and focus on the zone just below the heart. Let the impressions of Hod and the rhythms of Nezah recede. Listen to the silence behind each activity of the lower psyche. Allow yourself to enter the stillness of Tiferet. Continue as long as you are able.

Practice this twice a day, morning and evening.

19. *Emotion*

We have now a picture of the natural man. A complete Tree composed of the body and the lower psyche, he more or less mechanically obeys its laws. However, no man is without the upper part of the psychological Tree or the beriatic and azilutic Worlds which lie beyond it. These are present at full power although a man may not be aware of them. In the case of the upper yeziratic Tree there is a dim recognition of a non-material inner world. This is seen in moods, thoughts and dreams which obey laws quite unlike the outer world of physical reality. Such a realm is difficult to define because being yeziratic by nature, it constantly changes its form, resolving and dissolving moment to moment in an endless flux of inner states. Men since the earliest of times have tried to understand this invisible realm and some have constructed a model of its chief elements and their relationship. The Kabbalistic schema is an example and we begin by setting out in sefirotic terms, the two upper or inner levels of emotion and intellect.

First it is important to realize that emotion is quite different from feeling. They are too often mistaken as being the same thing, whereas they are quite separate functions. Feeling belongs to Hod and Nezah, that is, it belongs to the psycho-body's reaction to internal and external physical stimuli. It may be traced to an embarrassment in the gut due to hunger or to a sense of well-being after energetic exercise. This would be on the Nezah side. Or it could be related to Hod in the exhilaration of a novel game, or the excitement generated by the stimulus of danger. All this and most of what we often call emotions are instinctive reactions to our surroundings, or internal bodily secretions and tensions. A man, for instance, might consider himself deeply in love. Passion he most certainly feels, and tenderness too, but more often than not when the honeymoon period has passed he finds himself looking at other women seeking to recapture the same intensity. This is the realm of feeling which belongs to the animal kingdom and includes all our attractions and repulsions, likes and dislikes. Observe a cat; it also has moods, is affectionate, jealous, sulky, aggressive, the whole gamut of what we commonly regard as human emotions. The animal part of man is not emotional. Emotion belongs to quite a different level of experience. It is as the two sefirot state, concerned with Judgement and Mercy and these are faculties no animal possesses.

First let us look at the emotional triad on the Tree. Judgement sits on the pillar of form, and Mercy on that of force. Judgement is passive, Mercy active. Judgement is receptive while Mercy is applying. These positions give us a clue to their qualities. It must also be remembered that they are opposites and complements, and act as the expanding and constraining combination on the Tree. They oversee Hod and Nezah and feed into the self of Tiferet. This latter configuration creates the central triad of self-consciousness, this is the Soul or Neshamah in Kabbalah. As such it will be perceived that the soul is emotional by nature which may explain why it is regarded as feminine in the Kabbalistic tradition. Taking the analogy further the soul is occasionally referred to as Eve and the spirit as Adam. However, before we can discuss the nature of the soul and spirit we must become well acquainted with the pairs of sefirot concerned with Emotion and Intellect.

Judgement in the human psyche is the outer emotional aspect of a man. This is that part of him that assesses, values, checks and constrains his emotional life. Being on the passive column it reacts rather than initiates, responding emotionally to what it is presented with. For example, a man is being interviewed for a job. He wants it badly and knows he must perform well in order to win it from a short list of competitors. His instinctive lower Face drives him to try hard but if he did not have the emotional discipline he might well overplay his talents. This discipline is

Gevurah, his emotional judgement of the situation controlling the impulsiveness of Nezah which feeds Hod's need to talk. Second by second his Gevurah enables him to parry the skilful questioning of the interviewer. Constantly the enquiry tests his Gevurah rather than his Hod which may know the facts. For the company wants a man with discrimination and nerve—both talents of a well-developed Gevurah. For his part the interviewer must have a fine Gevurah himself or his conclusions will be inaccurate. Observe a good TV interviewer, see how disciplined he is as he applies his Gevurah–Hod–Tiferet triad to the person he is interviewing. The best always have the hint of emotion, the hallmark of a human being.

Outer emotion is the response created by an imput coming down any of the paths focussing on Gevurah. Thus Binah or Understanding is emotionally implemented in the life of that person, Hod is instructed to react under emotional discipline, and Tiferet is informed of judgements made in response to its own insight or Hesed's power. Every one of these interactions has the quality of control, constraint and contraction. This means that Mercy is never without discrimination, that Understanding is not just the cold hand of Law, and that Hod need never get out of hand or the self be without the ability to define limits. This last point is most important because one might say that without the emotional faculty of Gevurah a man could run amok intellectually or instinctively, and most important, allow his self to over-dominate his being. A king or president who insists on holding all the key offices in government becomes a tyrant. Even the self has to be contained.

By Gevurah we negotiate our daily business. With it we select good from bad (according to our understanding or Binah), advance and retreat in relationships, and decide the merits of things, events and people. It is a moment-to-moment operation. Split second analysis is its metier. This is quite different from Hodian comparisons based on data computation. Gevurah is emotional. It judges by the criteria of Binah and forms an opinion the instant it is in possession of the facts in relation to the frame-work of understanding. Take the case of a soldier under fire. His instincts wish to make him run—anywhere—but his Gevurah in the light of his understanding of battle conditions holds him in place, until he sees a situation when it is safe to move. An inexperienced soldier is easily killed. In the First World War it was reckoned if one could survive the first week in action one might out-live the war. Here is an accelerated development of Gevurah and it is not without reason that tired seasoned troops are more formidable than fresh but untried ones. This does not mean wars should be encouraged, but it is worth noting that comradeship is a well-known phenomenon of an emotional nature. Indeed, at the battle of Arnhem in the Second World War, an extraordinary level of courtesy was observed amongst the paratroops. This control of Gevurah and expansion of Hesedic emotion is due to a life-and-death situation which calls on Tiferet. Here is the soul triad sometimes called 'Charity'.

The control of Gevurah is vital to the emotional life of a man. It is from this sefirah that he allows himself to act. This may appear strange, but when it is seen that Gevurah is the emotional gate controlling the power of the upper part of the Tree it will be realized what a critical role it has to play. Remove the constraint of Gevurah and the force of Hesed will drown a man in a surfeit of fervour. One who cannot contain his deepest emotion frightens people away. Few can take the overwhelming power of Jupiter, the god ascribed to Hesed. It needs Mars to order and direct the energy or the vast reservoir of emotional vitality will be quickly exhausted. The armour of Mars is a symbol of protection, from force coming from outside, and constraining that within. His sword is the emblem of clean instant judgement and his shield that of passive resistance. When Mars, the ruling principle of Gevurah, takes the initiative there is trouble. Traditionally he always loses the battle. A soldier's job is to defend, not to be aggressive. This can be seen in a person whose judgement becomes destructive criticism. Mars is power under discipline, ready to resist evil and define the good. Without Gevurah we would be easily deceived, not know how to defend, be unable to make decisions or enjoy the thrust and parry which enables us quickly to assess who is friend or foe. No intimate is accepted without the test of Gevurah.

From the first moment of acquaintanceship the judgement faculty is operative. Only after a series of probings, tests or even battles, is the relationship defined. Moreover, this process is never finished. Enemies and allies, old and new relationships are constantly under the scrutiny of Gevurah for nothing remains static in the yeziratic World of psychology.

By Gevurah a person constantly makes judgements which formulate his attitudes. Observe yourself while reading these lines and you will perceive the constant aye and nay of Gevurah. It has a flavour belonging neither to Hod nor Nezah. Nor is it intellectual in its manner. Its response is emotionally instantaneous and martially precise. Bigoted it may be, because of Binah or Hod influence, but its tone is emotional. It is from this centre that we judge ourselves and others. On its own it becomes overbearing and constricting and for this reason Hesed is its vital emotional complement.

Hesed on the active pillar is the expansive partner to the con-tractive Gevurah. In the psyche it is the inner emotional power of man. Without this dynamic a person would have no wish to grow. He could of course still remain alive within the context of the lower face but there would be no richness or profound meaning in his existence.

Hesed is situated directly beneath Hokhmah, the head of the active pillar. From this supernal sefirah inner emotion receives a great impulse. This is reinforced by the Lightning Flash descend-ing from Binah via Daat. Such an input gives Hesed an enormous might and traditionally the sefirah is also called by the names of Greatness and Magnanimity. The western translation of Mercy is good, because to be merciful one has to be in a powerful position, and this Hesed certainly is.

We observed in the section on the body that Hesed is the principle of expansion either by release of energy or the building up of cells. In the psyche the same operation occurs, although in its own terms. To take first a negative illustration, suppose a man has no ambition, one can be sure that his Hesed is not functioning normally. This may be due to an over-constraining Gevurah or to the dispersal of his power directly through Nezah in the form

of unbalanced sex or repetitive habits that drain his Hesedic
resources. A man who over-eats or drinks too much draws off
vast quantities of Hesedic energy which weaken his will to really
do something with his life. These are simplified examples but they
define the difference between a man who devotes his life to an
art and its perfection and someone who repeats every Saturday
night in bar and bed the same distribution of energy pattern. The
Hesed-orientated man has a concern for greatness, not necessarily
for himself, but in his love of growing larger in experience and
depth. He may practice the violin, or surgery, business or boot
mending. It does not matter. The significant point is that he
wishes to improve, to perfect both his craft and himself. Such a
man will not work just for money, but will put in extra hours in
order to fulfil himself. A pianist practises day after day, a doctor
accepts that he may have to get up in the middle of the night, a
painter or a writer may work for years without any sign of
recognition.

The motivation here is love. Love of the work and the expanding emotion it brings. No man works for nothing. In this
case the wages are psychological and the profit is the gain in
emotional width. Moreover, such is the abundant power of
Hesed that everyone benefits from its evocation and development.
The sciences as well as the arts gain from people orientated in
Hesed. The discoverers of radium, the Curies operated for many
years under bad and dangerous conditions but the deep emotional
power behind their work kept them going, as it did for all the
people who attempted to build flying machines and still searched
for a solution in spite of failure.

A painter like Rembrandt had no craving for fame when he
produced his best pictures, neither did van Gogh whose Hesed
was so strong he could hardly contain his love for anything he
became attached to. This brings us to the function of Gevurah as
the complement to Hesed. In the example of van Gogh his un-
governed inner emotion was too vehement for his good. To
give everything to the poor was indeed Christ-like but in fact
counter-productive. Likewise cutting off his ear and sending it to
a girl he admired was being over-generous with himself. Gevurah

checks such excesses. By its constraint the pianist can focus and discipline his love of music into a balanced and controlled performance at a concert as well as to keep him at his daily practice. Because of Gevurah, the mother, while loving her child can chastise it when it is naughty, and yet not terrify it out of its confidence in her. Likewise a teacher can command authority because the disciple knows that even in severity there is the presence of love.

On a more personal level one can observe Hesed at work within oneself. The love for someone else deepens over the years, and despite minor misdemeanours we regard that person with ever-widening affection. This extends also over great distances so that when we meet, the connection seems never to have been broken. Differences, quarrels, and even estrangement occur, but the underlying Hesedic emotion is there, and can heal the wound. That Hesed is the complement of Gevurah was shown very clearly when some British troops in North Africa, bored with their diet of bully beef, threw their rations over into the German trenches and the Germans replied by throwing back their field rations of sausage. Such is the ability to switch from one side of the Tree to the other that in Christmas 1914 British and German troops sang each other's carols and played football together between the trenches. Had there been a permanent centering in Tiferet, a miracle would have come to pass, but alas this is only possible if individuals are so focussed, and most of us are usually fixed in Hod, Nezah or Yesod.

Hesed it will now be seen is a powerful factor. Usually unseen or suppressed it is one of the major influences in our lives. Without it there would be no progress in the practical world of technology or in the psychological development of man. Most political ideologies originate in Hesed and although they usually degenerate into the predominantly Gevurah Hod activities of political parties, their intention is for the benefit of humanity as a whole. The love of one's homeland is a very good example of the scale of Hesedic emotion. It is concerned with larger matters than one's personal life, even to the point where one's death is to be offered. The British fighter pilots of the R.A.F. in 1940 operated off this sefirah, men with no heart cannot fight or indeed accomplish anything beyond their own interest.

For obvious reasons religion is a Hesedic activity. It is concerned with the expansion of the heart and the search of the devotee to relate to something larger and greater than himself. Here is the capacity to receive and give great love. Mercy resides in this place, so too does the higher and inner force of love. People operating off Hesed emit and shine in spite of themselves, revealing in their generosity the meanness of more ego-centred people. However, without the balance of Gevurah, naive tolerance can allow many things to go on when they should be curtailed. The head of a religious order is responsible for his disciples. If he is without the corrective of Gevurah all sorts of evils can occur. Many an esoteric school has been destroyed from within by the laxity of its leader whose excessive mercy is taken for, and eventually becomes, real weakness. Hesed out of control is well illustrated by the myth of the god Jupiter who blasted a princess he loved by his unconstrained magnificence. It is great and good to love and be loved, but according to the Kabbalah even God had to apply the pillar of form to the pillar of force or the Universe would expand into useless diffusion.

Hesed in the psyche is emotional inner power, contained by the outer emotion of Gevurah. Together, they are the emotional expressions of the two side columns. Looked at another way, they are the emotional wings of Tiferet which reconciles them in self-consciousness. As a pair of functions they are vital for development because they create the small intermediary triad between the upper and lower faces of the yeziratic Tree known to us as the Neshamah or living soul.

20. The Emotional Side Triads

The two side triads defined by Gevurah–Tiferet, Hod and Hesed–Tiferet–Nezah are functional by nature. Adjacent to the lower face of the yeziratic Tree they perform active and passive duties between the psycho-body organism and the psyche proper. Like the enzyme and hormone triads of the body their job is to act as a catalyst, the pillar of form triad as the conservative element and the pillar of force triad as an innovator in the person's emotional life.

Most mature individuals do not live entirely in the lower face of the psychological Tree, they have an emotional world. However, this may not necessarily be of a particularly high order. In many people the general level of consciousness hovers mainly between Tiferet and Yesod, that is in the animal triad with an optimum involvement of Gevurah and Hesed. As a working configuration of sefirot and triads, the emotional activities go on in the psyche much as the gut and heart operate, that is, without our leave. Here is the edge of the Unconscious.

On the form side of the Tree all the experiences received by the person are analysed and formulated into psychological complexes, that is, in groups of fixed associations and memories. These are experienced, recognized or not, in a man's attitudes both to himself and life. This set of emotional valuations is based on the data collected by Hod and the judgements of Gevurah, the two formulatory principles relating their findings to Tiferet which completes the passive triad of emotional attitudes. These passive complexes can be both useful and useless, depending on the situation they are applied to. The reason for this is that they are inherently resistant, being on the form side of the Tree. In, for example, a laboratory worker such emotional fixity is valuable, for scientific criteria must be strictly adhered to, but if the same man is confronted with a non-rational subject, such as magic, his formalized emotional posture cannot accept its other-world premise.

The same occurs in personal relationships when one partner breaks a shared emotional format. For ten years a marriage has worked acceptably. Suddenly its emotional stability is shattered by one partner taking a lover. From that point on the marriage dissolves or reforms because, as the triad indicates, only within a formalized process are certain things possible. The passive emotional triad is conservative by nature. However, it tries to preserve not only the external emotional connections of work, of social and private life, but maintains within the psyche a system of related emotional complexes which have been built up since childhood.

From this triad we get most of our resistance to new ideas. It has its ready-made patterns, its tested methods, and it dislikes the infiltration of untried things. Repression originates here.

On the credit side this triad gives a person emotional resilience. For example, some strange situations, revolutionary ideas and disturbed personal relationships could destroy a man without this stable system of emotional attitudes. Disciplines learnt over the years are not only useful to carry out tasks but act as a bulwark in bad times. For instance, after a disastrous love affair, a man may immerse himself in his work to carry him over the emotional abyss. Likewise such a firm emotional base can be the platform for a set of mature beliefs and possibilities. No painter, writer, or in fact anyone, can develop without this backlog of emotional experience to build on.

On the other side of the Tree is the active or opening emotional triad. Here we have the initiating of new experience. While the resistant triad checks for overbalance, this side allows the need to explore wider emotional fields. It also makes possible the release of emotional energy. We see how this is achieved when we consider the sefirot involved. Nezah is the instinctive mind and Hesed love. In the opening phases of a new relationship between two people when Tiferet may meet Tiferet, the miraculous opening out of the heart occurs. An old love is quickly chased away by a new love, says the mediaeval Book of Courtly Love. Emotional scars preserved in the passive triad may not be healed, but they are smoothed over as the active triad, working through Tiferet and the adjacent Nefesh and Neshamah triads begins to influence the emotional formations of the last experience.

The positive emotional triad engenders an open endedness and enables fresh attitudes to enter, vitalizing the psychological and physical organism. This is certainly observable in relationships. In work, the same thing may be perceived. Although more common in the arts, in that they are on the whole concerned with the active column, the sciences also have their use for this triad. A research scientist must be prepared in his emotional attitudes for change and experimentation. If he is not, he becomes closed to any possibility of discovery. Kekule, the discoverer of the benzine chemical ring concept, came upon the idea while dreaming in front of his fireplace. 'Let us learn to dream,' he said to a group of scientists. This level of illumination was only possible because he was operating on the expanding, rather than the contracting emotional triad.

As will be seen the yeziratic World lies between Beriah and Asiyyah. If the emotions are cloudy no light of intellect can shine through. Until a man becomes emotionally disciplined and yet open, no progress can occur. Take the case of any creative work which has come to a standstill. The vision is obscured. One feels dark turbulences in the psyche and only old worn-out ideas come to mind. Something has to be dissolved and something completely new be born. It is an emotional operation which can only be cured by the psyche centring on Tiferet. How this comes about can be manifold. With some people it is rest from the problem, with others, they have various techniques for contacting the self, ranging from a walk round the block to deep meditation. Either, or any way, the consciousness is shifted from the dulled ego at Yesod up the path of honesty to Tiferet where at the focus of paths and triads, especially of our two active and passive emotional complements a synthesis may take place. In creation or discovery, this can happen instantaneously as old and new emotional attitudes blend, then trigger an idea that the balance allows to descend from the upper sefirot of Understanding and Wisdom, perhaps even Knowledge.

In more mundane circumstances this dialogue between the two functional sides of emotion occurs all the time. It is a process of constant dissolution and resolution in attitudes which go to make up our emotional life. On the passive side our formulated complexes aid the psyche by giving it patterns to respond by, and on the active side, the positive complexes continually prevent the psyche freezing solid into an emotional atrophy. The inter-balance is critically vital for psychological growth. If the passive side becomes dominant the person inclines towards the outlook of a bigot, and if the active predominates that of a libertine—the bigot always valuing by the criterion of fear, the intemperant by that of elation. This extremism is not that rare. We see it in politics with the 'law and order' militants on one side and the provocative revolutionaries on the other.

The norm of course is to be in the middle. When centred in Tiferet the psyche can make either side perform its correct duties. By being dominated by neither triad the self is serviced by both, each checking the other's bad tendencies and supporting the good. When they are functioning properly the mechanism of the psyche, like that of the body, runs smoothly as experience is processed by each triad. This brings about the phenomenon of learning which is the prerequisite of spiritual evolution. Besides feeding into Tiferet, both triads relate directly to the Neshamah. This connection has a crucial bearing on the soul's progress. Pivoted on the self and supported by outer and inner emotion the triad of the soul or self-consciousness is closely assisted by the two functional triads. Whereas the half awakened man of the Nefesh triangle is only dimly aware of his psychological processes, the self-conscious man can make use of them rather as a doctor does his stethoscope or a painter his brush. Instead of being ruled by his various complexes, the self-conscious man makes them work for him, as they continually add to his sensitivity and appreciation of the subtle realm of emotion. In Jungian psychology these triads belong to the personal unconscious.

In essence these two triads are difficult to describe, but if they can be defined in their own language of allegory, they might be likened to the ebb and flow of tides within the psyche, which continually build, erode and modify the shore line contour of awareness. Penetrating below the surface waves of the sea of unconsciousness, their subliminal currents greatly influence the way we live, but it must be remembered that though they are deep, at the bottom is the solid ocean floor of Asiyyah, while above hangs the vast heaven of Beriah. Both of these worlds penetrate and meet in the waters of Yezirah. However, with an ark built on the boat-like plan of the Tree of Life, one may become another Noah and ride out any storm or flood.

21. *Intellect*

The outer and inner intellect correspond in the psychological Tree with Binah and Hokhmah. As the functional members of the supernal triad they occupy a cosmic role in the Tree of the Psyche. Situated at the head of the active and passive columns their job is to formulate and to initiate in the realm of thought. Thought must not, like emotion and feeling, be confused with ordinary thinking. The latter is a Hod function which collects and correlates data for Yesod to store in the Foundation of a man and in his brain cells. This day-to-day information may be the basis of real thought, but more often than not it is the body of facts most easily accessible in the communications network of the psyche. All the paths store information as does the Hod of every minute Tree inherent within each sefirah. Such data can manifest in emotional complexes or instinctive reactions. A learned body reflex is one example and a skill in tactfulness another. This experience-acquired information is quite different from the realm of thought.

The realm of thought, as is implied by the position of the two intellectual sefirot on the Tree, is the zone of interaction between the Worlds of Emanation and Creation. One might say that here ideas manifest out of nothing. One moment there is the void, then a concept or realization emerges. For obvious reasons this is a rare phenomenon for most of us, however original we might regard ourselves. Indeed most of our ideas are borrowed and sometimes even stolen, the ego taking the credit for someone else's work. The whole of the history of ideas operates this way. Occasionally one man or a group come up with something new and they are imitated *ad infinitum*, the latter-day genius often claiming to be the first with the thought. Many great inventions were not the direct result of the inventor's concept but were modifications and developments on someone else's flash of insight. George Stevenson did not invent the steam engine as many believe; it was based on the experiments of James Watt. Neither can the modern discoverers of the atom claim all the credit, for the idea of an individual unit goes to Leucippos, a Greek philosopher who lived twenty-five centuries ago.

Nearly all the knowledge we possess today is based on the understanding and wisdom of what amounts to perhaps a few thousand people spread out over the centuries. We fly today, shuttle rockets to the moon, can carry on long-distance conversations and see far beyond our Milky Way to other galaxies, assuming that we all know more than men did before our time—but in fact this is only information about things, not direct knowledge of them. One may view the thousand-fold magnified image of molecules on an electron microscope, but know nothing beyond the borrowed information of learning. Real thought is quite different. Its mark is originality, and that is by definition as well as quality. It may not be the first time a man has come to that conclusion, but it is so for the thinker, and this makes it unique.

The scholar may solve a lifetime of questions with prefabricated formulations, which may or may not be right, but Einstein in his youthful creative period contributed more by his originality. Nor is thought confined to science. The arts have their genii and one recognizes them by their power and outstanding freshness. The English painter, Turner, opened up a new way of looking at the sky. People saw, through his vision, an atmospheric realm more real than any pretty set pieces of classical painting. The Impressionists merely followed the old man's lead, taking the credit for an approach practised forty years before. No need to mention Shakespeare whose works, besides being skilled in all the other sefirot, contain the wisdom and understanding of a very profound man. Even lesser masters exhibit the quality of thought: the poet, John Donne, for instance had many important thoughts on love and death. Closer to our own time musicians like Igor Stravinski broke the sound barriers of conventional music and allowed the negative realm of chaos as well as harmony to enter our perception. This initially upset many people who preferred the soothing anticipation of sonorous progression. Such originality always disturbs as it shakes people out of the slumber of long-held and often outworn concepts. Christ and Socrates paid the price for their societies' peace. Their ideas were dangerous, but they could not be destroyed because they belonged to another world, even though society might kill the thinkers.

Let us begin our study of the realm of intellect by defining its outer and inner aspects. Like the emotional sefirot, Binah and Hokhmah are on the side pillars. On the passive column Binah, Gevurah and Hod tend to concentrate, while Hokhmah, Hesed and Nezah radiate. The column of force expands from within and the column of form compresses from without. When observing the active principle we usually see it manifesting through something that originates from beneath or from within the surface of an object, event or person. It is power, enlivening, activating, and moving, whatever it passes through. On the other hand the passive column expresses itself in the outer form of the thing, event or person. As the resistant principle it seeks stability, constancy and inertia in order to maintain itself. Form is the outer configuration of consciousness, as force is its inner dynamic. Consciousness itself, as defined by the central column, is omnipresent in the active and passive, both the side columns being a relative manifestation of the Creator from which all things come. In terms of the Tree of psychology, Outer Intellect like Outer Emotion, is concerned with formulation, while Inner Intellect and Inner Emotion are the dynamic impulses emerging from inside the man. Some traditions consider the inner aspects as higher, but in the Kabbalah no sefirah is considered in any way superior to another as they are in fact all One.

Taking Binah first, we can see how the name Understanding could not be anywhere but on the column of form. To understand is wholly to observe the real basic structure of something. In this, the first sefirah of form, are set out all the principles that must follow. True, Hokhmah supplies the energy, but Binah clothes it with matter even if it is only the materiality of a formulation of an idea. Such a concept is not to remote as imagined—Einstein's

MC^2 = E equation on the relationship of Matter to Energy is a hard fact. As the word 'hard' implies, it has substance. It also contains the energy of Hokhmah that is even more powerful than a hydrogen bomb or even an exploding super nova star. This is the realm of intellect, which, as will be noted by its position on the Tree between Azilut and Beriah, is eternal.

Understanding is the third sefirah to be created in the sequence of the Lightning Flash. As such it has a direct connection with both Keter the fountainhead, and the full potency of the active principle of Wisdom. Moreover, it is the jumping-off point across the Abyss of Knowledge, through the World of Creation to Mercy. It also has direct influence over Judgement. It will be seen from this that it commands, in its passive way, a very powerful situation. One might consider it rather like the constitution of a nation, such as the American Declaration of Independence, with its statement on basic rights and duties. In essence such Binah law may be very simple, as in the case of the British road code which says that no one may cause danger or obstruction on the Queen's highway. A person may have to drive on the wrong side of the road to avoid an accident or even back across it if they have good reason. These misdemeanours are the breaking of minor rules in order to obey the greater law which is designed to keep the Queen's highway clear for everyone.

Understanding is Outer Intellect, that is, it is the formulation of universals. This can manifest in a set of commandments upon which a whole civilization can be founded. Or it may be, on the personal level, the recognition of recurring phenomena which make one conclude that this must always happen. An example of this could be a midwife, who after delivering babies over many years, comes to understand every symptom of labour and sign of actual birth. This sort of understanding comes about slowly through practice as the psyche is steeped in experience. The same occurs in a doctor whose familiarity with diseases is so great that he can diagnose at a glance.

From a less specialist view all of us simple skills. First we learn them, through Hod, then we practise via repetition—that is Nezah. Having got to a level of competence we refine the craft into an art with the discipline of Gevurah, adding later the power of Hesedic love to work. When we have practised for a very long time, understanding dawns as regards the general rules, how, where and why they may apply. We may even come to understand their purpose in our lives and indeed in the whole scheme of creation. This is when the entire Tree of our being is involved and our work is directly connected with our fate and perhaps destiny.

An instance of this can be seen in the lives of great men. Rembrandt was a talented miller's son. He trained as a craftsman painter and became a fashionable painter of portraits. However, he became more interested in the human face than just getting a superb likeness. He began to set down the truth about his clients and they were upset when he portrayed them as real people instead of the Yesodic image they wanted of themselves. A gross burgher wished to be seen as a rather refined gentleman with his immaculate lace collar. He did not want his warts recorded or the slightly avaricious turn of his mouth. Rembrandt lost his customers and his fortune, but he did not care. He painted and painted and began to produce his most penetrating works. A whole series of self-portraits over a lifetime reveal the increasing depth. Nothing was spared as he looked into his own face searching for the key to his nature. His eyes are quiet and steady even though in the later pictures his painting becomes less precise at the edges. This is strange when one considers that the skill and experience of a lifetime were concentrated into every brush stroke. But Rembrandt was more concerned with principles than effects, each canvas not so much a startling composition as a single statement that summed up the whole person. This is Understanding.

A more common example is the understanding that comes with time. As we grow up, many things that were a puzzle to us as children are understood in youth. Likewise with middle and old age. Patterns emerge out of time. Cross-references connect, odd events and dozens of unrelated phenomena begin to focus into an overall design. We see how fatal happenings could not have fallen out any other way and that in some small way we may have contributed to a great enterprise, which in turn was a critical point of decision in history. The scale of this vision is not usually appreciated except in times of national crisis, and then only in hindsight, when all the hidden links are locked into what can now be seen as a grand strategy. A man who can see on this level while events are actually happening, has understanding. If he can perceive the factors leading up to the present and foresee what will follow then he understands the inevitability of cosmic mechanics. Here is the essence of Binah, the passive formulator of great laws.

Without the rest of the Tree, Binah would maintain a rigid universe, with every occurrence unfolding with clockwork efficiency. Fortunately Hokhmah and Keter and all the other sefirot mellow this supernal passive sefirah and prevent its tendency to formalize. In human affairs this isolation can happen and we see it in ultra-orthodox religions which possess great laws but no mercy to soften them. A tradition with a dominant Binah really lays down the law and enforces it all the way down the conservative pillar of the Tree through the severe discipline of Gevurah and the zealous attention to detail in Hod. Here is a warning that understanding is not enough.

Inner Intellect is deep thought. Its quality is originality, absolute appropriateness and profundity. This is indeed the hallmark of Wisdom. Situated at the top of the active pillar its performance is quite different from Understanding. Whereas Binah always carries the element of constraint as in the Commandments which say 'Thou shalt not do this and Thou shalt not do that', Hokhmah carries a positive charge. This is well demonstrated in the first utterance of God in Genesis when He said 'Let there be light'. Out of this statement streams not only all that is to be but also the power and essence of Wisdom.

Hokhmah is the first direct contact with Keter in the Lightning Flash. As such it is the prime active sefirah, pure potency in the relative Universe. It is all potentiality, the father principle ever ready to initiate action. This power flows into Binah, down to Hesed and into Tiferet. The impact of such force is enormous. From this second note of the Universal Octave all the succeeding notes emerge carried along by its cosmic vitality. As one of the supernal triad its influence underlies every active process in creation, its power felt even in the most minute event. In human terms one word of wisdom can change the direction of a man's life.

Inner Intellect in most people is quite silent. And yet out of its depth, at the right point, there rises perhaps a simple thought that illuminates a situation. This may happen in the solving of a scientific problem, as seen in the sudden flash of insight of the chemist Kilkule before his fire, or of inspiration in the arts experienced by many painters, writers and composers. Its effect is always creative as might be expected from its position at the head of the active column and situation between Azilut and Beriah. From such moments of illumination, the light demonstrates the single or many possibilities regarding the subject being contemplated. To be sure the phenomena of direct wisdom is rare, but nevertheless it does operate in human life as a hidden inherent sanity that may come, as the saying goes, 'out of the mouths of babes'.

As will be recalled, the upper parts of the Tree are fully operative although the lower face of the psyche may not be consciously aware of them. This does not mean they do not have their say in a man's life, and modern psychology agrees with the Kabbalistic premise of the total man, calling it the Unconscious. From the point of view of Hokhmah, Inner Intellect will travel, if its conscious manifestation is needed, down any path leading from it, giving Understanding, Beauty and Mercy the veracity of Wisdom. Hokhmah is recognizable behind the very Hesedic sermon on the mount where the power of Wisdom underlies Love. Such a statement as 'Blessed are the pure in heart: for they shall see God' is loaded with Hesed and Hokhmah and carries the full active principle of the positive column. More directly still, the path from Hokhmah to Tiferet is a vital one in an individual man. From Inner Intellect can flow a potent realization. It exceeds even understanding, bringing about a level of comprehension often far above and in excess of the experience of the person involved. Thus a quite simple or uneducated man may receive the revelation craved for by a scholar or sage.

There are many examples of this throughout history. Baal Shem Tov, the Jewish founder of the Hesedic Movement in the eighteenth century, was such a case, so was Jacob Boehme, a seventeenth-century bootmaker, who experienced over a period of seven days the mysteries of the invisible world. Neither Boehme nor Baal Shem had particularly strong intellects, yet both operated from Hokhmah. This is made possible in psychological terms by the flow of the paths down from Hokhmah to Tiferet and then on to Yesod, where the revelation is formed into an image on the ego-consciousness of the psyche's foundation.

The language or symbolism is not of this world, as the awesome vision of Ezekiel clearly demonstrates. Here the yeziratic World formed a complex picture that obeyed no laws familiar in the asiyyatic World. Such elaborate symbolism has its own key which ordinary Hodian logic is totally inadequate to provide. A man needs to be raised to that level of himself on the Tree to comprehend it. Perhaps the most famous of these experiences is that of Mohammed, the prophet, who rode on the back of a winged horse with a woman's head and a peacock's tail up through the hierarchy of Heaven and into the presence of the veiled Godhead. Similar accounts are found in the Merkabah period literature of early Jewish mysticism and the Book of the Secrets of Enoch. In Kabbalah such Hokhmah revelations are called Prophecy. To reach such a high level of comprehension requires direct experience, acquired by long and diligent spiritual practice or through the grace of God. Such matters are of a totally individual nature and cannot be discussed with real meaning except in very general terms.

How then can we at least grasp something of the ordinary psychological nature of Hokhmah? Perhaps if we reflect on our own personal experience we may recall a moment when the inner intellect manifested. It might have been during a very quiet moment. A profound thought may come in the middle of an ordinary conversation, even during the chores of daily life. Its quality is quite distinct. Its immediate impact will last for days and will influence all subsequent decisions and actions if it is not ignored. This, however, happens at our peril, because such important realizations are not random, but only occur when relevant to some important point in our lives. Many people can look back over their personal histories and recall in detail one or more cross roads. Often it will be remembered that such events were often preceded by a shift in their view of themselves or the world about them.

Unlike understanding which tends to work through receptive observation, Inner Intellect usually points a way, tells us how to solve a problem or take up a completely new position. We may not even verbalize the thought. It can be a deep penetrating look at the situation around us or even into ourselves. It is like the illumination of a whole landscape by sheet lightning which reveals roads, hills and houses previously unseen in the darkness of the ordinary state. Nothing is the same after such a moment, however softly it may steal up on one. An exhausting job procrastinated becomes intolerable, and a change must occur if the integrity is to survive. Perhaps a relationship has reached a point when something new is needed. A moment under the tuition of Inner Intellect may trigger a totally unthought-of solution. Out of the blue a completely different angle emerges, changing a partnership well set for a lifetime, into an event of distant history. On the big scale, this is the power of ideas and we know that some conceptions have indeed altered the face of the world. The proverb comparing the power of the pen to that of the sword is a Binah recognition of this fact, and one should not underestimate the potency of thought within the realm of our personal existence. It may come upon one at any moment. It is present all the time but we do not usually acknowledge it. As ordinary mortals we cannot cope with Wisdom all the time, but without the guidance of Inner Intellect emanating from life about us or from deep within us, we could not live.

Here then is the Intellectual combination of Understanding and Wisdom. Together they are the supernal heads of the two outer pillars. Between them is the column of equilibrium, Will and consciousness. As the active and passive principles they indicate and formulate thought. Out of them comes the Beriatic World. They are the parents of creation in the macrocosm and the great male and female principle on the human level. It has more than once been said that the Universe is a great idea and this is a fairly accurate description in the light of Hokhmah and Binah. It must be remembered, however, that these two polar sefirot are aspects of one intellectual singularity which is in turn but a facet of Keter the Crown out of which all emerges. Even so, as no sefirah, including the Crown, is superior to any other, so each sefirotic pair operate equally at a particular level, none takes precedence. In man the same is true. Although made up of many parts and several bodies he is an exact replica of all men, the mirror image of Adam Kadmon, who is himself a likeness of the One who called, created, formed and made him.

22. *The Intellectual Triads*

The twin Intellectual triads described by the passive Binah–Gevurah–Tiferet and the active Hokhmah–Hesed–Tiferet configurations perform functional tasks in the psyche in much the same way as the atomic ions do in corresponding triads in the physical body. Whereas the ions by their positive and negative charges aid the body's metabolism and electro-magnetic organism, these psychological side triads perform a similar task, but in a different materiality between the soul and the spirit. As intermediaries contacting the beriatic and yeziratic Worlds they are directly connected to the lower face of the Tree of Creation.

Such a position makes them extremely powerful although by no means any more important in the context of the psyche. Their role, as will be guessed, is very deeply embedded in the unconscious of a natural man having profound effects on his state at a level well outside his personal consciousness. An example of this is the case of a man's cultural outlook. A Chinese sees the world in the light of the history of China, with his own country naturally at the centre of things. An Englishman does likewise and indeed is slightly disturbed when he sees an American map of the world with the United States in the mid-section of the sheet. These are small matters but indicative of many influential things we take for granted. Indeed so deeply rooted are some of these concepts that whole empires have fallen because of the unconscious assumptions of its people. Roman, Chinese and British imperialism worked through many generations who accepted the mythology of their civilization without question. Here too is the power of the American Dream and the Soviet Utopia. The ideas may be good, bad or indifferent, accepted or rejected, but they have great impact on the people living under them. In an individual such a realm of intellectual concepts is part of his psychological heritage and operates through him, often without his being aware of them until he meets another set of concepts in someone else's psyche. How do these intellectual functional triads operate? We will take the passive side first and illustrate it with the old chestnut joke of the rabbi and priest arguing over who has the best religion. On reaching an *impasse*, the priest, seeking to invalidate the rabbi's high moral stance, asks him whether he has ever eaten pork. The rabbi blushes with shame and nods. 'It's nice, isn't it?' says the priest, rubbing salt into the wound. The rabbi, after a moment's thought, regains his composure and asks the priest if he has ever slept with a woman. The priest's face whitens. The rabbi smiles and says, in an act of reconciliation, 'It's nicer than pork, isn't it?' Here we have a pair of loaded Binah–Gevurah–Tiferet triads in conflict. Indeed most humour is the juxtaposition between side triads with the punch line resolved in the central column.

Contained in the passive triad is an amalgam of intellectual formulations inherited from the individual's race, nation, family and education. These are mixed with conclusions drawn from a man's personal experience, and his relationship with them. Thus we see that this triad is created by his Understanding, his Judgement and his self, the combination crystallizing into a framework of concepts which structure his thinking. An Irish Catholic trained by the astute Society of Jesus will have at his command not only the irrational charm of the Celtic mind but the dogma of the Church and the ability to argue a tight case. His Intellectual platform is very stable and resilient by nature and his Jesuit training soon shows in any conversation on matters of religion. Like the passive emotional complexes in the triad below, this side Intellectual function operates as both a conservationist of old and a resistant to new ideas.

A man may say he is a lapsed Jew or Catholic, but the concepts of respect for law will show in his life style even if he has to become a radical in order to obliterate them. The depth of the influence of this or the opposite triad must not be underestimated. Men have died for the precepts embedded in them. Sir Thomas

More was beheaded by Henry VIII over a matter of divorce and Che Gevara was killed in the South American jungle fighting for world revolution. Both men died for a principle—the first a martyr for the passive triad and the other a hero for the active one. Both behaved according to their ideals.

Another way of looking at the passive triad is to consider it as a constellation of accepted propositions. As a series of intellectual processes, some will be related into groups, while others will have little or no connection. These propositions may be totally distorted, perhaps by an unbalanced judgement or misunderstanding, but they will still function. The phenomenon of Nazi Germany well illustrates this point. A good party member could take part in the death of thousands of Poles, Russians and Jews yet he could be a perfectly good husband and regard himself as a model officer of the Gestapo. This may have come about because of the deep racial level Hitler evoked with its sense of Nordic superiority blended with the man's identification with it. Thus he easily conformed to the madness around him. After all the whole nation was affected, so his work was quite socially acceptable. This is because in him, and many Germans, the passive side of the Tree was dominant. There is no built-in corrective on the passive column on its own and very few people are centred enough in Tiferet to take the full responsibility for their actions, to stand up as an individual to an obvious imbalance of the nation's Tree of Life.

On the positive side this passive Intellectual triad retains the overall form of a man's training so that if he is a scientist he can draw on its working principles to solve problems. It is here that the philosopher operates, testing out ideas, checking them against tried precepts. In more ordinary matters our experience is formulated and valued in this triad and its findings made available to the self when needed. One may not be aware of its presence but its form controls our prejudices. This triad is like a submerged range of mountains over which we sail, the currents of our emotional mood profoundly influenced by the peaks below.

On the other side of the Tree is the active complement to the formal structure of our Intellect. Here the intake of new ideas from above or below is possible in the expansive and dynamic triad created by Hesed, Hokhmah and Tiferet. One might say that genius works in this place, for expansion in the intellectual realm can only manifest through this triad. An idea is born, but it has to be processed, that is, its force must be demonstrated, then formalized on the other side of the Tree if it is accepted into the psyche.

The proverbial flash of illumination takes place in this triad. Hokhmah delivers the insight to Tiferet while Hesed carries its power into the emotions. Anyone who has had an inspiration knows the elation and opening up of inner vision. But illumination alone is not enough, it is quickly lost unless it is passed into Tiferet and out again for assessment and formulation by the passive triad. Understanding, directly across the Tree from Wisdom receives the insight by way of the normal Lightning Flash sequence and this feeds into the top of the passive Triad. Easily observed processes are rare, and most of the enlightening conclusions we come to in the deep part of our psyche pop out on the screen of Yesodic consciousness at the most odd moments. We are in fact thinking all the time, and this does not mean the moment-by-moment conveyor belt of Yesodic dreams. One indeed might be buying groceries or talking when the thought comes into consciousness about some question we have been considering. It is usually important to our lives and development and is invariably a brick in the edifice of a whole area, within our passive intellectual triad, by the input and acceptance, of a completely new conception.

An example of this is common to many creative people when they leave college. It comes, for instance, when perhaps a young painter realizes his ideals about being the world's greatest artist have to give way to the fact he is talented but not good enough to compete in any major art league. The shift of ground, if it comes in at the conceptual level, does not blast the ego. The advice of Wisdom is accepted by Understanding. Judgement and Mercy both confirm and release the self as the active Intellectual triad helps to rearrange the formal configuration of ideas on the passive side. The self perceives this major change and in an emotional catharsis, the person often feels a lot better at not having to live up to his idealism. It is usually at this point, when correctly handled by Tiferet, that the dreaming ego comes to heel and the person begins to paint something worthwhile.

For obvious reasons this triad has great creative power. Adjacent both to the active pillar and the central triad of the Spirit the energy generated is enormous. In the realm of the psyche this is the power of ideas emerging from deep within a man. On reading the great dialogues of Plato one gets the impact of this triad even though it has been formulated by its passive complement. The same is true of certain works of the Kabbalah, especially the Book of the Concealed Mystery which, though almost unintelligible to the ordinary mind, is like the thunder of truth behind a cloud of words.

It is indeed very difficult to describe this triad because its potency cannot be spoken about without being misleading. The nearest one can approach is the direct experience of our creative process which carries with it the illumination and extension of the intellectual grasp. This does not mean a Hodian increase of information but a profound widening of the total outlook. Here is the vital dialogue between the conservative principle on the passive side and the revolutionary input on the active. Between them comes the Central great triad of the Spirit composed of both. This combination forms our overall intellectual backdrop of the World. Usually we incline to the conservative side because few of us can face the threat of change in our ideas. However, there are some who prefer to lean the other way, and these include our greatest thinkers, saints and artists. Such people are usually regarded as radicals in their time.

Both the Christian Church and the Orthodox Jewish Synagogue, focussed primarily in the passive triad, had trouble with their members who operated on the active side. Indeed St Thomas Aquinas and his Jewish contemporary Maimonades had the task of setting out a compensatory Theology for their respective traditions because there was much original thinking at that time as the result of contact with Greek and Arabic thought. The great cathedrals built all over Western Europe at this period were also the result of a vast influx of this same creativity. These massive structures may be Binah–Gevurah–Tiferet in flavour but the origin of their conception is Hokhmah–Hesed–Tiferet. It has been said they are models of Creation in stone and to stand on the circular maze at Chartres and look down the huge nave is to catch a glimpse of the Beriatic World of which these twin functional triads are the flanks. Indeed, it has been suggested that the ground plan of Chartres conforms to the dimensions of the Tree of Life. Whether this be true or not does not matter, because it is more important to realize that a similar structure exists in the psyche.

Crystallized between force and form the complex structure of our intellect is designed to house the Spirit, which is what it does on the Tree. Moreover, the complex is adjacent to the two emotional side triads supporting and feeding into the self-conscious synthesis called the Soul. We have here the traditional model of the temple with the lower face as its outer courtyard, the inner court being of Tiferet and the Holy of Holies beyond. In the terms of our study, psychology from this point on begins to take on a spiritual flavour. This is because we are at the frontier of Beriah. The upper face of the psychological Tree is the lower face of the beriatic World. Only consciousness can participate fully in Beriah and this is confined to the great central triangle of the Ruah or Spirit which roots down through the Soul triad of the Neshama into the self which is the individualized Divine spark in all men.

23. The Psyche as a Whole: A recapitulation

So far we have examined the anatomy of the psyche by slowly climbing up the yeziratic Tree. Now, before we explore the Nature of the Soul, we must appreciate the psyche as a working whole so that we can observe how it operates and contributes to the two upper triads of the Soul and Spirit. First it will be remembered that the yeziratic Tree participates both in the asiyyatic and the beriatic Worlds with the small conscious triad of the Neshamah as the only true yeziratic element between the upper and lower faces. Moreover, it must be recalled that a man may operate his psychological Tree consciously or unconsciously, the conscious being the process of developing his soul and himself into a supernatural man. This evolution will be discussed later after we have seen how the natural man functions in ordinary ego consciousness almost entirely within the lower face.

Let us begin with a general survey of the psychological Tree and its dynamics. Taking the Tree as a whole we can see that it is all of one piece despite its many parts and levels. This is because it is a unity, the various aspects merely the relative attributes of the one, that is, the original model of Adam, Adam Kadmon the Universe and the One. As a complete unit no part can operate without affecting the whole. This is manifested through the three pillars, the four worlds, the sefirot, the triads and paths. Being so complex an organism it has a wide variety of functions and subtleties. This is demonstrated in the Tree of the physical body which possesses a vast number of interlinking processes and structures capable of extraordinary flexibility and capacities. In the Tree of the psyche the same integrated system occurs, although the energy and substances involved are largely invisible to the physical eye. Furthermore, like its material expression the body, the psyche is an interdependent organization within the context of its Tree, so that no feeling, emotion, thought or spiritual event happens in isolation but relates to the whole organism.

Having recognized that the Tree works as a single entity it is observed that the law of three operates throughout the psychological organism. This is perceived in the various active and passive processes in the psyche, on the large scale in the pillars, on the small in the sixteen triads. All of these triads, be they conscious or functional, have the reconciling principle in their contact with the central column.

Starting with the lower face the sefirah of Malkhut makes the direct connection with the body Tree through the asiyyatic Tiferet of the central nervous system. The sefirah of Yesod is simultaneously the knowledge consciousness of the body and the Foundation or ego of the psyche. The twin sefirot of Hod and Nezah balance each other at the bottom of the pillars of force and form and operate as the voluntary and involuntary functions of the ordinary mind which is focussed by their convergent paths in Yesod. They also have path connections with the nervous system and can operate the body even when the Yesod consciousness is asleep, in other words when the path to Malkhut is closed down to minimal circulation. Tiferet, the pivot of the Tree, is the self of a man.

While the self may be the centre of the psyche ego it may not wish to acknowledge it. This is because ego, by education and experience, acquires a persona which it wears on the path between itself and the outside world of Malkhut, and an inner Yesodic image which obscures the path of honesty between the ego and the self. This shadow side grows as the foundation of the person's Ego is formed. Primarily built up of things it does not like about itself, the ego suppresses them so that what might be considered the Mr Hyde to the charming Doctor Jekyll of the outward looking persona emerges. In mediaeval terms, this is one's personal devil who lies in wait on the path from Yesod to Tiferet. Because of this complex the ego often assumes the role of master of the psyche, thus usurping the self's role.

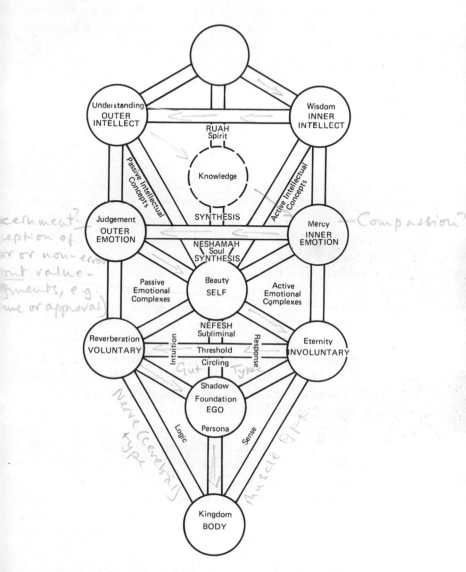

PSYCHE IN DETAIL

Connect with Table on p. 25

Having an influence on the lower face of Yezirah are the three body-types of the nervous, the muscle and viscera which take effect from the lower face of Asiyyah, that is the autonomic Yesod. These constitute the vegetable man who lives a more or less mechanical existence be it on a farm or in a university. Such people are quite predictable and nothing particularly new happens in their lives. They are content.

Contained in the lower face of Yezirah are the four ego-types of logic, sense, intuition and response. These four triads can be subdivided into introvert and extrovert, the ones attached to Malkhut being the latter, the other pair obviously inner by their connection with the self. Thus there are twenty-four aspects indicated, four ego-types each operating through a body-type and each extroverted or introverted.

Below the path between Hod and Nezah is the triad of 'circling'. This together with the Great Triangle of Hod–Nezah–Malkhut may be considered the vegetable or routine part of the psyche. However, the triad formed by Hod–Nezah–Tiferet, known traditionally as the Nefesh or Animal Soul, is the level of awakening consciousness. This state is quite distinct from the repetitive cycling of the mind and brings the ego into contact with the self. This does not mean a sustained self-consciousness because the path between Yesod and Tiferet may not be clear or permanently open. It requires a certain degree of courage and determination to break through the shadow ego and centre consciously in Tiferet.

Beyond the lower face are the twin function triads of emotion. These active and passive sides are the working complexes of a natural man's unconscious. Through the interaction via Tiferet and the path links, a synthesis of emotional attitudes both open and closed is created, and these underlie our approach or retreat reactions. Such instant response is emotional by nature and helps to create the moods behind the activities of the lower face. Simultaneous to the downward feedback is each triad's contribution to the Neshamah or Soul triad. This is the conscious refinement created out of the acceptance and rejection, expansion and formulation processes of the emotional complexes actively or passively operating in the side columns. The soul receives this uplifted input from the sefirot of Tiferet, Judgement and Mercy, that is, the Self and Inner and Outer Emotion.

Above the emotional functional side triads are the intellectual triads connected with the sefirot of Understanding and Wisdom. These perform in much the same way, but as complex groups of concepts, associations and memories. The chief difference, besides being mainly intellectual in flavour, is that they are less personal than the emotional triads and have an objectivity not always connected directly with the person's external life. This is because the sefirot of Binah and Hokhmah are directly related to Beriah and Azilut. Indeed these triads have a cosmic flavour. Their job is to process input from above and below, the active side to handle the revelation, the passive the formulation. Between them they create the deep structure of a man's life and influence, consciously or unconsciously, the fundamental principles upon which he bases his psychological existence. Both relate to the triad of the Spirit which is the conscious synthesis of them, and to the descent of the Will and Grace of God from the Azilutic World above.

The whole Tree functions as one. No part may act independently. Flows may choose different paths but the law that governs circulation, although allowing many combinations, has a finite pattern of possibilities. Likewise with the triads which, while highly flexible, still obey a distinct set of rules. Even the sefirot have their limitations determined by the whole. Gevurah may become dominant for some reason but Hesed, its complement, will eventually check the imbalance, aided directly by those sefirot whose paths flow into Gevurah, with the backing of the whole Tree which works for the common good of all.

Here then in brief is a recapitulation of the psychological Tree. Our next step is to see how it operates in its own terms as a whole. For this we turn to ancient and modern definitions. These speak in the language of archetypes, the tongue of the yeziratic World.

24. Archetypes

An archetype is the model upon which something is based. It is the immutable set of laws that make a thing, an event or a being conform to a basic pattern. The archetypal relationship between men and women, for instance, is repeated in every generation. The laws are as unchanging as the inevitable characteristic pattern of a salt crystal emerging from a drying solution. There may be variances, but these are well within the margins of that archetype. Archetypes are usually recognized by a yeziratic image although their origin lies in the eternal World of Emanations.

In Kabbalistic terms an archetype exists in Azilut, is created in Beriah, formulated in Yezirah and manifests in Asiyyah. The first chapters of this book describe the process from Adam Kadmon down through the Worlds into the individualized earthy person like you and I. Adam, being in a likeness to God, is the most comprehensive of archetypes. There are, however, many other, lesser archetypes.

The prime archetype is Oneness. There is no division in All in spite of the incredible complexity within, because All is contained and permeated by the One.

In Tree terms the symbol of the Crown through which flows the Will of God is the penultimate archetype.

The second archetype is the trinity composed by Keter, the Crown and the active and passive sefirot of the Great Father and Mother of Hokhmah and Binah. This supernal triad carries within it the manifest archetypal World for all Universes. What develops out of the Realm of Emanations is rooted in its unchangeableness. Below, the beriatic, yeziratic and asiyyatic Worlds create, form and make their subarchetypes which are expressed in terms of their own Force, Form and Consciousness. In the world of the human psyche the yeziratic archetypes are quite recognizable as expressions of the Tree. There is the One of Adam, that is mankind, the two, of male and female principles and the various psychological formulations of all the sefirot and triads.

The idea of archetypes has been known since ancient times and even the most primitive mythology and folklore recognizes their existence. Tales about the creation of the world are cast in yeziratic terms and imply through their powerful imagery the operations of beriah working out the will of Azilut. Nature gods, and elemental deities may appear to be redundant in our modern age but they personify powerful factors which even advanced technology has to take into account. A hurricane sweeping across the United States killing hundreds and destroying billions of dollars worth of property commands much respect even in the atomic age. Such storms are even given a girl's name by the U.S. weather bureau. This is an acknowledgement that the phenomenon has a distinct identity. Early man did precisely the same, only he saw it for the archetypal principle it was.

In the early religions of man, archetypes were defined by the various gods. Some peoples had highly complex hierarchies of archetypes, others simpler, and the Hebrews only one, with no yeziratic image at all. This greatly disturbed Israel's periodic conquerors when, on entering the Holy of Holies found nothing but an empty chamber. This was in recognition of the commandment, 'Thou shalt have no graven images.' Here was the warning against being caught in any of the relative worlds and an invitation to make contact with the Creator direct.

In the general Mediterranean area the gods became divided into greater and lesser deities. The Olympians in the Greco-Roman world were the archetypes of major cosmic principles, while the numerous lesser gods and goddesses personified minor functions in the scheme of things. The goddess Vesta, for instance, was the deity of the fireside hearth, a domestic archetype in many cultures. There were also very minor gods like Tiberinus who personified the river running through Rome, but these were very local identifications.

As already mentioned some of the Greco-Roman gods have been used by Kabbalists to define the cosmic principles embodied in the Tree. These were very clear images full of the qualities of Yezirah and the content of Beriah. As ready-made entities they were rich in mythology and visual information, and their placing on the various sefirot increased the knowledge of those using the method. Those Hebrew Kabbalists who did not wish to be influenced by gentile culture used the archetypes of the Biblical patriarchs to describe the lower sefirot. Abraham was related to Hesed because of his great love of his Creator, for he was the friend of God. Isaac was placed on Gevurah because he lived his life in strict discipline and this was sometimes called the 'Fear of Isaac'. Tiferet was manifested in Jacob who was always concerned with the Truth, while Moses was ascribed to Nezah because of his power, and Aaron to Hod in the light of his eloquence. He spoke, it will be remembered, for Moses before Pharaoh and later as the priestly clan, for the Children of Israel. The archetype represented in Joseph was connected with Yesod, the sefirah particularly related to sexual matters. This referred to Joseph's encounter with Potipher's wife. Malkhut was symbolized by David, the spiritual and yet earthly king. Other Biblical archetypes were also placed on the Tree using the sisters Leah and Rachel, for example, as Binah and Malkhut, with Israel, as Jacob was later called, at the Tiferet position. There are in Kabbalistic literature, it will be noted, several combinations of Biblical personalities each expressing in the qualities of their lives the sefirot in human terms.

This use of archetypal imagery to convey principles has two characteristics. Firstly, that the beriatic content never changes, and secondly, that the yeziratic form is constantly modified to relate to a particular time and place. Thus it is that certain ideas, common to all humanity, recur in widely spaced geographical locations, and at different points in history, and are, despite their varied form, recognizable as the same thing.

A good example of this archetypal phenomenon is the goddess Venus who represents the female sex symbol. She occurs in her wide variety of attractive guises in every culture, from the most primitive, to the most sophisticated. In ancient times the Venus principle was simultaneously embodied in the Greek Aphrodite, the Phoenician Astarte, the Babylonian Nana, the Assyrian Isktar, the Norse Freya and the Indian Lakshmi, to mention only a few. All the facets of the same archetype were sensual, lusty and desirable. Men saw her as the ideal of feminine beauty and women modelled themselves on her prototype. The worship of her continued right through mediaeval times with the love for the noble maiden, and the peasant mistress. The Renaissance is pervaded by her image, both in art and fashion, and this continues to this day in the current movie image of Venus and the endless renewal of fashion each season, which dresses and undresses each generation as it passes through its age of Venus. In Kabbalistic terms this is the sefirah of Nezah, Eternity or repetition, and all the processes to do with instinct.

Much later, when the Tree of Life was used in the unkabbalistic practice of magic, yet another set of archetypes was placed on the Tree. These were again expressions of the various sefirotic principles but in the language of pure Yezirah. Magic operates in the world of forms, the magician calling on the sefirot of that realm to aid him in his work. Such operations consist of creating forms and forces which will either draw him up into Beriah, or manifest below in Asiyyah. In plain everyday experience, the latter magical operation is carried out in propaganda and advertising which seeks to make the mass psyche do something in the world of action and hardware. Most of us practise a form of magic when we attempt to influence some person or event. This can range from a work of art to an evocative remark which exerts a definite pressure. It is commonplace, but it nevertheless follows the principles of magic, that is, the effect of yezirah on Asiyyah.

In so-called High Magic, the magician, like anyone who understands the laws of human nature, uses these yeziratic laws to build up a charged form. The theatre and cinema do this as a matter of course, to create sometimes a very potent atmosphere. The magician attempts to obtain the same effect but makes it powerful enough to move Asiyyah into action and form. To do this he has to know what laws to apply and how to evoke them. This requires a long apprenticeship, because to miscalculate the forces used may cost him his life. Perhaps it sounds dramatic to say this, but the yeziratic world, it should be remembered, is the world of psychology, and madness is a risk to any who play with magic for fun or personal power.

The trained and balanced magician is in fact evoking in his operation, for various reasons, the Tree of his own psyche. This is aided by the magical images ascribed to each sefirah. As archetypes their evocation connects him with the powers of Yezirah and if he has the nerve or discipline, they will operate through him. Possession of a man by a spirit is accepted in primitive societies and it is not as uncommon in Western man as one might think. Whereas a magician seeks to call and control the archetype he has evoked in himself, some people one meets in ordinary life are in this state without being magicians. We call them obsessed when they have our contempt, and single-minded when they evoke our admiration.

The various magical images on the Tree are yeziratic formulations of the sefirot. They also bear a distinct resemblance to the Graeco-Roman gods except for Saturn in Binah, which although the traditional image of old Father Time, is also the passive receptive principle embodied in the Kabbalistic archetype of the Great Mother. This image is carried over into the magical tradition. In the case of Tiferet the image is three-fold, that is a sacrificed god, a child and a king. These archetypes express different yeziratic aspects of the sefirah. The same is true for Yesod which has a naked man for its symbol.

Interesting as this is, how does it relate to our study of man and in this section on his psychology? The point is that we can begin to see how the same archetypes recur when dealing with the psychological world. In ancient Kabbalist tradition various angels are associated with the sefirot of Yezirah and these may also be evoked if there is control over a personal yeziratic World; which few people have. To acquire this inner stability entails long and disciplined training under a teacher who really knows what he is doing. No one in a hurry need apply. Nor is it advisable for people who cannot cope with ordinary life. Indeed, the ability to

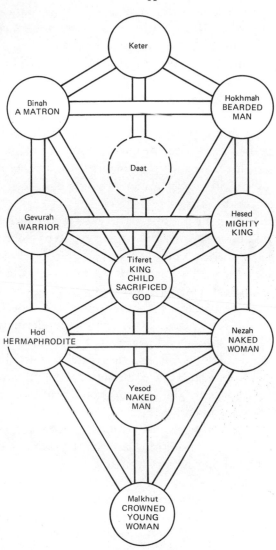

A SET OF MAGICAL ARCHETYPES

handle one's mundane affairs well is a prime qualification for Kabbalistic practice. Besides this, Kabbalists, while acquainted with magic, do not use or encourage it: Kavvanah or prayer with intent is permitted, but not magic. Most magicians are not Kabbalists.

The archetypes of Yezirah already exist in the psychological body. They are inherent in all human beings and manifest as constants in the gods, myths, and visions of man. Dreams are pure Yezirah, be they in sleep or the ever-distant mirage of a life-time's work or love. As such they manifest the archetypes in the individual psyche in many guises even though their essential character remains the same.

In the cases of night dreams archetypes reveal themselves in characters and situations, sometimes using events of the day before, at others, old memories. These are the yeziratic players and props through which the archetypes work. Occasionally the roles are clearly differentiated and one may easily recognize the lush yeziratic image of Nezah or the hero-like figure of Gevurah. Hesed, for example, may manifest as a powerful ruler figure while Hod, as the clever chameleon, for ever changes his role. Tiferet has a unique role because it is also the Watcher who observes in the dream as if from a high place, the antics of Yesod which is the image one has of oneself. The two supernal sefirot can manifest in a variety of ways, sometimes as the great enclosing principle of Binah the Mother or as a powerful Father figure in Hokhmah. The dialogue, conflict and resolution between the active and passive pillars is the underlying subject of many dreams.

In the external projection of the yeziratic world the archetypes play a very big part. Every young man seeks Venusian perfection in a girl, and women, for their part, look for the male equivalent of Nezah in a beautiful and vital young man, while both sexes try to emulate these ideals in dress and manner. Likewise the Father and Mother archetype is a blessing and a bane for most people. Some attempt to project their need for parental love, perhaps denied earlier, on to others, who in turn may take pleasure in acting out these roles, working out their own parental relationship. The supernal pair of archetypes, by their position on the

Archetypes　　197

Tree, are particularly powerful as they also include the male and female elements in every man and woman. The Gevurah archetype, when projected, may be seen in the worship of heroes or men of courage and decision. It can also be observed in a person working through his own Gevurah in an excessively tough period in his career. Hesed can be the reverse with a man playing the active role of the generous benefactor, or negatively in looking for someone to fulfil that archetype, even if it takes the form of public or private assistance. It is interesting to note that the Gevurah aspect of such people vehemently demands a Hesed reaction as their right. The projection of Hod is seen in the nimble operator, the wheeler-dealer both in ourselves and in others. We secretly admire the crafty, the astute and even the clever Hodian crook. Most detective stories are based on the good and bad archetypes of Hod with whom we identify almost instantly as our Hod is easily excited.

The Yesod archetype, we have said, is our imagined picture of ourselves, which is usually the synthesis of all the other factors. Depending on the ego's inclination, this image is beautiful or ugly, brave or cowardly, intelligent or a fool. One usually hovers somewhere between these poles, but all are magnified, larger than life to us. Indeed this is true of all the archetypes in that they seem to be richer than any asiyyatic reality, more dramatic and volatile. This is the quality of yezirah which can enhance the forms it makes and project them deeper in to Beriah or further out into Asiyyah.

All who have been deeply involved with anything or anyone, know how that interest or person takes on archetypal profundity. A devoted doctor feels he is connected with the ideals of Hippocrates, and a man in love sees his girl as the epitomy of feminine beauty. The power of the archetype holds the imagination, although perhaps for different reasons; the doctor's for instance, may stem from Hod, and the lover's from Nezah. It is common experience to have an ideal and this is fed by the Arts which meet a yeziratic need of the psyche. Obviously it is a power that can be used for good or evil. The rise of Adolf Hitler depended on the archetypal projection of the German people. The same technique was used by Churchill in the war against Hitler with the British bulldog image. Many generations have made the most extraordinary efforts under the evocation of an archetype. The Church has the Mother principle to thank for the power of the Virgin Mary, and Judaism, in spite of its lack of images, has the Father projection of Moses and the Patriarchs.

As we saw in dreams, Tiferet, by virtue of its position on the Tree, is a man as himself. While inwardly it is the all-knowing guide and adviser, externally it can be projected as the Christ or Buddha figure. Not the Divine Father, nor an ordinary human being, this archetype is the most powerful for man, because while being of a high order, it is graspable, if only by a glimpse of what is possible for a man or a woman, who are true to themselves. In many spiritual traditions the externalization is the Master or Teacher so that many people dissatisfied with the pettiness of their egos go in pursuit of their own projected selves. The discriminating ones find a teacher who releases them as soon as they have made stable contact with their Tiferet. The unlucky ones, clinging to their own archetypal projection of their guru, are stuck to his nature and tied to his fate instead of their own. This causes trouble when they discover their worshipped master is only too human, and they turn violently against him, before seeking someone else upon whom to project their responsibility for themselves.

In the case of a relatively stable person the archetypes check and balance each other, although in times of crisis the sefirah, trying to correct the imbalance, will exert a strong influence on the disturbed psyche. An example of this is the classical marriage situation in which the husband is excessively on the form pillar and the wife the reverse. In these encounters the reversed active and passive roles increase the female archetype in the man and the male in the woman with the result that the woman becomes more aggressive and the man defensive. This usually occurs when the archetypal roles of husband and wife are not being fulfilled by one or both partners. The solution is for both to centre on the middle column and see themselves as human beings, warts and all, through the truthful eye of Tiferet. Only then can a real marriage, an acceptance of the whole man and woman occur.

Archetypes, as will be seen, have a powerful and not so much unseen, as unnoticed, effect on our lives. Their yeziratic form and force surrounds us in the clothes we wear and why, the mass media in what we watch or listen to, and the kind of lives we lead in the community of our choosing. The world of Formations is vast. It operates throughout the Universe as angelic principles, and is perceived via the human psyche, in archetypal forms and powers. It may be evoked on the level of a whole civilization through its beliefs, arts and customs.

In the more parochial area of communities it is used to project an ideal, in one example, as the successful business man, in another, as the liberated hippy. Both are archetypal images which may possess a person. On the individual level the yeziratic World is the form and energy of his psyche, and the archetypes of his nature play their roles within him as the yeziratic focus of various complexes. In Kabbalistic language, each sefirah draws to itself all the experiences, memories and associations sympathetic to its quality. Like is drawn to like, so that about each sefirah there collects a mass of psychological form or energy which builds up over the inherent cosmic archetype of that sefirah, into an archetypal image peculiar to that person. This intermarriage of cosmic and personal patterns is law, inasmuch as what is greater affects what is lesser and vice versa. This also applies to inner and outer, and vice versa. Therefore, if we wish to understand ourselves more, we must examine the archetypes common to all men and perceive what our own are, and how we respond to them. With this knowledge one begins to have command, and in the watery World of Yezirah it is a vital element in our training.

25. The Archetypes and the Unconscious

In the case of natural man only the lower face of the psychological Tree is conscious. The upper triads and sefirot are operative but remain out of conscious view in what is called by some contemporary psychologists, the Unconscious. This is the state of most of the human race and is regarded by those traditions concerned with the evolution of the soul as psychological sleep. In the Kabbalah it is called 'being in Egypt'. The implication is profound because it suggests that the mass of humanity has very little direct control over itself, and is directed from within as well as from without, by forces as powerful and influential as the physical environment.

The concept of the Unconscious is thought to be a new one but in schools of development in East and West the idea that man has an inner but unrealized aspect of his nature has been known and discussed for many centuries. Indeed many of the spiritual disciplines are specifically designed to open up the channels to this inner realm. The Dervish dancer's spin, many of the Buddhist and Christian meditational practices are techniques by which a man may enter Paradise and Heaven, the allegorical names for the upper parts of the Tree. In the Kabbalah there are a variety of methods each designed to meet the need of a particular physical and psychological type.

For a natural man, or one who is not particularly interested in his spiritual development, the situation is different. He is not cut off from the possibility of making direct contact with the upper face of his psyche, but this may only happen once or twice in his lifetime and he may discard the experience as a touch of irrationality, a moment of imbalance despite the extraordinary illumin-

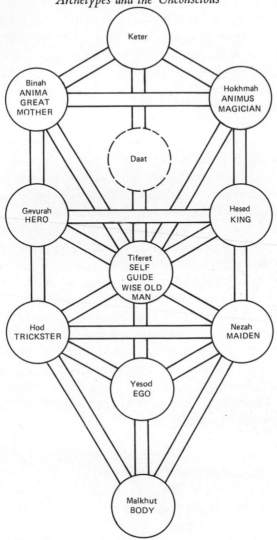

JUNGIAN ARCHETYPES

Occurring in dreams and projected into life these yeziratic images are common to all men but in terms of their own culture. The most obvious manifestation is in the folktale. Jung went so far as to name his own guide Philemon.

ating quality it shed on his life. To face the full truth is difficult and
most people prefer to repress or devalue the vision that reveals
too much about themselves. They, like Esau, in Gen. 15:32,
would rather sell their birthright for the immediate satisfaction
of a mess of pottage. This places them in the strange position of
living in the twilight world of ego which confuses dreams with
ordinary life, and reality with them both.

In modern psychology the two medical pioneers Freud and
Jung each defined this relationship between the Conscious and
Unconscious in their own way, and much credit must go to both
for drawing conventional science's attention to something religion
and philosophy had been concerned with for millennia. The terms
Self and Ego are not new, nor is their meaning and relationship
to one another, to people involved with spiritual development.
This is most important to remember because while Freud and
Jung made what appeared to be innovations, they were in fact
rediscoveries of ancient ideas, and Jung was to acknowledge this.
In this book some apparently Jungian terms are used because they
are twentieth-century definitions for basic Kabbalistic concepts
and should not be mistaken as Jungian in origin. However, the
restatements by the Jungian school have close correspondence to
the Kabbalah and therefore a blend of the terms for our time and
language is inevitable. For my part it is simply a question of
credit where credit is due, both to the ancient and modern study
of man.

The Unconscious is that part of the Tree which lies beyond the
threshold of the conscious. Set on the Tree, consciousness is for
most people, Yesod and Malkhut, that is, the ego and the body.
The extreme range of the ego when fully alert is Hod, Nezah and
Tiferet, but this as a rule only occurs in a moment of passion or
crisis or in some highly stimulating situation. Normally the ego
hovers in a dim and fluctuating awareness with the adjacent
sefirot of Hod and Nezah out of sight. They operate subliminally
performing their tasks of life maintenance. This is true in fact of
the whole Tree, which controls the intellectual and emotional
processes of a person, despite his unawareness of their workings.
One occasionally catches a glimpse of this when conclusions or

emotions suddenly arise in the ego. At times they even surprise the person concerned, in that he had no idea he had thought about this or felt that. The Unconscious works in spite of us.

Before we penetrate into the World of the Unconscious, we must first define the Conscious. On the Tree, Yesod is the screen on the middle pillar into which both outer pillars flow. Focussed there are the three body types and the four ego-types or aspects of the lower psyche. Added to this is the direct relationship to the body and the self. All these converging paths make the ego the seat of consciousness in the asiyyatic World. This gives the ego a strong sense of physical realities and, with its function as the Foundation of the Tree, makes it believe it is the main perceiver of the Universe. For a man with little or no experience of the other three Worlds, Yesod is the only level of reality he knows and so all his assessments are based on the kind of foundation he formed as a child. If he is a savage, the jungle may be his world and if a New York executive, business is his universe. There are of course savages and sophisticates who see beyond their environment, but these are few and if we are honest, most of us are confined to a quite small circle of friends and environments. A man can be a traveller, but most professionals are remarkably closed to the ways of other people. It is only the occasional traveller who really sees anything. This is because for a brief time they are shocked into Tiferet while they are out of the Foundation image of their normal environment.

The ego, as will be recalled, is a complicated formation made up of all the influences of the lower face and things learned since birth. It is by no means one homogeneous piece, but is composed of hundreds if not thousands of factors, some related, some not, in a loose configuration of complexes. Consciousness, which operates through the middle column, does not illuminate the total ego but brightens and dims according to the attention invested by the person. Moreover, only certain areas of the Foundation may be involved, so that at any given moment particular complexes are in ascendancy while others may be receding. This phenomenon is easily recognizable in the moment to moment of daily living. As with language, one may have a great or small vocabulary, and some of its words or complexes may only be used on rare occasions. This creates the picture of a working area in the ego with a system of backup complexes constructed of skills, memories, values and all the information and techniques needed for ordinary living. These can range from making a cup of coffee, to the ability to perform delicate operations, like brain surgery.

As will be recalled the ego wears a face called a persona which is a functional device to meet the world. A man can have several personalities to suit different situations and can acquire more, or adapt his masks, if he has not identified with them as the real him, as sometimes occurs. He also has the shadow personality that hides behind the ego which influences his ego consciousness negatively. As traditional devil stories tell us, it whispers from behind, tempting and slandering from just inside the Unconscious.

The threshold dividing the Conscious from the Unconscious is variable. Just as the ego's awareness can extend, shift or contract, so the liminal level of consciousness can deepen or become more shallow. This brings about some very interesting phenomena. When the attention of the ego is focussed on a problem, its range of concentration is narrowed to a bright point. When this occurs the thoughts passing through Yesod are observed but largely ignored as they are usually random and without any apparent pattern. Conversely, when the ordinary mind is allowed to wander, topics rise and fall, but sometimes, a question that has been hovering just below the subliminal level, rises and surfaces into the ego consciousness to be restated or answered, having been solved by one of the upper sefirot. Such moments of reflection are useful to see what preoccupies the Unconscious.

From the point of view of the ego this fluidity is vital. If Yesod were to freeze solid one would become a robot, or go mad with a fixed pattern of responses to both the inner and outer worlds. This occasionally happens to people who become locked in a psychological prison by their disbelief in anything outside their Foundation. For development, the ever-changing screen with its rise and fall of complexes is a great asset. It enables the entry of new experience and ideas, and the outward expressions of new inner realizations. These are fed into Yesod along all the converging paths and by the input from all the adjacent triads of body- and ego-type. Also included are the major influences of the impressions and pressures coming from the Malkhut of the body below and the observation and suggestions coming from the deep within of Tiferet. This gives one some idea of the reason why the ego considers itself so important, because for most people, it is the only sefirah in view and they regard it as the cause and not the effect of their psychology. If we recall the allegory, the ego is likened to a servant in charge of a house for an apparently absent master. He leads himself to believe that he owns the house, but a closer look at the Tree reveals that he lives in the basement and the master, who resides in an upper room, is always watching his performance. If the right time comes the master will take the servant upstairs and show him all the treasures of the top storey where the landlord of the master resides. This will be spoken of later.

The ego then, is an ever-fluid receptacle composed of force, form and consciousness, which Kabbalists call the psychological Yesod. Its job is to screen what has been absorbed and reflect an image of current physical and psychological events in the light of its foundation. Through it all conscious experience passes, and out of it come the manifestations of the Unconscious. Ego consciousness is personal and particular, giving a man a sense of personal identity into which can rise, under conscious demand or unconscious pressure, the will of the psyche, be it instinctive, emotional, intellectual or divine.

Leaving Keter aside because it is beyond the world archetypes, we will set out on the Tree the Jungian archetypes of the Unconscious. This will give us yet another insight into the psychological World of Yezirah. Hokhmah is the Great Magician or the Animus, with the Anima or Great Mother in Binah. Daat has no real archetype as it does not actually exist even as an image. Hesed takes on the symbol of a Great King, with a Warrior Hero in Gevurah. Tiferet may have many archetypes, including animal forms which appear in dreams, while Nezah is sometimes seen as a girl or youth. Hod is the Trickster and this image is common to many folk stories.

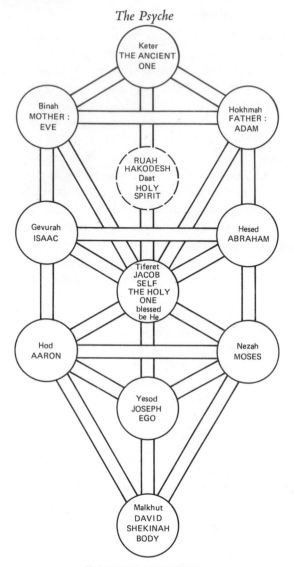

KABBALISTIC ARCHETYPES

According to tradition there are several arrangements of Patriarchs on the Tree. This is one. On the passive column is Isaac's Fear of the Lord, on the right Abraham's Love of God. At Tiferet is Jacob who was concerned with Truth while below is Joseph, the ego of many colours who brought Israel down into the land of Bondage. During meditation the Kabbalist takes both Fear and Love into account as he tries to bring about a Union between the Holy One and His wife the Shekinah in Yesod, thus drawing the influx down from the Ancient One at Keter.

What do these archetypes do, one now asks? First as the human yeziratic counterparts of cosmic principles within the psyche, each acts as a focal point for various complexes. Thus instinctive impulses and experiences collect round the active and passive poles of Hod and Nezah, while emotional and intellectual equivalents accumulate about their respective sefirot. These in turn are operated on, and work through, the related side triads, sometimes acting at a distance on Yesod and occasionally directly into the ego. Let us take examples. We have seen how men and women react according to the male and female archetypes, either projecting them on each other or by living them out, and we have also noted how a community may cast a man into the role of saviour-leader. This may also occur in an individual when one of his archetypes is out of balance and dominates him.

An instance of this is the puritan who seeks what he calls 'Justice' with a ferocity far greater than is necessary. He will appear sometimes as a zealot in religion and a fanatic in politics. This is the righteous warrior working through him and it is so powerful that he usually loses the personal touch and declares that only the law matters. Such men can turn into hunters of witches or political dissidents. The bookworm scholar archetype is a classic case in university life. Here a man knows his subject with incredibly Hodian detail, yet is totally out of touch with the rest of humanity. The Hesed archetype is often seen in clubs and bars, buying drinks all round even though he may not be able to afford it, because the jovial aspect of himself has him in its possession. The professional saint is another Hesed example. The Casanova lover is an easy Nezahiam archetype to identify and so is the 'femme fatale'. These Venus possessed people have great power to charm and yet no personal relationship is possible for them because of the overloaded emphasis in that sefirah.

In the balanced psyche the archetypes make life meaningful. They help us to respond to the Arts and grant the power to influence other people. They can also manifest through one's profession investing the ego with the role of doctor, priest, artist, soldier, or any other role which tempts one of the sefirot out of balance. An ego under this kind of pressure is to a greater or lesser degree possessed. The force or form emerging out of the Unconscious can take the ego unawares, because without the balancing sefirah of Tiferet it may not always know it is carrying the high charge of an archetype. A person in this state may consider that he is acting under authority from on high and is usually categoric in his statements. He will of course attract followers because the power of his archetypal-driven ego fulfils their need. Moreover it will violently repel those who reject its view, anyone in opposition becoming an instant heretic. History is littered with such people and their activities both good and bad. Their chief characteristic is that the leader always has a grand cause. In the truly great and balanced man humility acts as a counterbalance. Such people possess the common touch, while the demagogues rarely have much contact with ordinary life. 'I love humanity but I can't stand people' is their unspoken motto.

Archetypes operate in the Unconscious. As yeziratic entities they perform through the World of Formations. These may be passive or active, and manifest in every psychological inflection in our lives. Most of the time we do not see their influence but our thoughts, emotions and actions are inspired and viewed by ourselves and others in their light. Observe any social occasion and the psychological games played, or any professional encounter. One or more of the archetypes will be present. Even in solitude the symbols of our Yesodic world are archetypal in their roots and vocabulary. We live for the most part in Yezirah, mainly in the tiny area prescribed by Yesod. Nearly everything we see within, or without, is recognized by its connection with an archetype. Our chief acquaintanceship with the Tree is through the archetypes, because no single thought, emotion or action is sufficient to define a sefirah. Only time reveals, in perhaps a concept, gesture or act, what has really been going on inside us. This is why ceremonies and symbols are so important to man, be it the token of a kiss on the personal, or the pageantry of an inauguration on the national, level.

In the case of Natural man the archetypal world has no obvious manifestations, because he is immersed in its fabric so deeply that he does not know he uses and is used by it. All round him their power is evoked in dress, custom, status and language. He sees their symbols everywhere in ships, planes and cars. Advertising plays upon his archetypal keyboard, shooting, via the Yesodic imagery, into the subliminal world of the Unconscious. If he goes out and buys a particular soap powder without any thought, what other influences are impinging on him, not only from outside but from deep within, quite unknown to his ego awareness? To understand this we must penetrate the threshold of his personal consciousness and see how the Unconscious is constructed and operates.

26. The Threshold of Consciousness

For the Natural undeveloped man, the Unconscious is separated from and joined with his personal consciousness by a distinct but volatile threshold, beyond which lies the Individual Unconscious. It is called individual, as against the Jungian Personal Unconscious, because its sphere, centred on Tiferet, only touches on the ego-persona with its lower perimeter, while the rest of its circumference passes through Hod, Gevurah, Daat, Hesed and Nezah. It is quite a different orientation from the ego Consciousness which connects Tiferet, Nezah, Hod and Malkhut. The four triads encompassed by Tiferet, Yesod, Nezah and Hod are the threshold between the Personal Consciousness and Individual Unconsciousness in Natural man.

If one considers the Personal or ego Consciousness as ordinary mind it can be seen that for everyday purposes it can draw on enormous resources. It has the ego type triads and the four lower face sefirot. Three of these are involved with the Individual Unconscious and one, Tiferet, is connected with the deeper level of Unconsciousness beyond the Individual, namely the Unconscious of all humanity, called the Collective Unconscious by the Jungians. This will be discussed later.

The threshold between the Conscious and the Unconscious is a critical balance: and through it flow many things in both directions. All that is consciously experienced in the world passes into the Unconscious via Yesod, or subliminally via the Malkhut–Hod, Malkhut–Nezah paths to Tiferet. Whereas the conscious response to external events is easy to recognize even though much of what we take in is subliminal. Many impressions of sound and sight received and processed by Hod, are completely unknown to

Yesod. We cross a busy road thinking about something else while Hod guides and protects us in a constant monitoring of ear and eye. The slightest danger, if we are not too immersed in our Yesodic world, brings our ego consciousness sharply back to where we really are, as Hod and Nezah alert Yesod, which in turn moves our Malkhut body out of danger. Nezah also operates subliminally, sensing by attraction and repulsion our relationship to things, events and people. We may not like somebody in spite of their charm because of something we feel in our bones. This reaction may not be at all conscious and only manifests when the person does something odd. 'It doesn't surprise me,' Nezah says, though one often cannot explain why. Nezah is not so articulate as Hod.

It could be said that the path between Yesod and Tiferet is the hot line between the ego and the self. When it is fully open the whole of the psychological organism shifts onto a different footing and the man becomes self-conscious which brings a completely new set of possibilities. Alas, this is rare in natural man and he seldom glimpses direct flashes of the inner world, but then this is his choice. Most of the time natural man hovers on the threshold between the Conscious and Unconscious, occasionally catching sight of himself but usually living in his ego which, on the whole, is concerned with looking out to the world of Malkhut. While this is important for his existence and experience he has no command and little knowledge of the inner world. If he is reflective, he will observe the thoughts, feelings, and images, flowing through his Yesodic mind. He may recognize the switchings from Hod to Nezah and back again as he moves between active and passive roles, but none of this is of any practical use if he cannot recognize that he has a self other than the ego. In this situation he is at the mercy of all his states. He is controlled by the various triads and sefirot which are themselves subject to inner and outer influences. It is only when a man is centred in Tiferet that he can say he is truly in charge of his fate.

The threshold rectangle of Tiferet, Hod, Nezah and Yesod is composed of the horizontal triads of animal and vegetable consciousness, and the functional side triads of intuition and response.

CONSCIOUSNESS AND THE UNCONSCIOUS

Pivoted on a central sefirah, each field of operation extends to the axial sefirah above and below. Also shown are arrows of sefirotic input which may be initiated from either end of a path. The central sphere acts as an intermediary between the inner and outer worlds of consciousness.

These describe the various activities of the threshold in its various shifting levels and active and receptive operations. Taking the vegetable triad, this sub-division of the upper asiyyatic triad is concerned with the current cycle of thought processes and feelings. The path names give a very good indication of this. The path between Hod and Nezah is called, from its Hebrew letter designation and root meaning, 'to flower and decay', that is, to appear, then fade. This is a vital and continual phenomenon of the mind. The path between Hod and Yesod is called 'Mouth' originating from the Hebrew letter peh, and its complement in the Yesod–Nezah path is called 'to ape, or imitate'. These combined paths create with their sefirot a fair picture of the work of this triad. Moreover, if one carries a Kabbalistic principle further the word 'Nakaph' which is formed by the letters of these three paths means 'to go round in a circle'.

This principle of connecting the Hebrew letters on the Tree into sequences of paths is a special study and while it may seem a trifle glib, its veracity has to be fully tested before it can honestly be denied. Such a project is outside the brief of this book, but to take another example, the letters on the great asiyyatic triad of shin, nun, tov form the root of the words 'cycles, day, year and sleep'. Likewise the animal triad letter-paths make the Hebrew root of 'to lock in position'. This gives us some idea of the function of that triad and the threshold complex when ideas, emotions and actions pass into the working repertoire of the psyche. As a current set of complexes they lie just below the subliminal level to be called on when required. All of us utilize this and take for granted the ability to recapture from the far side of the threshold memories, reactions and techniques left untouched for years. An example of this is the fact that one rarely forgets how to swim or ride a bicycle. To forget is to allow the experience to recede behind the current activities and interests, circulating round the vegetable triad. A skill once learnt is simply switched from one circuit to another on the Tree.

The two side triads are functional aspects of the threshold. They perform the task of bringing memories into the consciousness of the ego and also out into the lower side triads for practical application in Malkhut. As intuition, the Hod–Tiferet relationship makes the essential connections which bring Yesod into awareness of what has been intuited from the Unconscious while the Nezah–Tiferet combination relates the unconscious response about something, and brings about a reaction in the Personal Consciousness. It might be said the passive side triad collects and relates data and the active values them, both above and below the threshold.

For obvious reasons the threshold is complex, with flows, circulations, alertings and dimmings, going on all the time. One can see why clinical psychologists have a difficult time because the various phenomena have many sides and configurations, depending on which sefirot, triads, paths and levels of consciousness are being used in the subject's Tree.

If we take one example, such as the phenomenon of repression, it will be seen that a person may, because of an inhibitor idea embedded in his Foundation, try to deliberately forget or subdue a sexual desire. Here an instinctive desire is blocked off by part of the ego's shadow aspect eclipsing the Yesod–Nezah path. With such an inhibition present in a man, his Tree has to compensate its natural flows. The man then shoots the Nezah energy over to Hod, talks excessively, openly or silently, but files the guilt unconsciously felt into the shadow part of his ego. This little personal devil is simultaneously projected out into the world via the Hod–Malkhut path, because the man does not like, consciously, to recognize such desires in himself. Thus his own repression is projected onto others and he sees sexuality in whatever he comes across, only to reject it from his ego, whose Foundation perhaps contains some unfortunate experience which though forgotten still resides in the subliminal 'locked in position' triad.

The cure is the opening up of the path between Yesod and Tiferet. If the man can see the ego's problem from Tiferet, he can alter the Foundation, and so release the devil which he has created. The task of the psychotherapist is to act as a substitute Tiferet, just as a teacher in an esoteric school acts as the temporary self for his disciple. After a real contact with Tiferet has been established the teacher and the psychotherapist have to step aside and let the man's own self take over.

If one takes the threshold as a whole it is the intermediary zone between Consciousness and Unconsciousness. Into it, influences from within the psyche and experience from the world outside come together. Using the allegory of a pool, the conscious aspect is the surface of the water. The threshold is the twilight zone just below the surface into which things float or swim up, and into which things sink and disappear. The bottom cannot be seen. This is a fair picture of the Unconscious.

In our daily lives the process of rising and falling thoughts, feelings and habits, is taken for granted and we regard the phenomenon of memory quite casually. The action of remembering and forgetting is most important because we would go mad if we had to consciously remember all we know. We are safeguarded from this by the threshold which takes out of sight what is not needed and passes it on up the Tree to the paths and triads concerned with the matter. On demand the Hod, Nezah, Tiferet triad can call back the memory, with the help of Malkhut or the central nervous system, which stores physical data throughout the body.

The threshold therefore is a kind of clearing house, through which we learn. For example, a medical student learns the theory via the Hod–Yesod–Malkhut and practices on the ward with Nezah–Yesod–Malkhut. Ego has to actually be aware of theory and practice so the Hod–Yesod–Nezah triad of circling must be operative. When the lesson begins to be established in Hod and Nezah it shifts, because the self has been watching, keeping the ego alert, into the Hod–Tiferet–Nezah triad where it is 'locked into position'. Here it sinks just beneath the subliminal threshold where it is readily available or allowed to sink deeper into the psyche to be called on perhaps years after the lesson has been learned. During this time, the lesson is associated with other lessons, and related to the emotional and conceptual levels of the Tree, where it forms perhaps a key link in a group of complexes, that at a certain time may bring unconscious emotional, or intellectual, pressure via the threshold to the notice of the ego. A case of this is the doctor who refused to do operations which he considered immoral. A strong Roman Catholic background, in

Kabbalistic terms a well developed upper Tree, would have such an effect on a doctor asked to perform an abortion. To a greater or lesser degree, we are all subject to the same law, according to our education and inclination.

What is accepted through the threshold is governed by the kind of Foundation we have made in our Yesod. We all have our Yesodic screen through which we view the world and ourselves. This is the limitation of our ego. Included in the selection system are both useful and useless devices. These range from perhaps good taste and manners, to quiet bigotry towards certain accents and dialects. More serious are the unknown selectors, picked up during our formative years, which have either been forgotten or deliberately suppressed, because they are unacceptable to the conscious ego. We all have these elements present in our psyche, some of which we accept too easily and others which we reject without real cause.

As such they operate from the Unconscious and through the threshold without actually letting the ego know. The case of forgetting to do things for people we don't really like, even though we won't admit it, is a common example. So is rationalization about things we have done. Here the ego smooths over and justifies what the impulse just below the threshold has made us do. Projection is a clear example of the Unconscious by-passing ego via Hod and Nezah straight to the outside world of Malkhut. There are many classic cases. For our study they are interesting in as much as they reveal the activating of the upper part of the Tree. A man's mind is not just his ego consciousness. Beyond the threshold lies a very powerful hierarchy of minds which have a deep interest in the man. Indeed so much so, that the Jungians use a term called 'the Wrath of the Self' to describe the work of Tiferet in its attempt to stop a person doing something against his nature. This, for example, may be an unconscious self-inflicted minor accident, which draws the ego-consciousness's attention to a collision course of much more dangerous proportions. It is not an uncommon phenomenon that several small incidents prelude a disaster. This can often be the all-seeing Tiferet sending Yesod an early warning.

The threshold zone of Yesod, Hod, Nezah and Tiferet is in a natural man the field by which the upper part of his psychological Tree communicates within him. It may be direct, through the sudden or gradual input of thought and emotion, which manifest as dim awareness of pressure, or abrupt upsurges; or it can be through dreams when the ego consciousness allows the Unconscious to use the viewing screen of Yesod. Either way, the Unconscious has more effect on us than our egos will acknowledge. This is very significant because it indicates the depths of our self knowledge. It is interesting to note that while the most stupid of us are convinced that we run the course of our lives by our own will, the wisest amongst us submit the will of ego totally to Tiferet. This implies a quite different way of viewing the psyche. Whereas a natural man may realize that he is subject to his Unconscious he may not be particularly interested in explaining it, because life is good and uncomplicated. For the person who wishes to develop himself the Unconscious has to be brought into consciousness, so that greater depth and profundity may enrich his life. That the natural world is beautiful there is no doubt, but for some people the supernatural world is more fascinating, especially if it is possible to participate and enjoy both. Here is the marriage between Heaven and Earth.

The task for the Kabbalist is to push the threshold of consciousness up the Tree. Change the Unconscious into the Conscious. By this process the relationship of a man to his Tree is reversed. As he moves slowly up the central column balancing the left and right pillars of himself, he moves out of the realm of psychology into the realm of the soul. As such he may approach, while still bound by Earth, the gates of Paradise, where on either side stand the angels with flaming swords, known to us as Gevurah and Hesed. Beyond lies the still existent Garden of Eden, our original home.

27. The Individual Unconscious

In the natural man, the Individual Unconscious is that which lies beyond the far side of the conscious threshold, and yet is, or has been, within his individual experience. During the course of life many thoughts and emotions pass through the ego, most of them only dimly perceived as fleeting inner overlays to the view of the outer world. For the natural man the external world is of greater interest so that his psychology is on the whole related to the events, things and people that he perceives with his senses. Much of this sense data, like his psychology, is not consciously observed. A person, for example, may know his route to work in great detail, recalling if he wishes, who he meets every morning and what sights and sounds he may encounter, all without having given them any deliberate attention. Indeed if something unusual happens, like someone being absent from the pattern, he will react, feeling uneasy until he sees that person (who has perhaps been on holiday or ill) is back again.

Here a complete world has been constructed in the memory, often quite unbeknown to the person who built it. If we flash back to scenes of our childhood the most extraordinary fineness of detail is recorded of texture, colour, height and distance. Sometimes even long gone child-like states of mood and idea are evoked. During these early formative years we soak in the psychological state of the household; the rooms may be shabby, but full of happiness, or elegant and cold. The relationship between adults and children can outwardly appear one thing, but in reality be another. No child can be fooled by appearances, although it may not be able consciously to perceive estrangement or love between its parents. All these impressions, like the unobserved sensual data, can go straight into the Individual Un-concious, to be attracted to the various associated emotional and intellectual complexes within the Individual Unconscious.

In Kabbalistic definition, the input, entering via the psycho-body sefirah of Malkhut, can travel up either of the outer paths to Hod or Nezah and pass into the psyche, without drawing the attention of Yesod. This is not at all difficult when one considers that the ego's consciousness is pretty dim as it watches the passing show of life. Observe people walking down any street. Their eyes are distant, half in dreams, half in the physical world. At work, if there is any need for concentration, the story is no better. Absorption limits the ego consciousness, as does boredom. Very few of us can maintain a wide range of attention for long. Sooner or later, we focus down into complete identification with what we are doing, or drift off into a Yesodic dreamland, of what we will do, or should have done.

For natural man, this state is a normal condition, although he will deny it vehemently, stating that he is in total command of consciousness, and does not realize the depth of his own psycho-logical sleep. If he were truly as awake as he considers he is, many of the troubles of his life, and the world at large, would not occur. Those who rushed to their own slaughter at the beginning of the First World War give some idea of the magnitude and depth of this state of mild hypnotism in which natural man is steeped. For the ordinary individual such a condition of unawareness is normal, and he absorbs a myriad impressions from the world about him, ranging from hardness of the chair he is sitting on, to the mass media, without realizing they are affecting him. Most of this influence is subliminal, that is, it either skirts his ego consciousness or passes clean through it unnoticed. This can occur because of various Yesodic screens which devalue, rationalize or repress what the Personal Consciousness cannot directly accept. All these devices may inhibit the person recognizing what he is confronted with, but they will not stop the experience passing into the Individual Unconscious.

An example of how such an event might occur can be seen in the end of a love affair which one partner cannot accept. Here the man, we will say, wants the relationship to continue, but the girl explains it is not possible because of his possessiveness. The man cannot understand. He is not possessive. She tries to explain, but his Yesodic ego devalues her evidence as he pushes the truth out of the Personal Consciousness. Afterwards the parting thoughts and feelings circle in his Hod, Nezah, Yesod triad for days. It is her unbalance he rationalizes. He reruns all their good times through his Yesodic cinema, cutting out any trace of trouble. The edited film is stored in the Individual Unconscious. From the viewpoint of ego nothing is changed. The girl is mistaken and he approaches her again only to be rejected. This creates more film that is examined frame by frame by the battered ego. If Tiferet is contacted truth can enter and the man see the affair is really over. In this light he can make use of the experience filed in his Individual Unconsciousness to run the next relationship intelligently. If not, he remains in Yesod, taking the whole thing personally. In this case the smashed ego lives on until in his next affair his Unconscious sets up the identical situation, for the cycle to be played again. This example is not confined to intimate relationships.

While the natural man is oblivious of Tiferet most of the time it does not mean that it does not exist for him. Far from it. Tiferet is the lynchpin of a man's Individual Unconscious. Junction of many paths, its range in the role of Individual Unconscious is described by the circle pivoted on Tiferet and passing through Yesod, Hod and Gevurah and Nezah and Hesed, with the circle closed at Daat. As can be seen the Individual Consciousness touches on the asiyyatic, yeziratic and beriatic levels of the psyche and these form a very powerful major configuration in the yeziratic Tree. As such it draws on the intellectual concepts, the emotional complexes and all the threshold activity. The contact with Yesod implies that the Individual Unconscious has more influence on the ego than it realizes, and observation in life shows this to be more true than people dare admit. The way we forget to do things that we have promised for people we do not really like, is an example we have already referred to. This promise is often over-generously made by the persona trying to cover up the unconscious dislike. Many people are convinced they are doing one thing, when in fact they are doing another, as their Unconscious pushes them. Here rationalization usually blocks out the awareness. The interesting thing, in many cases, is that the Unconscious makes them get into great difficulties which bring them constantly face to face with the lie they live by. Our rejected lover is a classic example.

On the Tree the sefirot and triads of the Individual Unconscious may work through Yesod or via the Hod–Nezah paths. In the Hod case a person may hear himself say things he did not mean (the traditional Freudian slip) or find himself doing things involuntarily under the prompting of Nezah which injects a sudden input of desire or repulsion. Observe any impulse, it often tracks back to one of the triads in the Individual Unconscious.

It might be interesting at this point to take a brief look at the phenomenon of madness because it demonstrates so well the relationship between the Individual Unconscious and the Personal Consciousness. In the case of simple schizophrenia a man lives in an imaginary world usually quite out of touch with outside existence. Here the imagery of Yesod is circulated round the Hod, Nezah, Yesod triad. In the manic-depressive the cycle swings from excitement to lethargy, as the active and passive sefirot take precedence. This alternation of action and exhaustion is characteristic of the manic condition and one can see from where the great power comes, for both psychic, and bodily expenditure. The same potential is present in a normal man, but the chief difference in the mad, is that the paths connecting Malkhut, especially the Yesod–Malkhut one, are malfunctioning, i.e. more or less blocked. This causes all the psychological vitality to circulate within the Hod–Yesod–Nezah triad, sometimes with the result that a chronic patient will sit all day in one position, his body quite immobile while a furious scene or dream circulates, from dawn to dusk, and all night, except in deepest sleep. We are all like this to a degree when acutely worried, and our world is quite as limited as that of a schizophrenic in this state. Again the chief difference is, that the sane, or relatively sane, can either come right out of the Yesodic state and into the external world to get a sense of scale, or do the reverse, with the same effect by penetrating deeper to make contact with Tiferet which always gives a truthful analysis of our predicament. Here lies our salvation in more ways than one.

In the case of mild neurosis, the Individual Unconscious may be too powerful for a weak ego to cope, so that the person says and does peculiar things. Such actions indicate that the Unconscious is trying to draw attention to imbalances. The remedy would require a psychotherapist's analysis of the paths and triads involved. As the substitute Tiferet he would help the patients make contact with their own Tiferet. With aid descending from the upper Tree, the malfunctions in, say, the passive emotional complexes would eventually be related to the active ones which prompted the malady. Many things repressed within the shadow side of Yesod when illuminated by the psychotherapist would then bring the patient's self into action, so that the path of honesty into the Personal Consciousness of ego would be opened. With this path cleared the problem is seen in its true proportions and its power is diminished. Afterwards comes a period of reconstruction in which a new Yesod has to be built for the shaky ego. This firm Yesod is vital for the psychological health, because it is literally the foundation of the psyche. In Kabbalistic practice the ego Consciousness has a definite place. Unlike other traditions which are concerned with withdrawing from ordinary life, the Kabbalist's task is to bring Keter down to Malkhut. That is why it has been said a true Kabbalist prefers to work with hammer and nails rather than perform magic. As one rabbi remarked: when he was young, he saw angels and devils everywhere. Now he knew more he did not see them at all. Kabbalah is not at all like its mythology.

What then are the contents of the Individual Unconscious? At a glance one can see that it contains the parts of both the upper and lower faces of the psychological Tree. This gives it access to the Personal Consciousness and the Collective Unconscious. Between these two lie a massive set of intermediary activities and formulations at the centre of which resides the self. As a system of dynamics there is the local conscious focus of the ego, the interchange zone of the threshold and the deep balancing mechanisms of emotion and intellect. These are synthesized downward, in the thoughts and moods percolating through the threshold and into ego consciousness, or upward, into the central triads of the Soul and Spirit. As the mid area, the Individual Unconscious is the point of meeting between that which has been conscious and has become unconscious, and that which was unconscious and is in the process of becoming conscious. All this relates directly to that individual and his life.

Examples of the exchange between the Unconscious and the Conscious can be seen in everyday living. The fact that one accumulates experience which is filed away and then subliminally used, is accepted without question. The seasoned man in any profession, who can diagnose trouble at a glance and offer a precise remedy instantly, is not uncommon. Perhaps less accepted is the notion that certain ideas deep within the psyche, do slowly emerge into consciousness. Instances of this can be seen in the questions of children about God or death. In adults it is more subtle in the gradual dawning of a recognition of law and principle. Most philosophy is based on the externalization of such abstracts, and certainly religious conviction originates in the Unconscious. If it were not so, there would be considerably more tooth and claw in the life of mankind. In the case of more mundane matters one can observe the manifestation of the Unconscious into the Conscious in the unfolding of a man's life. As time goes on, it becomes more and more apparent what kind of person he is. Here is the Individual part of the Unconscious. His every action, thought and emotion exhibit themselves in his ego, and others, if not himself, begin to recognize his nature.

Very young children are initially much the same, although there are obviously detailed differences. As they grow older their characters develop until there is no mistaking who is who. When they leave the standardization of school and go out into life the weak or strong, talented, dull, intelligent, quick and guileless individuals soon find their level. In some cases it is rapid, and in others, it takes a whole lifetime, but all have to come to terms with what they are, as the Individual Unconscious attracts to them their kind of life. Slowly over the years certain intimates, friends and professional colleagues collect round them, each one a direct reflection of the man. Indeed it is often the case that the person does not see that his circle is his externalized nature. The proverb that a man is judged by the company he keeps is a very useful observation.

A common situation, for instance, is when a person considers his acquaintances as less than himself and yet he still cannot find those whom he would consider his peers. Often such a man is as mediocre as the people he despises, yet they are his only friends. A hard lesson, but very indicative of the manifestation of the man's Individual Unconscious and not his ego image.

In the case of most people only the lower part of the Individual Unconscious is manifested. This is seen very clearly in the archetypal roles played at certain periods of life. The Yesod, Hod and Nezah stages are quite recognizable as universals, and yet everyone believes he is unique despite the fact that he is doing exactly as all the generations have done. This is the illusion of the ego. Curiosity, discovery, passion and rebellion against authority are common to all men. There is no real identity until a person makes contact with his Tiferet. When such a connection is well established one is a real individual, no longer subject to the tides that rule the mass of humanity. As such the person becomes a truly super-natural man.

In the case of the natural man, that is the person who by choice does not particularly want to evolve beyond the lower face, the Individual Unconscious acts as watcher and protector. The reason for the natural man's decision is because the process of psychological awakening requires courage, for not only does a man have to give up old patterns and values, and face the dark side of his personality, but he has to take full responsibility for his own actions. This commitment most people are not prepared to make. However, in spite of this they are still looked after by what some mythologies call a guardian angel. In Jungian terms this is the self, sometimes called the Guide. On the Tree Tiferet delineates the role of guardian very precisely, in that it knows what is going on anywhere within the radius of the Individual Unconscious. In such a position it will protect a natural man, if he pays attention

to its promptings, which manifest in dozens of internal and sometimes odd external ways. One example is that of a diplomat's
chauffeur who fell down stairs. Because of this his master took the
car out himself. Later the vehicle blew up with the master in it.
There are many examples of this kind of protection by the
Unconscious.

Of course one cannot listen to every inner whisper or take any
small incident as an omen good or ill, but nevertheless when
certain crises in our lives happen, we can often recall some sign
of warning of the oncoming event. Everyone has hunches or
intuitions at some time and these are the work of the Hod–Yesod–
Tiferet and Nezah–Yesod–Tiferet triads which have been instructed by the self to act on conclusions being worked on by the
side emotional or intellectual triads in the light of deep insight
coming down from Daat. An incident or intimation may be of
small import at first sight, but time often reveals that the realization at that point in the ego consciousness was a crucial turning
point, perhaps one of life or death. The proverbial tale 'For want
of a nail a shoe was lost, for want of a shoe a horse, then rider,
message, battle and Empire, all for the want of one nail', is a good
illustration of the laws involved at this level.

The Individual Unconscious is concerned with that individual's
life and everything to do with its past, present and future. One
life or even many lives are its range. In its orbit is the fate of that
person, although whether he chooses to live it out or not, is his
decision. The Individual Unconscious is the place where a man
joins humanity and the personal together in his own being. Here
is where the ego and the Collective Unconscious meet, both
upper and lower fields, innermost and outermost consciousness
coinciding in Tiferet, the self of a man.

28. The Collective Unconscious

For the natural man the upper part of the psychological Tree is the Collective Unconscious. Centred on Daat the circle enclosing Gevurah and Binah, Hokhmah and Hesed with Tiferet below and Keter above, contains the inherent knowledge, ancestral experience and cosmic nature of every man. Like the chromosomes of a man's body, his psyche includes the inheritance of his family, clan, people and race. The Collective Unconscious is that part of him which relates to things common to all men, that is Adam.

Adam is Humanity, and men and women are individual aspects of an earth-bound creature which is quite distinct from its co-habitants of the planet. While animals and plants are certainly conscious in their own degree, they appear to lack self-consciousness, that is, they are unaware of being conscious. While it is true that most of mankind is in a fauna- and flora-like state of consciousness it is possible for individual human beings to attain higher states of cognition and enter what appears to be another world. It is this that makes man unique.

The existence of other worlds is recognized by all peoples in their mythologies. Many myths are the product of the collective Unconscious of Humanity. Death is perhaps the most obvious contact with another world and whereas plants and animals are aware of death only man has more than a physical appreciation of it. Certainly the higher animals bury their dead, but there is no evidence of concern about an after-life which we find among even the most primitive people. The ability even to consider the dead in another, quite unseen, context is a concept of great magnitude. Its implication is cosmic, for with it goes the appreciation of non-physically perceptible intelligences and a whole realm of superhuman entities. This recognition of a supernatural king-dom arises in every level of culture, be it among isolated savages or highly sophisticated communities.

By historical times the study of the supernatural had moved from a simple fear of the dead and natural spirits to a respectful worship of abstract gods. As time passed the various deities were separated into hierarchies. In many cases there was an elite, such as the Olympians who carried out the main roles in running the Universe. They were often the same set of characters, each an archetype clothed in that culture's yeziratic form. An example of the most obvious archetypes were the Sun and Moon deities who occur all over the world. Others were the planetary gods and goddesses. While it can be argued that the presence of the planets in all skies is a possible reason, it does not explain the fact that commonly-held characteristics are credited to the same god. This suggests that something in the human being is not only responding to a constant within the psyche but to an external cosmic element which the recurring patterns in all mythology express.

Mythology might be considered as the yeziratic imagery of the Collective Unconscious. No matter what time or place, every culture has its gods, demons and heroes, the two former unseen, the latter the visible representatives of mankind. In the ancient world such beings were worshipped as pure archetypes; today we still worship heroes although they appear as pop stars or revolu-tionaries, and the gods also continue to walk the earth as entities just as powerful as of old. Mars and Venus still preside, as a glance at any newspaper will reveal. Indeed Mercury, the god of com-munication and travel, is more influential than ever, while Jupiter, the deity of both wealth and religion, is far from dead. The yeziratic World may give a principle many forms, but its essences remain the same. We can see this is so by observing the ever-changing mythology of our own times, as each generation restates and pursues its ideals, which, when seen in the long term, are the same as those it rejected in its parents.

Taking it from the other end, that is, within one man's psyche, let us look at the first principles of the Collective Unconscious Kaballistically. At the heads of the columns of Force and Form are the great Father and Mother of the Universe. Each represents the active and passive aspects of the supernal triad crowned by Keter. In archetypal images they manifest in a myriad ways in mythology, ranging from light and dark in Genesis to Sky god and Earth goddess in both primitive and sophisticated cosmologies. In terms of the human psyche they are the Adam and Eve aspects of ourselves, the force and form sides of our nature. As full members of mankind we are androgynous, that is, we have masculine and feminine attributes. In the body, subject to organic law, the organism is developed predominantly on one side or the other. Nevertheless the opposite sex is very much present within us and helps to create the powerful attraction between men and women and operate through their relationships.

The idea of both male and female sides existing simultaneously in one being is an ancient one and often occurs in symbolism. This is a yeziratic attempt to define that all is one, while at the same time indicating the positive and negative poles. The twin pillars of Jachin and Boaz before the Temple of Solomon demonstrated this idea, as do the principles of Rajas and Tamas or energy and inertia in the Hindu tradition, and Yin and Yang in the Chinese.

On the scale of the Collective Unconscious the male and female is manifest in the mass and in individual lives. Its most common form is the profound influence of family life. No one, apart from a few divine exceptions, is without a mother or a father. It is the most common experience of the natural world. To be without parents because of death, neglect, or estrangement, is one of life's tragedies and if a child does not have a foster-, or step-parent, it will seek, perhaps for a whole lifetime, for a replacement, so that it can come to terms with the archetype present within his own psyche. This pursuit of a lost parent may take many forms ranging through school teacher, gang leader, boss, to doctor and priest. Indeed so powerful is this need for a parent, that it occurs in whole communities. Kings, queens, presidents and prime ministers are all cast into the parent role. While the modern period has got past calling the Czar the Little Father, and Queen Victoria the Great Mother, we still react to our leaders as parental guides in spite of our sophistication. On the international scale the Pope is an acknowledged example, not to mention the classic Mother image of the Virgin Mary, where Mother Earth has been transformed into the Queen of Heaven.

These archetypes are deeply embedded in the human psyche. Being present in the Collective Unconscious they are with us from the day we are born. From that first breath we are totally dependent on two physical beings. At first, the mother and then the father take on, in the extending consciousness of the child, the likeness of gods. They are all powerful, granting benefits and dealing out punishments, that are ignored at our peril. For the most formative years they oversee our very existence and one can see why a person deprived of this experience finds it difficult to develop psychologically without having the full parental relationship played out. When adulthood dawns, and independence is possible, a natural rejection takes place. In animals the parents throw their offspring out as soon as they can physically fend for themselves. With human beings the process is not so simple because the psyche has also to be considered. Because of this protracted growth the physical need for personal assertion makes the adolescent push against often well-meaning parents. (Here is the activation of Nezah thus completing the great vegetable triad.) When sexual relation with the opposite sex begins, that is, when parenthood becomes a possibility for the erstwhile child, the break is usually accomplished and there follows the development of separate lives. Later, with the permanent union of a spouse the division is complete, and providing the parent–child connections have been worked through, the family relationship falls into a natural balance until the next cycle of generation.

In the scale we are considering the epic of the Mother and Father is common to every man from Cambodia to Iceland, from the jungles of Brazil to the London Hospital. It is universal. Moreover, as children to our parents, we are profoundly influenced by them and model our lives on their customs and practices. In being the next generation we not only carry the blood, talents and discrepancies of our forebears, but also the sins and blessings of our line. Indeed the Biblical statement on 'the sins of the fathers being carried over to later generations' is no mere poetic phrase but a very precise law of how deeds are carried over, sometimes for hundreds of years. From parent to child a myriad skills, mannerisms and ways of thinking about matters are conveyed and in just as faithful a manner as the DNA molecule passes on the pattern of previous generations of cells. On the whole this is good, because without it there would be no continuity, no tradition, no family, clan or people. Here is another aspect of the Collective Unconscious.

On one level, a man or a woman does not need to be trained to be a mother or a father, because it is inherent knowledge in the body and the Unconscious. All parents' actions and reactions, be they Red Indians, Russians, Tartars or Tibetans, are rooted deep in Hokhmah and Binah—the primal Father and Mother. This aspect of us is so potent that advertising uses the archetypes in their sales jingles. We may consciously reject the phoney TV image of the perfect mum and dad but the advert does its job subliminally. We unconsciously identify with two of the most powerful archetypes we have.

This cosmic pair crop up continuously, irrespective of time and place. One sees them in the tribal witch and shaman, and also in a modern Western hospital with the consultant physician and matron, both of whom command great respect based on a charisma not credited to ordinary people. This of course is partly because of the faith projected by the patient's dependence on them, and partly on the inherent response to the Great Mother and Magician archetypes within the patient.

To the sick the stethoscope unconsciously possesses the authority of a wand. Indeed such is its symbolic power that medical students make sure it is just seen poking out of their pockets; and every probationer nurse observes the extraordinary change that comes over them when they don their first uniform. This derives from the archetypal projection of Florence Nightingale—the Lady with the Lamp, a Great Mother image if there ever was one. Many patients would be quite disturbed if they saw their all-powerful medical Mother and Father in a social context. In the doctors' common room, and the nurses' restaurant, these paragons of modern magic and clinical care are only too human as hospital politics and intrigues quickly reveal.

In modern psychology Binah and Hokhmah are called the Anima and Animus. As such they have an internal function. As the male and female counterparts within one person, they collect round their polar foci both universal and individual experience. In a man his feminine aspect, or Anima, is the passive side of his nature. As the female side of him it compliments his active Animus. A good example of the workings of these two archetypes is illustrated in the beginning of a love affair. Here the Anima of the man and the Animus of the woman negotiate unconsciously while the lovers become acquainted on the yesodic level. Much goes on during the first week of a relationship, but most of it subliminally as the ego of each partner is too excited by the Hod–Nezah–Malkhut triad to handle anything normally. It is an extraordinary state. Everything is magnified. The girl appears as utterly feminine to the man and the man remarkably masculine to the girl's eyes, as each project their complimentary archetypes upon each other. Seen as a whole operation, the challenge and submission, the chase-and-catch-games of courtship are mutually enjoyed as Animus-Anima meets Anima-Animus, each partner matching the male and female need to fully complete their respective Trees of Life.

Individuality does not seem to be present although to the participators their relationship is very special, as are several million other relationships being acted out that day, all over the world. This is not to imply that it is not so, because every stone, plant and animal has its particular place, but to illustrate that the world of the Collective Unconscious has this quality of universality. Anthony and Cleopatra, Romeo and Juliet, Tristram and Isolde have their wide appeal because of the Anima and Animus principle within us all.

Besides Hokhmah and Binah the Collective Unconscious also includes the functional side sefirot of Gevurah and Hesed. These, along with Tiferet and Daat, are enclosed also by the field of the Individual Unconscious, being part of the supernal triad; the others, except for Keter, are within the ken of an individual man's experience. This means that Judgement and Mercy not only possess those things that are inherited from the Race Memory but also can acquire material absorbed from the conscious ego experience of the person. This relates to the functional intellectual and emotional triads pivoted on Gevurah and Hesed. Both the upper and lower side pairs contain personal memories. These, it will be recalled, are set out in intellectual and emotional complexes which gather round the archtypes expressed by Gevurah and Hesed.

Thus certain situations, such as a confrontation between an Irish Catholic and an Irish Protestant will usually (but not always) produce the same reactions as will certain emotional encounters which evoke perhaps long-forgotten memories. A visit to an old home provokes many things. Loves and hates, good and bad times, flow out of the Unconscious and into Yesod, to be seen as a personal 'this was your life' show. Behind these lie the great Collective Unconscious patterns of the family which often can only be seen in such retrospect. Occasionally people under some stress have to be taken back in time and deep into the Unconscious to come to terms with some event involving one of the concepts or complexes crystallized at an early period. Many a man has been motivated by a need to prove to his father that he was not a failure, even though his father has long been dead. It may root back to a single comment about his school work. This kind of motivation is a mixture of both the Individual and the Collective Unconscious. The classic joke about the Jewish mother is another example of the influence of the Collective Unconscious. When Mrs. Josephs was asked who her two small boys were, she replied, 'The one in the pram is the doctor and the other is the lawyer.' At least two thousand years of mother mythology lies behind that anecdote.

The archetypes associated with Gevurah and Hesed are the Hero and the King. Of both, very little observation is needed to spot the projected images. The natural man who, because of his personal choice, is confined to the lower face cannot be a hero or a generous king. This is the result of a law which states that unless you take responsibility for yourself fully in Tiferet, you are at the whims of both internal and external pressures. Kabbalistically one can see it cannot be otherwise, because without the conscious guidance of the self, the ego is without any stability other than its education and experience, which is always limited by its totally personal orientation. In this situation a natural man, who may be partially in touch with his self, can only react to his circumstance.

A hero is quite a different matter. He often goes against the common herd and performs deeds which at first ordinary men say are impossible, then marvel at. As an archetype it has a wide appeal. In folk tales the warrior and the knight have this fascination. Ulysses and Sir Lancelot relate directly to the Individual and the Collective Unconsciousness. Modern heroes like Lindberg, the first man to fly the Atlantic solo, and the first man to sail round the world single-handed, as did Francis Chichester, still catch the public imagination. Indeed nearly everybody on the planet Earth, who could get near a television, watched with fear and admiration Neil Armstrong as he placed the first human foot on the moon.

All of us had our heroes as children. We may grow out of the worship of footballers and film stars, but we still carry the hero archetype with us as we begin our careers. In business it is to be like the top executives we admire, in the Arts to have the audacity and conviction of our favourite practitioner, in the sciences the discernment and determination of a brilliant but maverick researcher who amazes our conventional colleagues with an extraordinary scientific breakthrough. Dreams perhaps, but men are more driven by their Unconscious than they realize. If Columbus had not wanted to play out the role of a daring admiral, then someone else with the hero syndrome would have discovered the new world. For mankind he has become the epitome of the explorer. In him and all subsequent explorers is the hero and the warrior. The Japanese Kamakazi pilots of the Second World War were reliving out the archetype of the Samurai, much as we often unconsciously identify with the hero cop, or cowboy, on the TV series. Such appeal is deep despite its impossible realization for the natural man.

The archetype of the king as part of the Collective Unconscious manifests again in many ways, as both personal experience and cosmic patterns blend in the complexes that gather about Hesed. Abraham is one kind of image. Here is a great man of God, an expanding entity with a powerful religious quality. Loving kindness accumulates about this sefirah. All the idealistic movements that relate to helping humanity, focus themselves here into individual action, based on Hesedic nobleness and generosity. These ideals root from a position of considerable strength. One cannot be magnanimous if one is in a weak position. The active pillar supplies the necessary dynamic bringing down the power of the supernal Hokhmah into the Individual Unconscious.

In the case of the natural man, to operate on this scale is rare, if not impossible in a sustained way. He is usually involved by being caught up in a popular movement. Many such events have occurred in the religious field, such as the thousands of ordinary folk who were drawn into the building of the great cathedrals in the Middle Ages. In our own time, just after both world wars, a desire for a lasting peace arose among the ordinary people of the world. The League of Nations and the United Nations were Hesedic in nature, both organizations attempting to maintain goodwill throughout humanity. The concept of love, the original basis for Christendom, was of this collective and Hesedic order, as was Islam, where men were brothers despite race, people or clan. Such an outlook on this scale is beyond the personal significance. No one can participate here as an individual except he become a symbol as did the late Pope John XXIII. Appeal is collective by nature, its archetype universal.

As part of the Individual, and the Collective Unconscious, the King image has a profound response. While not a Hokhmah magician with supernatural power, the Hesed archetype of King nevertheless imposes itself as a most attractive force. Men have always been fascinated by the idea of kingship. Many wars have been fought over a circlet of metal, which confers on the man who wears it the power of authority it represents. The president of the United States may not be a monarch by constitution, but he has all the majesty of an emperor. Indeed if a ruler has not command of powerful and rich resources his reign is meaningless as far as his people are concerned. The British monarchy has no political sway but the archetypal appeal still drew millions of people into a commonwealth when the Empire was at its zenith. As will be seen the mingling of the Collective and the Individual Unconscious occurs in Hesed as in Gevurah so that while the Queen of England and the President of the United States may be individuals they are also the Collective archetypal projections of their nations. Indeed they would lose this status if they disgraced the expected standard demanded by their people.

So far we have only dealt with the side pillars of the Collective Unconscious, but before examining the central column archetypes of Soul and Spirit it is worth mentioning one particular collective archetype, that of the Devil.

It will be remembered that in the Kabbalistic tradition there is the realm of Demons, the Kellippot or the World of Shells. Here is a situation in which a Tree is out of balance, or, worse, without a central column. In the first case a Tree may be over-active, or over-passive, creating frenzy on one side and grinding resistance on the other. Both situations can be seen in countries at war, or under extreme repression. A civil war contains both malfunctions, and events seen during such awful periods can only be described as demonic. On the personal level the phenomenon of madness, at either end of the scale, demonstrates very clearly the idea of being possessed. Indeed it follows well the notion that if one of the sefirot is unchecked by the others, and is operating directly through Yesod it can blast the ego and project directly out. This was observed in Adolf Hitler, whose judgement, without mercy or understanding to hold it in its passive position, was convinced he could never be wrong. The misplaced energy flowed down through Hod giving him an extraordinary ability to communicate through Yesod which was totally warped by the demonic aspect of the passive column. This leads on to the next and final stage of Kellippot, that of the fade-out, or blocking, of consciousness flowing down the central pillar. With little or no consciousness present, especially between Tiferet and Yesod, either side pillar can feed into ego at full power. In such a situation terrible things can happen, for there is no control. Unless the 'thing' it has now become, is over-ruled, or put out of action, it will continue to operate a destructive role until its considerable powers have run down in self-destructive exhaustion. The name the 'World of Shells' is a very precise description.

Into this situation comes the archetype of the Devil. We all have our shadow side devil but this is small fry and a question of personal selection and opinion, rather than real evil. Evil is disorder and the Devil is the collective image for it. Traditionally the Devil is made up of a hotch-potch of different creatures, usually malformed and with organs in the weirdest places. The image is universal to all cultures and has the same disturbing effect as when one sees a human monster in a medical museum. Indeed here is the work of the Devil and Kabbalistically one can see why. Over all order has gone and disruption and destruction set in. In a disease like cancer, when the organism as a whole is off-balance, the terminal phase is unpleasant to view and smell. It is not difficult to see why the ancient world regarded illness as demonic. The allegory is not only accurate but relates to the psychological body, if not higher, where a spiritual disorder may be at the root of disease in the body. It is said that physical illness is the last step of the person shedding a malady. Modern medicine is just beginning to catch up with the ancients in its acceptance that many diseases are psychosomatic.

The Devil might be called the universal archetype for disharmony, and as such has a job. As the evil antithesis of good, the Devil is opposed to God, the archetypal image of wholeness, or Holiness, which is the same word. While there are functions to eliminate unwanted elements, the Devil's task is to test order, tempt the good to make it stronger. Evil always has to be present to prevent the success of peace becoming the laxity of complacency. In the drama of Creation, as in every play, there has to be tension, and not just between negative and positive poles. The protagonist must be placed in jeopardy. Indeed we quickly lose interest if the beautiful and good and true are not threatened in some way. The paragon has to be tested so that honesty or courage, or whatever they represent, is seen to be real. We all know the hero is going to win through, even if it cost him his life, but that is not the point. It is how he handles the situation and how, in spite of all the odds, he proves and tempers his integrity—for all our sakes. A classic ancient or modern folk situation, agreed, but it does happen in real life, every day, and in Creation at large the same conflict occurs between harmony and disruption. The Universe is a drama situation and the Devil principle is the evil genius, but he is also the active instrument of the directing creator. Nothing is separate in Creation, nothing can operate on its own, because all is One.

The Soul

29. *The Sleeping Princess*

Tiferet, on the psychological Tree, was defined in a previous chapter as the essential nature or the self of a man. It was also called the Watcher and the Guide. All these names and many more such as the Atman, come from different traditions whose definitions blend into the Kabbalistic equivalent of Beauty. Some Kabbalists go further and call Tiferet 'Adornment' because it is the crystallization of the Tree's symmetry, and an empty focus containing all and nothing. From this viewpoint the self does not exist as a separate entity. However, in the Relative Universe the illusion of self is necessary so that the whole and its part may be related. Nearly all the major traditions speak of this paradox and Kabbalah is no exception.

For the purpose of our study we may take it that Tiferet is the essence of our being, in this case the self of our soul. While this is to be accepted in its context, one must remember the commandment, 'Thou shalt have no other Gods before me.' This refers to anything, including the sense of self which impedes the pathway up and down the central axis of consciousness on the Tree of Life. Until we discuss this in detail in a later chapter let us continue to see Tiferet in terms of the Natural man.

For natural man, Tiferet has little meaning. Most people are centred in Yesod and are quite content with ordinary consciousness and the ebb and flow of activity and rest between Hod and Nezah. Occasionally they will have a taste of Tiferet, during a highly charged state, or in a moment of particular quiet, depending on which side of the Tree they are, but on the whole it will fade into the Unconscious as a very lucid memory of being almost in another world. It is often, at the end of their lives, the only thing that stays with them as a distinct event, and though it may have appeared to be a trivial occurrence during a busy life, it is quite commonly the only thing worth remembering.

It is reported that one hard-headed businessman, when it came to evaluate his considerable achievements, only wished to recall a sleigh ride when he was a boy. The old sledge was the one thing he really loved among all his vast possessions, because it reminded him of that moment when he was fully alive. The rest was the frenetic machinations of an automaton. All of us have these lucid moments. They are a gift of Grace descending down the central column from Keter, through Daat to Tiferet. In such moments the path between Tiferet and Yesod is opened and Paradise is glimpsed for a brief instant. Paradise is the home of the soul.

For the natural man such an experience is extraordinary, because it has the quality of the fairy tale and myth. Through a crack in the skin of the hard tough material world he sees that magic and miracles are quite possible, that all the things he was told about, that he believed as a child, are in fact quite true. There are both a Cap of Invisibility, and Seven League Boots, but not in quite the way the ordinary world thinks of them. For a flash he perceives that guardian angels might actually exist, also that dragons and other traditional tests have to be passed. At this point the effort required to maintain such a consciousness is too much and the natural man slides into dreams once more, believing, as he must, in order to accept his life, that the ordinary world is the only real one.

During all these peak experiences the sense of self is both strong and non-existent. It is non-existent for the reasons previously stated, that in fact one does not, at the heart of hearts, exist except as the Totality of All. As for the other sense, the recognition of being a true individual, this remains indelibly impressed on the memory and is the key to many things. Unfortunately the natural man does not wish to know himself because it would mean giving up so many illusions created in Yesod, partly by his environment and partly by the identity his ego has assumed. To realize that one is nothing and everything, reduces the ego's status to less than nothing, and it will not concede this easily. Nor will it be willingly ruled by something it does not comprehend, especially when its hard-earned security is to be threatened. The ego will fight for its supremacy in the Personal Consciousness, because it sees itself as the centre of the universe. Everything quite literally revolves round it.

On the other hand the self manifests quite distinctly, although never directly, in the asiyyatic World. Via the Unconscious it influences us to a high degree, unless we are totally bodily orientated, and so no more than vegetables. Every natural man has within him a complete Tree. The difference between him and a supernatural man is that the connection is unconscious. Herein lies the difference between a man psychologically asleep and awake. However, there is always the possibility of awakening, and this occurs when the path of honesty between Yesod and Tiferet is opened. That is why the moments that make real memories have their clear and clean quality. One is awake for an instant to the supernatural world, that is, the realm of the soul.

In natural man the soul is asleep. Nevertheless it stirs from time to time in the Unconscious. In such periods, important changes occur in a man or a woman's life, perhaps a turning point in a career, or relationship, is reached, maybe a moment of reappraisal as regards the whole of one's life emerges. The scale of the event is quite different from just changing one's job or taking a new partner. Its nature is so deep that one only knows that behind the scenes of the subliminal threshold, some major readjustment is going on. For the natural man, that is most of us, such periods are an opportunity to break out of our Earth-bound situation. We can move into a new area, another dimension unknown in ordinary circumstance. Suddenly everything takes on significance as we begin to suspect that our outer world is a reflection of our inner state.

This is the work of Tiferet which having access to the whole of our psychological Tree can manipulate our actions without our knowing it, to indicate a change in direction. This phenomenon is used as a sign, both in psychotherapy and mystical tradition, of what is happening in the psyche and what should be done about it. In the case of the former it usually involves a study in order to find a remedy, in the latter a method of determining the next step of advance. An example of both is the parable of the prodigal son, who wondered why he was so unhappy living like an animal, when he had a rich father in a far country. The physical misery of his external existence showed him his inner state and the fact prompted him to return home where he was forgiven.

While the psyche might be considered the total working of the yeziratic Tree, the Soul, to be precise, is the triad composed of Gevurah, Hesed and Tiferet. This is because both the upper and lower faces of the psychological Tree belong partly to the worlds above and below Yezirah. The Neshamah or Soul proper, is the individualized aspect of the Creator and this can be seen by its focus on the nuclear sefirah of Tiferet. Neshamah means living soul. Some Kabbalists call the soul the Ruah, but if we refer to Gen. 2:7, the definition is Neshamah, while Ruah in Gen. 1:2, is called the Spirit which is of a universal order. This will be discussed later. The Neshamah, Genesis states, is that part of man which has been breathed into the dust of the ground, that is Adam. Here we have the human situation.

For the natural man the soul is the Sleeping Beauty as in the fairy tale. It is feminine in most traditions and as said is called Eve in relation to the Adam of the Spirit, that is the great triad formed by Tiferet, Binah and Hokhmah. These are allegorical names used to catch the flavour of that world which is yeziratic from our view. Many tales and myths use yeziratic language to express the journey of the soul. The epic of Gilgamesh is one and Cinderella is another. In the latter the soul is embodied in the ill-treated, but true daughter of the house, who is sent to live in the kitchen or the asiyyatic body, while her ugly step-sisters or malformed personas are shown to the world by the wicked step-mother ego as the real heiresses. With the aid of Daat, in the form of the fairy godmother, Cinders glimpses the realm of paradise at the palace. There she meets the prince who might be considered the self, whose father is of course the king represented by Keter. Aladdin has similar ideas contained in its text. So has St. George and the dragon and many of the Arthurian legends. All these yeziratic stories have a beriatic underlay. They are archetypal and appeal both to the Individual and Collective Unconscious, which is why they are repeated endlessly over the centuries, while fashionable children's stories are forgotten in a generation. The nature of the soul can be guessed at by the position of the Neshamah triad on the Tree. Situated between the beriatic and the asiyyatic Worlds it participates in both, being the intermediary for the two, while remaining separate. Below it and to each side are the two functional triads of the emotional complexes, while above, to left and right, are the intellectual concepts. These could be summed up as 'concrete' thought on the passive side and 'speculative' thought on the active. The emotional side triads could likewise be simply, but not fully, defined as 'certitude' in the passive form and 'trust' on the active side. These flanking triads feed into Tiferet which is the central pivot of the emotion sefirot of Gevurah and Hesed.

The horizontal disposition of the Neshamah triad makes it part of the conscious series of progressions up the middle pillar. Its relationship to the self is special, inasmuch as being neither asiyyatic nor beriatic, its nature is unique. This is why the soul is closely involved with the essential nature. In all men and women the self exists, they could not be without it. In the case of the natural person, it is the Sleeping Beauty, or Tiferet, which is the possibility of his individuality. This is recognized by the natural man in the expression 'to be one's own man', although he may not realize the full implication of what he says.

Everyone has an essential nature. We are born with it. It is uniquely ours although we may never realize it in Asiyyah. This is because we can choose to ignore it, preferring, like Esau, to satisfy our immediate need. However, there is another way to lose our birthright and that is by actually destroying our potential by committing crimes. Whether they be of active initiation or passive consent does not matter. Sin means 'to miss the mark' which is self-explanatory.

The soul of the natural man is composed of his essential nature and his judgements and mercies. These sefirot operate in both the Individual and Collective Unconscious. However, the soul triad is not quite like any other, because it is the synthesis of a man's inner life. While the lower face participates in the asiyyatic World, it must do all those things the psycho-body must do to live, and the upper face exists and must concur in the laws of Beriah, the soul need not conform. It can opt for one and ignore the other or vice-versa. The history of the human race is full of examples. Some, like Attila the Hun, only used the lower face to exploit physical force, while others like the earlier Christian desert fathers, chose to withdraw from the asiyyatic World and explore the upper face of spirit. That is the prerogative of the soul, its right to select. In the Kabbalistic tradition both worlds are accepted, the soul acting as a go-between between Earth and Heaven.

In natural man the Neshamah lies dormant. However, it is informed of what is going on by its adjacent triads. This creates, over a period of time, some changes, rather like that of growing old even though one may slumber through a lifetime. The effect is what might be expected, in that the sleeping soul becomes flabby, or rather does not really develop any capacity of account. Because men are old it does not necessarily make them wise. Occasionally one hears of people being old souls, the implication being that the person, although young in years, has been on the earth's surface before and has acquired his knowledge in a previous existence.

This concept of reincarnation, like those of the great eastern religions, is spoken of in the Kabbalistic tradition and is called Gilgulim or the Revolution of Souls. According to the Zohar, the soul is sent down from the upper regions into the asiyyatic World to perform a task both for the universe and itself. If it does not accomplish this, it is returned several times until it does. While this makes much sense of people's varied lives, explaining why some know more and others nothing, it does not give the whole picture. In the branch of the Kabbalistic Tradition this work belongs to, the view is held that a person only really exists in the present, living at various levels between Heaven or Hell, according to his state of responsibility for himself. Thus a man may be released or bound in the very instant of his actions according to his level of consciousness. This precludes any past credits or debits and brings him closer to the total situation of all men. In the moment NOW everyone, dead or yet to be born, is simultaneously alive in Adam, who is a reflection of the One, for whom there is no time. Such a realization perfects and can illuminate the deeds of Gilgulim.

Returning to the relative and therefore partial view of Gilgulim, the soul, it will be seen, is not directly affected by the decease of the body. On death the lower face of the yeziratic Tree will die as the upper face of the asiyyatic body. With it dies the ego and its Personal Consciousness. This, in the relative context, implies the possibility of reincarnation and the ability of the soul to survive, in some form, during an interim stage, before being recycled down into Asiyyah or drawn up into Beriah. It also emphasizes the uniqueness of man.

Man, as against animals and plants, possesses a part that is not earthbound. He can actually escape, whereas flora and fauna are confined to the planet, being continuously cycled between the two poles of life and death in Nature's circus. Nearly all traditions talk of this possibility, be it in terms of being born again or escape from the Wheel of Life. Man, therefore, has within him the ability to detach himself from the level of pleasure and pain. He can leave the world of toil, be released from the curse of Adam and return to Paradise. This can be accomplished by the awakening of the Soul, the cultivation of its consciousness and the realization of its proper place in the Universe.

For the natural man this opportunity is a myth. He knows of it, vaguely remembers it, is reminded of it by stories fed into him as a child, before he became involved in the World. Children and old people are aware of it, but they are too early or too late to do anything about it. The best time is when many skills and much knowledge have been acquired and the vigour of the body is in its prime. But the natural man usually ignores the various signs that remind him of the presence of his soul. The Unconscious prompts or the self indicates, even creates, situations that blatantly point out the path of correct growth. More often than not, the natural man and woman ignore the generous opportunities offered, and become too deeply engaged in the external world to encourage any inner growth. When they have passed their prime and their strength begins to wane they find that all they have acquired has no real meaning. Status is a sham, possessions become a burden and even personal relationships often lose their significance as the sex drive diminishes. A pretence is kept up, but sterility sets in on life.

Only those who have cultivated some inner world seem to continue to grow, while the rest fall into reminiscences about former glories or recriminations over failures. The same stories are retold and the cycle of memories becomes stereotyped. Eventually these in turn resolve into a physical-mental vegetable existence before death.

It is different for those who have made some sustained contact with their inner nature. The Soul is not affected even by bodily disease. It can soar, sometimes despite intense physical pain, and live within the kingdom of the psyche on more than memory. In such an evolved person the past becomes an investment, the present more real than ever it was, and the future full of potential. This is the range of the soul that lies sleeping in so many of us. The princess, the story says, is still waiting. When the kiss comes, after the prince of consciousness has cut his way through the wood blocking the path from Yesod to Tiferet, the whole palace will awaken, with the princess, from deep sleep.

30. The Breath of God

While the natural man wanders through the jungle of the animal and vegetable kingdom his soul lies dormant. It grows with life experience but only in an unconscious manner so that what is learnt is only dimly recognized, as a dream between sleeping and waking. Left to itself the soul would be terrified of the world about it, as an embryo child would be if faced with the harsh world outside the womb. Indeed it is not a dissimilar situation in that the gestating soul has to be both protected and nourished. To accomplish this, the upper and lower faces of the psychological Tree contribute their attention. In the case of the lower face, the intake of experience is passed across the threshold of Personal Consciousness into the Individual Unconscious, where it is separated out and stored in the respective emotional and intellectual triads and paths. From these reservoirs it is, when occasion arises, drawn upon by the soul which synthesizes a psychological amalgam for the use of, in the natural man, the Individual Unconscious. Situated on the Tree above sits the great triad of the upper face composed of Binah, Hokhmah and Tiferet, with Daat at its centre. As the Neshamah is named the triad of the soul, this great constellation of sefirot may be called the triad of the Ruah or Spirit.

In Biblical terms the Spirit is the breath of God, spoken of in Gen. 1:2, 'the Ruah of Elohim moved upon the face of the waters'. It may be seen as Beriah hovering over Yezirah. In man, the image of the Universe, the same situation occurs. Just as in the creation of the macrocosm, the microcosm gestates through the four worlds with the Spirit above the waters of the psyche, and Asiyyah below, as the earthy body of action and elements. Even in quite ordinary human experience, we have observed the levels of differentiation, although one does need some knowledge and a trained eye to detect the differences.

What is the Spirit? One might well ask, no book can give the answer. All that can be conveyed is by implication, and from here on this study of man can only be a speculation. The reality may only be realized in consciousness.

What then is spirit? For the natural man it is something cosmic; that is, something vast, and beyond the ken of the ordinary natural mind. For most men, the nearest they come to appreciate and stand in awe of Spirit, is when they look up at a clear night sky and see the Milky Way stretching from horizon to horizon. In such a moment they sense the great deep of space extending beyond the moon and sun. For perhaps a brief minute they perceive the distance between the nearer stars and the stellar cloud banks of our own galaxy. Maybe they even begin to grasp, as they see the pale disk of our neighbouring nebula Andromeda, the idea of another cosmic order and beyond this, the unimaginable fact that there are as many galaxies as there are stars in sight. This realization is awe inspiring and it is not without reason that the path between Tiferet and Keter is called 'awe'.

Such experiences as that of glimpsing the scale of the Universe are not as uncommon as is thought. All normal men and women have such moments deeply embedded in their psyche. The power of such a perception is that it carries the quality of recognition, but of what, the natural man does not know. To stare up at the stars with the eyes alone tells one nothing, but to perceive the response deep within one's being is another thing altogether. Far below the surface of Personal Consciousness, and even beyond the Individual Unconscious is something in everyone that is akin to what is permeating the vast space overhead. On looking within it is perceived as deep and wide and as full of mystery. Moreover, this inner space is filled with forms and forces as potent as those in the intergalactic void surrounding us. This is Spirit and yet it is only on the asiyyatic level, because as we look up into the realm of planets, stars and galaxies we are only seeing the earthy manifestations of higher worlds. Even the biggest telescopes, visual or radio, only detect the asiyyatic world, the former the material and the latter the energy aspects, of the physical universe. This gives some idea of the true nature of the cosmos, in that we only see a fraction of a quarter of manifest existence.

What does this all mean in terms of man? How does he even rate notice in the enormous scheme of things? It could be said that man has a special role to play in the universe. If one takes the mechanical parallel of the hair spring of a fine watch, Nature, as regards the earth, may well be a small but critical regulator of the planet's function within the solar system. Indeed the distance, velocity, size and character of all the planets have a small but distinct effect on the sun as it circles the Milky Way. Again while our sun may not be very important as a star, it, like the millions of blood cells, is one of a vital collection, supporting the Milky Way which in turn is part of a crucially balanced cluster of galaxies within a vast cloud of nebulae. To us, this makes man less than insignificant, but we must remember that man is more than mere size, he has the capacity for cosmic consciousness. This factor makes him crucial because he brings into Asiyyah a completely different dimension. While consciousness is by no means rare in Asiyyah, for all things from stones to suns possess a physical awareness, cosmic consciousness is of another order. Only man, in his incarnated form, has the ability to be cosmically conscious. For the planet and indeed the whole solar system the implication is enormous. Within its orbits the solar system contains a minute but unique organism as vital to it as brain cells are to us. Through these tiny microbes called human beings, the solar system has a level of consciousness denied to any star-planetary system without a mankind. The human race is small and on a planetary scale the life of one generation is about as long as a cell's generation in our body, but its presence is not insignificant or accidental. We know that on our level a slight change in chemical balance can upset our metabolism. How much more must the effect of several hundred million people be, to the earth. Moreover evidence shows that the demand by the planet for more human beings is increasing. The dinosaurs fulfilled one planetary function, the woolly rhinoceros and mammoth another. No doubt the earth is responding to the requirements of the solar system, rather like our body informs itself that it needs more iron, or water, oxygen or light. Man, unlike the plants and animals, contains all the worlds, he has a wider purpose than being just a sensitive converter of asiyyatic energy and matter, as the rest of Nature is. His job, it seems, is to bring a higher level of knowledge down to Earth.

The purpose of natural man is to husband Nature. At the moment it appears he is making a bad job of it. However, it may not be so accidental that he is polluting the planet. Only the long-term view will show. While it is true as a species he is not very old or experienced at being on the planet's surface, he is watched over by the Upper Adam, who, no doubt, as the self in an individual's life creates such problems in order to improve a growing situation.

Besides acting as steward to the vineyard of Nature, man also has the duty of cultivating himself, both for his own benefit and that of the planet, the solar system and indeed the whole Universe. For this reason he has an inner as well as an outer world to explore. Because of the perfect construction of man he can rise through all the worlds and return to the source of all. No man or woman is denied this possibility, except the person who has so long ignored the realm within, that he is virtually becoming less than an animal, plant and stone. This is the deepest Hell, the ultimate Kellippotic situation in which nothing but an empty shell remains of the person, even the demonic energy gone.

Everyone, except the hardened criminal, recognizes the emotional nature of the soul, but few can grasp the universal Intelligence of the Spirit because its scale is vast, cosmic and ordered in a manner no natural mind can comprehend. However, if we place it on the Tree, we might at least catch a glimpse of what Ruah might mean.

The Ruah triad is composed of Hokhmah–Wisdom, Binah–Understanding and Tiferet–Beauty. At its heart is Daat–Knowledge. Herein resides a strange secret, in that Daat does and does not exist. It might be called the invisible door of the Universe wherein the Lord may enter and disappear, and where a man might make union and vanish into his Maker. Daat means to Know. It does not mean to know about, as Hod or Yesod do, but to know, that is, to also *be* that Knowledge. This is the essence of Daat and explains why in Christian Kabbalah it is called the Holy Ghost, that can descend from the Father at Keter to the Son at Tiferet. For the natural man the triad of Ruah exists, but deep within his Unconscious. It is fully at work, but he is unaware of it because his consciousness does not extend most of the time beyond Yesod. Occasionally he will touch Tiferet and then, if it is appropriate, he will catch a glimpse of the Ruah scale as Daat flashes him a momentary illumination, which is unforgettable. Such moments are recorded in many great novels, such as Lermantof's 'Hero of our Time' seeing and sensing through the mountains he is viewing, the vast cosmic scale of things. Closer to our own period the action novelist Hemingway touches on the realization when he makes a character sense the whole world is moving as he makes love. 'And Adam knew Eve'—that is, contact is made through Yesod and Tiferet to Daat. Such an experience of male and female union creates an awareness of all mankind. In such a moment the miraculous can happen and often does. In this meeting place of Beriah and Yezirah the creation and conception of a child occurs. From that point on a fertilized cell has the possibility of growing to become a living, breathing, eating, sensing, feeling and thinking human being with a complete life and death of its own to live out. This is a cosmic event involving all the worlds above and below the Daat of Yezirah which is precisely half-way between the Crown of Azilut and the Malkhut of Asiyyah. 'In the beginning God created the Heaven and the Earth'. No one's life is without cosmic significance in the Universe.

The triad of Ruah appears to most of us as a distant influence. This is equally true both externally and internally. However, this does not mean it does not have an intimate effect on our lives. Taking the external first, it is very obvious that any catastrophe in the macrocosm would profoundly disturb us. For example, should the sun expand or grow hotter or cooler than it now is, the earth would be no longer in the temperature belt that can support organic life. A shift of only a few degrees up or down would burn or freeze us all. We take utterly for granted the narrow limitations we live in. Indeed most people who complain that it is too hot or cold, forget that the full range possible in the universe at large, extends from absolute frozen zero to millions of degrees of heat. We are very lucky to be where we are, or is it luck? Consider how man's situation is contained in the ecological pyramid of Nature. This organic scheme is precisely balanced and regulated, so that a myriad adjustments can go on at all levels without too much disturbance to the general rhythm and form, and as such it is characteristic of one of the minor cosmos's of which the Universe is made up.

As there are complete Trees of Life for each World so there are cosmoses, or orders, in the Universe with each level containing and being contained, one above and one below the other. In that manner we get galaxies containing stars, each of which probably holds a collection of planets, which in turn encloses our earth which envelopes in its great electromagnetic field and atmosphere, the realm of Nature. This biosphere itself is divided into micro-orders of man, animals and plants, all of which are composed of cells, which are themselves made up of molecules. These molecules are constructed of, or contain atoms that are but the containers of particles and waves of energy and matter. The whole of this complex ladder is grounded in a total void, that is, the same Nothingness that contains the Total of All Creation. Such are realization about the relative universe in its full implication is cosmic. A person experiencing it would be in the Ruah triad.

Psychologically the triad of the Spirit is of the same magnitude as the comprehension of the physical universe, but in Yezirah. It is that part of man which meets Creation on its own level. Our study of archetypes of the Collective Unconscious gave us some taste of the cosmic nature of its order and we can see how it is possible for a man, who attains that degree of experience, to perceive the Universe in a very different way from natural men who live primarily in the Yesod of Personal Consciousness. However, in spite of the natural man's remoteness from this level of

Creation, it has the same degree of rulership over him as does the outer asiyyatic universe, for the great triad of Ruah is the inner space background to our being. It is the firmament of our psyche. As such its influence is like that of the sky, not always to be seen, but always there, ever present, acting as a distant but powerful back drop to the local activities of our psychological solar system. The parallel is apt, if one remembers the position of the mythological planets on the Tree with the sun at Tiferet and the moon at Yesod.

If one can grasp just the fringe of the scale of this triad it will be perceived that from here comes the cosmic purpose of mankind. In these terms, one can see not only the destiny of the human race being controlled from this triad, but the meaning of peoples, each of which fit into a set of family relationships, each of which fulfil an aspect of mankind's task on earth. Nations rise and fall according to a cosmic purpose, each one moved by a spirit inside them that roots back to the Ruah triad. Astrologers argue that celestial forces working on the mass psyche cause such movements as great emigrations while historians contend it is economics and politics. It makes no difference, because the inner and outer universes concur. The external and internal firmament is the same. A mass, or an individual man, becomes an instrument of destiny because it suits some cosmic design. Such unconscious men of destiny are not as rare as one might suppose. The man who invented the safety pin, or Marconi, or the Wright brothers, might well have been oblivious of their cosmic role, whereas men like Christ or Buddha knew well what their tasks were. Here is the difference between the natural and the supernatural man. The natural man is used, whether he likes it or not, by cosmic intelligence, while the supernatural man volunteers, is called, then chosen to perform the task. For him the important point is to actively submit and aid the Spirit so that it can descend directly to Asiyyah into a place or event prepared by that man. This is why on meeting such evolved people there is a strange and beautiful atmosphere about them. They have made themselves a channel for the Ruah and this is attained by making their Tiferet the conscious focus of the soul and the Spirit. They have the Presence in them. In such a state of grace they can be simultaneously conscious, in the upper face of the World of Formations, and in the lower face of the World of Creations. In this, their self—the Tiferet of Yezirah becomes the Malkhut of Beriah, the Tree of pure Spirit. The Breath of God is upon them.

31. The Divine for Natural Man

The supernal triad of the yeziratic Tree for a Natural Man is his contact with the Divine. The reason for this is that the Keter of the psyche is the Malkhut of the Azilutic Tree. One might say that contained in this single sefirah, when all the Trees of each world are interleaved to form a ladder between Heaven and Earth, is the maximum a man can experience while still embodied in the flesh. For besides being the Keter of Yezirah and the Malkhut of Azilut this sefirah is simultaneously the Tiferet of Beriah. Such a potent combination might be considered the God of a Natural Man.

Gods, as against the Absolute, are more common in our experience than we realize. By definition a god is what we worship, and indeed most of us do worship various deities, besides the one we nominally subscribe to when we go to church or synagogue. A vernacular saying, 'for six days thou shalt worship the Bank of England and on the seventh God' is not so far from reality. Neither is the idea that the many things we devote most of our lives to are in fact our gods. Some of us, for instance, worship status, others money or power, and others security. Food is a very important divinity to many, and includes an elaborate ritual. Sex has perhaps the biggest congregation of devotees of all. In themselves, none of these things are good or bad, they are part of life and must be met and experienced. However, as the first commandment states, 'Thou shalt have no other gods before Me.' This is setting out a scale to be lived by, a richness and fulness that does not exclude, but includes, all human experience. The chief problem is that men—and women—forget to remember from whence they came and to where they must return.

When a man is only operating in the great vegetable triad he worships only that which he desires and is excited by. The scientist, for instance, who believes in nothing else but data, is a devotee of Hod, while the *bon viveur* is committed to Nezah. Yesod also has its converts in their surrender to either their own or another's graven image. One sees this kind of zealot in the entertainment world very clearly, but it can also occur in the establishment of a community. Dictators use the power of Yesod to create a human idol. In ancient times various emperors actually said they were of divine status and demanded that they be worshipped. This to us appears to be ridiculous, but observe oneself and what one surrenders to and you will find you have your own pantheon of gods, ranging through car, home, job and partner, all of whom stand in the way of making direct contact with one's own essential self, not to mention one's origin.

Nor is the worship of gods confined to the lower part of the Tree. Men have revered theories, given their whole lives over to them. Art has been more than one person's god, so has law, discipline and many other idols identifiable with the form column. On the other side, power, love and even wisdom, have followers, all of whom believe that the active principle is God. None of this is, or can be, the Ultimate, because by nature they are the servants of the Absolute. When Abraham left his father's idol shop he went because he could find no real deity other than the All Inclusive Absolute. Such a Being is non-existent in the Relative Universe, and yet the Absolute is manifest in all He created. Returning to the Kabbalistic idea of Unmanifest Existence we will recall that beyond the first Crown of the Great Tree of Life stretching between Heaven and Earth are the Three Veils of Unmanifestness. Here is the silence behind everything, the still background against which and within which everything moves. Without Negative Reality nothing could become positively real, that is, come into existence. On the human scale no music could be played without silence being present. While other sounds fill the room, music cannot be heard in its proper form. If any other noise is as loud or intense as the melody, its nature is destroyed. Such is the critical balance between positive and negative existence.

Keter is the Hollow Crown through which flows the Will of the Absolute. On the yeziratic Tree, Keter is simultaneously Malkhut, or the body of Azilut, and Tiferet, or the Essence of Creation. Through it stream three Worlds which descend eventually into Asiyyah. The quality of such a composite set of sefirot in one place cannot be imagined, but one can guess its nature will be one of godlike being, and indeed it is called in the Beriatic Tree, Michael, the Archangel, whose name means in Hebrew 'Like unto God.'

For the Natural man the Crown of his psychological body is his god. From it springs the source of his soul. The supernal triad of Yezirah is the archetypal origin of the realm of Formations. To an animal the Keter of Asiyyah is its god, that is, the Great Tiger, or Great Deer depending on what species it is. For natural man with a greater conscious potential, this same asiyyatic Keter becomes the yeziratic Tiferet of his self. This individual self is in turn the Malkhut of Beriah, while his yeziratic Keter becomes the Tiferet of Beriah. To advance further, a man must develop his soul. This will allow him to rise up the Tree of his psyche into Beriah where he can come in contact with the Divine via Daat. Here he may, or may not, choose to go on to ascend into the Azilutic triad. If he does, he can attain his Divine World and have complete reunion with the Absolute, or, as an alternative, choose to return to the world of natural men to teach and point the Way. This explanation makes sense of Christ's remark after his death, that he was going to ascend to 'your father and my father', the implication being that there were different levels of Divinity. It also explains the view in several traditions that teachers return, from time to time, to earth, to remind men of the Source of their existence.

When one considers the Azilut triad with its three supernal sefirot the sheer weight of the names gives some idea of its relationship to natural man. Several blessings, both in the Christian and Jewish religions, contain the words Wisdom and Understanding together with the name Spirit or Holy Ghost. These attributes of God, along with the ritual of raised hands in the blessing which evoke the two side pillars, call on the Presence of Azilut.

Many sacred buildings designed to remind the natural man of his God describe in their architecture the Divine Triad in their spires, cones and pyramids. All of these descend from a high point in the sky to the earth, or, as can be seen the other way, rise up from the mundane ground level to form a peak which some call the Holy Mountain. Most cathedrals have the two pillars embodied in their western towers, but what is often not seen are the upward pointing tympanum triads of Azilut capping fronts, windows and doors.

To the natural man abstracts like the Trinity, be they Father, Son and Holy Ghost, or Brahma, Vishnu and Shiva, mean little, but the idea of a vast mountain with the godhead at the summit does carry a meaningful weight in yeziratic terms. In the psyche such an exalted archetype exists and while the deity may have no definite form other than an immensely old man (the Ancient of Ancients is one Kabbalistic definition) it does give, as it did the Children of Israel (Natural man) before Mount Sinai, a trembling sense of awe. As the Bible puts it, 'a fear of the Lord'.

The Azilut triangle is the realm of Emanations. In the yeziratic Tree it is the level at which all Formations originate. To the rest of the Tree the archetypes here appear as changeless, that is, they are, were, and always will be, the same in relation to the endless resolving and dissolving going on in the Worlds below. For any being incarnated in Asiyyah, such as ourselves, the Azilutic triad of Yezirah appears to be Eternity and indeed it is, because this is where we were formed after being created in God's image in Beriah. Moreover, as long as we remain attached to the recycling processes of Asiyyah, we will indeed be eternally repeating within the two lower Trees. This is the other meaning of Eternity. Most of us regard eternal life as highly desirable, but this is not quite the same as perpetual existence. Eternity means to reproduce endlessly, to return constantly, to recur and in terms of life, this could mean no variety, no 'alternative', which is the complementary word opposite to 'eternity'. Eternal life might not be what is imagined. Indeed we may already be living in an endless roundelay of lives. Many traditions state this in the symbol of the Wheel of Life.

For those who wish to be released from the curse of Adam and the continuous return to the dust from which we were made, the soul has its possibilities. In the triad of the Nashamah is the ability to rise up the Tree and out of the Great Exile. This is a crucial step which can change the whole course of a person's life. The choice is there, for everyone. No man, if he wishes it, can be prevented from attaining entry into the upper face of himself. However, from the first moment he is truly committed to be a supernatural man; he must go on until he reaches the Azilutic triad. 'He has set his hand to the plough'. He cannot go back. The natural world can never seem the same once he has tasted Paradise. Nor can his life be lived in the old way once he has glimpsed the presence of Heaven within his own psychological being.

32. The Soul's Awakening

So far we have dealt primarily with the natural man. Now we leave him to live as he must on the earth. However, this does not mean we neglect him, because he is still an essential part of man incarnate. We ignore the natural man in ourselves at our peril. As our physical basis he has to be clothed, fed and housed. As said, in the Kabbalistic tradition we must be able to competently handle the affairs of ordinary existence which includes a profession and a personal life. Such conditions, it must be stated, are the prerequisite for balanced Kabbalistic work. No one can expect real development if he is unstable. To attempt to climb the Holy Mountain without practical skills and psychological reliability is to court not trouble, but disaster.

How then does the awakening begin? It often roots back to the earliest memories of childhood when the person, perhaps even as a baby, suddenly came upon himself as if out of a dream, into a world in which everything about him was extraordinarily real and clear. Abruptly quite mundane situations became pregnant with a sense of something bigger and deeper than what appeared to be happening. The senses were acute, each sound, smell, touch and sight having a richness and significance far beyond the role of information bearers. Such moments are unforgettable and indescribable, but they are retained in the memory and collected with others that occur from time to time into an album of special events stretching over a whole lifetime.

For most natural men this is as far as it goes, but the quality of such moments is never lost, although it might be deeply buried beneath the layers of worldly desires and cares.

Childhood and its own peculiar magic is intimately connected with the awakening of the soul. Besides the wonder at nature with its variety of plants and animals and the first feeling of awe as the child suddenly senses the distance of the stars when it looks up at the night sky, there is the realm of the fairy tale and folklore. These stories, like those of the Bible, have a deep effect on the psyche. It is as if the soul were being reminded of something it once knew and had lost sight of. Some psychologists suggest this is the appeal of the archetypes of the Collective Unconscious, while those of a spiritual tradition might say that indeed old memories of a previous existence, natural or supernatural, are being evoked. The precise answer does not matter. More important is the effect of the characters and themes of the stories.

Every culture has its folklore and whether they be Norse, Red Indian or African, the same motif is repeated. There is always the hero and the princess, the ogre and the miraculous object or person whose aid is required to solve the problem facing the hero. In the British tradition the tales of King Arthur are full of battles and intrigues, but most of all, despite the mediaeval flavour of style and courtly ideals, the story of the seeking of the Holy Grail has a strange appeal. To the natural man Sir Lancelot has much attraction with his courage and skill in arms, but to another side of a child's nature, a much deeper element, Sir Galahad, the knight who fully accomplishes the mission of finding the Grail, also has a fascination. This is true about the lamp in Aladdin and the crock of gold at the end of the rainbow, and many other supernatural objects or persons who intrude into the ordinary world of the child. Such puzzling, non-practical entities are dismissed by most people as they grow into adolescence, but to some, they remain part of an accumulation of questions adults cannot or will not answer.

With youth comes passion. The age of Nezah takes over from the curiosity of Hod. But for the person who has not forgotten his moments of awakening, the album begins to fill with a new kind of experience. The first kiss and love affair is etched deep. Dreams and all the Yesodic mirages whirl the body and psyche into confusion, and yet here and there are those moments of clarity, of stillness, even in the midst of violent feelings that remind the person of incidents of similar lucidity experienced as a child. Much poetry is written and music made, mostly about love or rebellion, and for the vast majority this is where they join the tribal gatherings which seek identity in politics, pop culture, or car rallies, any event where others have a common cause. The real power behind such occasions is often not ideals, or the declared intention of the happening, but the youthful need to meet and compete. Nothing is good or bad. It is just the rutting period of that generation.

For the person who is still puzzled with, and still unsatisfied by, the world of the natural man, the situation is difficult. He turns into what has come to be called an 'outsider'. This is not the social misfit who desires to belong to the in-group but has no skills or personal attractions to be accepted by them. Our outsider quite genuinely feels isolated from the crowd, not by them but by something in him that rejects the tribal conventions of whatever community he lives in. Life for him is tougher still for he has few friends he can talk to about this problem and his women are often irritated by his eternal questioning about life's purpose. 'Life is to be enjoyed' they say. He agrees, but surely there is more to it than making love, money and status. He is usually rejected in time as an ineffective wierdo, which to the society he exists in, he is, because he has no obvious objective, unlike his peers who at least want a sports car or a decent set of spears.

The female outsider has an even worse time because she is expected to conform to the conventions of her time and place, which usually results in either a bad marriage, or no marriage at all as a resistance against the pressures applied to her, not only by parents and set of friends but Mother Nature, who is interested in producing the next generation. This gut impulse rises periodically and both sexes, when just past what is considered critical ages for mating, often take partners out of quiet desperation. For the natural man this is by no means a disaster, but for the outsider it can bury for several years the important questions asked in childhood and youth. However, when the offspring of the 'outsider' mother and father become independent, the enquiry usually begins again. If it is strong enough, it will alter the pattern of life either increasing or destroying the bond of marriage. This is often a characteristic sign of awakening. In some cases the reasons for separation or divorce are inexplicable, in that sometimes there is no obvious reason for the breakdown of marriage.

The awakening of the soul can come at any time in adulthood. It cannot come before, because the full stature of the person has not been reached. A young man or woman may know of the soul, be aware of its powers, but they have not yet the experience to handle the delicate, and often crucial crises that befall someone seeking a spiritual path. This does not preclude young people from practising, but they need to be under the seasoned guidance of a teacher who can carry them over difficult periods. The process of awakening is not for everyone, and traditionally only those who will not be put off by the intentional cold-shouldering of a teacher can be accepted for the first stage of work.

However, before the stage of being under a discipline is reached, many tests have to be passed, because the tales told about the journeys of heroes in search of the miraculous are quite accurate. Various psychological dragons have to be killed and the person's metal proved, mostly to himself. It is not enough to read the right books or even belong to a study group discussing esoteric ideas. They have to be practised in life. In Kabbalistic terms—the meeting of Heaven and Earth. For the outsider the trail is full of distractions and diversions. At times he will be apparently lost and yet, often, as in fairy stories, something occurs, either externally or internally, that gets him out of a nasty scrape. After a while he begins to recognize that something is watching over him. At first he suspects all sorts of strange beings like angels, and then, in time he will discover it is himself, that is Tiferet. When sufficient contact is sustained and he begins to glimpse the whole of his lower face, many new things begin to happen.

A traditional saying states, 'when the disciple is ready the teacher appears', and this is often the case, in that he sees something that was there all the time. It is usually in the form of a person he has known for some while or suddenly meets, who stands, at that point, one degree ahead of him. In such a relationship, he who knows a little more pays his debt to his own teacher, by imparting the knowledge to his new-found pupil, at that moment in time. In this way the seeker who has been looking, sometimes for what he does not even know, recognizes the thing he has desired and is connected to a long chain of people evolving through a whole generation and on back into remote history. Moreover, he is the link forward into the future of the human race. At this realization, the scale of the operation can overwhelm a person.

Sometimes he quits because it is too much responsibility. He prefers to dream of waking up without doing any work. Such people occasionally drift back into the natural man's world. Unfortunately they still cannot join in. They know too much. Often they return to commit themselves, but sometimes the situation becomes tragic as they try to bury what they know in the usual ways of trying to forget.

For those committed to finding a path there ensues an initial honeymoon period of egoic spirituality. The reason for this is that Yesod takes on the outer personality of the tradition connected with, so that the man or woman wears its uniform and adopts the speech and mannerisms of the devotee. This being the first stage, that is the Hod, Nezah and Yesod complex, the person talks a great deal about it, desires to convert everyone, rejecting any other way as false or inferior. Indeed so passionate is the identification with the tradition that everything is taken personally regarding it. Fortunately this phase passes for most people, but there are some for whom it does not, and this is often due to their ego claiming the tradition's authority for personal use in status or power. Later, as the truth of Tiferet asserts itself the problem resolves one way or another.

The process of awakening is not easy for it takes patience and determination to maintain over long periods. Over the millennia the great traditions have evolved their basic approaches to meet the needs of different types of people. These fall into the first, for the man of action—that is the Malkhut–Nezah–Yesod triad person who learns by doing, by ritual and skill. The second for the man who works predominantly off the Hod–Yesod–Malkhut triad, who prefers to work with ideas. And the third type, the

Hod–Nezah–Yesod orientated man who is interested in feelings. He is usually more introverted than the other two and inclined towards the devotional approach, which requires the right atmosphere and a secluded situation. All three approaches are based on the body-types of the great vegetable triad. They can be seen clearly in the Christian monastic tradition where a monk may work as a carpenter, or pray continuously or contemplate theology. Judaism, Islam, Hinduism and Buddhism have their equivalent to accommodate each type of man.

There is, however, a fourth path in the cultivation of the soul and while it is often associated with the relatively modern Gurdjieff and Ouspensky esoteric school, it is by no means exclusively theirs. It is in fact related to the ancient concept of the spiritual householder, and is indeed acknowledged as such by Gurdjieff. Its form is that it is a composite of the other three ways, but that unlike them, it operates in direct contact with life. Both the Kabbalists and the Sufis, the inner traditions of Judaism and Islam, use this approach and one might well meet a Kabbalist selling baby clothes in London or a Sufi architect in Bagdad. To be in the midst of life is the essence of both teachings and yet to be able to create a holy space wherever they are, is also a pre-requisite.

For the 'outsider' who has made a connection with a long-standing tradition, several things can happen. He can go along with it to find out if it suits his needs, or move on to another, having at least identified his question and its possible answer. This can lead to a new problem in that he can wander from teacher to teacher to hear different versions of the same answer so that he never really commits himself to any approach, and these people make no progress. In some cases, the person drifts through a whole lifetime becoming much more confused by different terms and techniques for the same thing. This phenomenon relates to the commandment 'Thou shalt not commit adultery' which refers to the weakening, by mixing, of any pure relationship with anything, be it a person, tradition or God. The only solution is to be fully involved with one line and follow it right through. Nothing less will work.

A person who has accepted a particular way of working on his soul is in a unique position. Once he has crossed the line of decision the whole quality of his life begins to change. The first thing that often happens is that he loses his natural man friends, who begin to regard him now as a serious freak, and often he quits his job, if he is not dismissed first. This is because there has been a profound shift in his psyche. At first there is confusion as his normally ego-orientated psyche battles with the acknowledgment of what is important to his life. He feels yet more of an outsider and at moments he thinks he must be crazy. His erstwhile friends are no help, because his change of state is a threat to their ego-balanced world. He is too penetrating, too deep and confused to be trusted in the old way. They can no longer understand his way of thinking, even less his actions.

This state is well described in the opening to Bunyon's *Pilgrim's Progress* and Somerset Maugham's novel *The Razor's Edge*. Such a period can go on for a long time. The ego fights a long and hard war to save its status, because surrender means to loose its illusionary rulership of that person. Lies of the most extraordinary ingenuity are told by the ego, couched in the most reasonable terms. The shadow side of Yesod manipulates the lower psyche in ways Machievelli would have been proud of. It is a life-and-death conflict. Whether by self-help, or outside aid, the ego-will has to be broken. This may be done in Wild West style by riding it hard as some esoteric schools do, or in the English manner of gradually adding halter, bridle, blanket and saddle. In this way the ego submits to gentle reining. Such technique requires an experienced teacher, and the pupil must be worth the attention. No instructor will waste his valuable time on a man without a real aim. This is why, although Kabbalah, or any tradition, is in principle open to all, people are put off. A man must really want to work on his soul. To be less than totally committed to any path is not only useless, but as pointed out, sometimes dangerous. This does not mean that a person should not knock, ask and seek. There is a way for everyone. At some time that is his individual fate and destiny.

33. The Disciple

If a person wishes to develop his soul, he has to implement the desire consciously. This requires a sustained effort over a long period under discipline. It is possible to attain entry into the upper Worlds without help, but it is not recommended, because if access does occur unexpectedly, the person is often too disturbed by the power and strangeness of the experience to make use of it. This is why training is insisted upon by all traditions. A prepared person is not only familiar, if only in theory, with the upper part of the Tree, but he is ready to hear and see things that a natural man would find totally unacceptable. Miracles and magic, for instance, are denied or explained away, by the natural man, in terms that have no bearing on what really happened because the logical mind cannot grasp the idea of the operation of laws in a World other than Asiyyah. The social anthropologist who has no experience of Yezirah or Beriah will see Witchcraft as trickery or self-deception, at best as psychological illusion. With his scientifically trained Yesod he can only see what relates to his own foundation.

Decision, discipline and effort are the prerequisites for the man or woman who wishes to develop his soul. These are aided by the various traditions which have within their historical line schools which train such aspirants. These schools vary according to the needs of the time and place. However, while some remain fixed in their traditional approach, like the orthodox Jewish Kabbalah, others adopt the oral tradition to meet contemporary requirements, as this work does. Generally there is a balance between the two, the inner content of both always related to the same Teaching.

When the aspirant commits himself he begins to change his whole way of life. In Kabbalistic terms, he starts to alter his yesodic foundations. This is a major task because much psychological rubbish has to be lost. The initial period is crucial because, as Christ observed, to get rid of one devil may open the house for more and worse. Which brings us to the dangers of the induction phase.

In most traditions the line of responsibility is handed down from from teacher to disciple. The purpose of this is to preserve the teaching and to pass on the spirit. The Sufis call it the 'Baraka', which has the same root word as the Hebrew for blessing. However, traditions contain human beings and occasionally when a teacher dies without appointing a successor of high calibre, those remaining try to preserve the form of the Teaching. Alas, this is rarely successful. With time the dead teacher is elevated, more by hero worship than understanding, to sainthood, while caretaker leaders, despite their apparent modesty, take on authority. Slowly the Teaching loses its life as its inner content is forgotten. Theory turns into mere words, and practices into empty repetition. The outer form is perfect, and as such, is often mistaken for the real thing. However, the results are the precise reverse of what the original teacher intended, for the work of liberating people gradually turns into one of binding them closer to a mechanical way of life, however spiritual it sets out to be. There are many examples of this in historical and modern times. All the great religions have suffered from such phenomena and so have many small and unknown communities originally dedicated to the development of man.

Fortunately these situations produce their antidote. Both Buddha and Christ were, in their historical sense, trying to get back to the original Teaching of their traditions, which had, at that point, become too rigid. Christ never denied Judaism. He rejected the tendency towards conservatism for its own sake. It must be remembered that his first followers were Jews, not rebels or converts. It is also sad to note that the phenomena described above happened in his sect within living memory of his death.

Examined objectively, such events reveal that the spiritual path

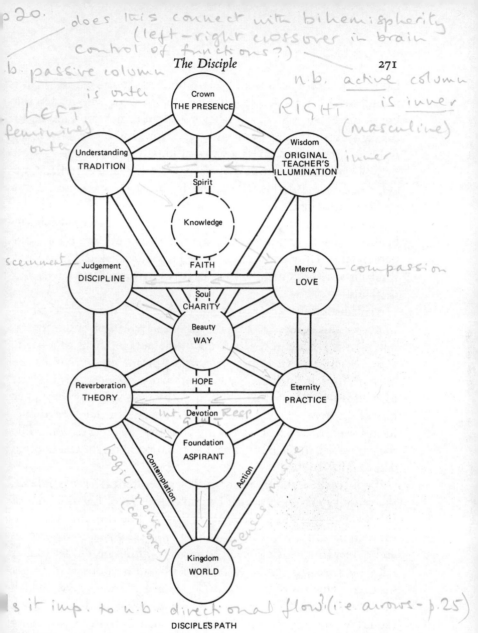

DISCIPLE'S PATH

Here the aspirant climbs the Tree of Development, passing through a series of initiations. During their course he must always keep to the central pillar of equilibrium, never deviating to left or right, that is into too much activity or pure form, as he ascends from the lower face of the natural man, through the Neshama and into the great triangle of the Spirit.

has its traps, temptations and corruptions. As in the natural man's world, there can be deceit and self-deceit in those who profess the life of the Spirit. One must be ever-watchful, for the track up to the Way proper is strewn with test problems to be solved. In Kabbalah these are seen as a series of initiations.

Kabbalah has two kinds of initiation, internal and external. One generated in the psyche, the other by outer circumstance. Both are self-instigated. They have nothing in common with the notion of ritual as many people half-acquainted with Kabbalah believe. Such ceremonies belong to the Magical Tradition, and here again a clear distinction must be made, Magicians are not Kabbalists, although they have borrowed Kabbalistic terms and methods.

Kabbalistic initiation is related to life. Be it the private aspect of prayer and contemplation or out in the world of business each initiation is precise in that it is about the development of a particular sefirah, so that step by step the aspirant slowly climbs the Tree of himself. In this way he continually balances and perfects each stage, passing from sefirah until he passes out of the upper face of the lower Tree and into the lower face of the Tree above. In this way the ascent is safely made from Earth to Heaven while the man is still in the flesh. The first initiation as might be expected is through Malkhut.

If it is recalled, the Malkhut of the psychological Tree is Tiferet, the central nervous system of the physical Tree. For the sake of convenience one can regard Malkhut as the body. In this initiation the man becomes acquainted with his physical vehicle by exercises and observation. Using what happens to him daily he no longer takes his senses for granted. Nor does he allow himself to forget his body which is drawn to his attention by certain tasks, which may range from hard physical labour to fine and delicate work requiring the utmost sense attention. Such exercises as working faster or slower are common to many traditions, as are those which bring a man to a sudden halt or make him jump, so as to expose habitual postures and attitudes.

In some traditions dances are used which are both harmonious and deliberately irregular, and are designed to bring the body into the field of consciousness. Special breathing and the various body postures found in the Muslim and Hindu traditions are examples of the Malkhut initiation, as are those found in Christian monasteries. In branches of these traditions there are variations, again designed for a specified historic time and place. Occasionally one finds practices which have no meaning even though they are carried out with great precision. This is often the case of a school which has lost contact with the original aim and cannot see that its purpose is no longer relevant to the age, or the people, who dutifully perform a long-dead ritual.

The work on the body is continuous even if it is to learn how to sit perfectly still for half an hour a day. This cultivates will, which is later to be applied, rather like a rock climber has to acquire stamina if he is to gain the summit of the peak he is scaling. To control the body is not easy because we are full of old and bad habits. These must be identified and cured while simultaneously learning how to master the many sub-roles of the body. The ancient Hindu analogy of a chariot and horses is a good one. A driver has to learn to control the left and right animals from his position in the vehicle. On the Tree the Driver or Yesod is standing in the chariot of Malkhut and working with Hod and Nezah. This brings one to the education of the driver.

The driver is ego. Founded on all the Yesodic residue of years the Personal Consciousness has to remove slowly many ideas, memories and habits useless to the person. This is difficult, because, the ego, backed up by its shadow side, will fight to maintain its established position. A person cannot normally cope alone with this crisis situation because it literally threatens his foundation. Therefore, like the psychotherapist, the role of guide is taken up by someone experienced and competent, who is senior to the disciple. This person may be acting under the instruction of a living teacher if he is not one himself, or he may operate under his own Tiferet. Either way, he occupies for a while, the Tiferet role in the disciple. In some traditions the organization acts as an archetype, but this projection is often very dangerous because no real responsibility is taken by the instructors who have not been properly trained themselves. Individual human contact and responsibility is vital. At no time must the name of the tradition or organization be invoked, because the phenomenon of possession by an archetype can occur both in the disciple and the so-called teacher. There is no authority except what lies within the disciple. The teacher must not usurp permanently the Tiferet of the aspirant. He does so at his own peril, for he not only stands in the way of the disciple's growth but blocks his own path of development.

With the acquisition of knowledge about development and the growing consciousness of the body, the personality begins to change. People not involved in the cultivation of the psyche observe distinct changes of character in the aspirant. Whereas before they suspected some difference they now see distinctly new traits in the 'outsider'. It affects various people in different ways as their egos adapt to the new foundations they are laying. Slowly, and occasionally quite abruptly, a completely new personality emerges, with a new set of bodily gestures and psychological postures. None of their old friends recognize them and their ways are soon parted, either because there is no longer any common ground, or because the aspirant is going through the previously mentioned honeymoon phase in which he outwardly demonstrates all he knows. This usually causes a violent reaction among natural men who regard such people as arrogant or just boring.

Converts often take up a superior position, seeing the worldly as fools or just Nature fodder. From this point on, communication breaks down, and any useful contact that might have existed is broken. Such a phenomenon is common among the recently converted. A secondary characteristic is when they meet anyone who disagrees with their half digested ideas. Out of this comes the bitterest of conflicts, that of belief, and we see throughout history the most bloody wars fought over issues on which both sides in fact agree. This is the world of ego, or Yesod, that while absorbing and accepting the highest ideals into its foundations, nevertheless takes the whole to itself personally. At this point one can see why a rule of silence about many esoteric Teachings is applied at the early stage.

To a man at Tiferet the veracity of tradition is valid as long as it takes him up the central axis of consciousness on the Tree; but the person grounded in Yesod can only see it egocentrically. According to the Kabbalah the Torah, that is the Teaching, may be comprehended in four ways, literally, allegorically, metaphysically and mystically. These relate directly to the four Worlds. Yesod is part Asiyyah and part Yezirah so that while the ego can grasp an idea in one World it is capable of seeing it in another, making the parable literal and the practical example into illusion when embroidered by the imaginings of Yezirah. Either way Yesod's view is subject to the limitations of the ego's very personal outlook.

Fortunately after a period, if growth has occurred, the imbalances tend to correct themselves. If they do not, that person or organization has to go on struggling with the ego until it is overcome. This can happen either gently or violently, at both the communal and personal levels. The power struggles and doctrinal rows that plague some so-called occult societies illustrate this point well.

In the case of the individual who has managed to control his ego to a certain extent the sign of a conscious foothold in Tiferet is apparent. This means he can cross the normally unconscious threshold between Hod and Nezah and so begin to convert the lower part of his Individual Unconscious into self-consciousness. This is a delicate and continual process in which the mind of Yesod has to be assisted by the flanking action of the receptivity of Hod and the activity of Nezah. In this interaction between the pillars the consciousness is lifted up the path of honesty from Yesod to Tiferet. In order to do this the development of the two-side sefirot is needed, the first being the initiation and training of Hod. In this way we progress, but in reverse order up the Lightning Flash.

Hod is that part of the psyche that collects and imparts information. It is also intimately connected with the voluntary processes, that is, the willed application of the body originating from Yesod or Tiferet which it also supplies with data. In the case of our disciple, his Hod has to absorb a vast amount of completely new knowledge. Out in the world he was taught facts in relation to a sensible reality. In an esoteric tradition, however, he is expected to believe in and study worlds he cannot see, hear, smell or touch. If he is in the pursuit of wonder workers and phenomena he is in the wrong place and should go to the market place if he wishes just to be amazed. If he wants to develop spiritually he must work and his Hod has to master the whole theoretical system of the tradition he is following. If he is a Christian he must learn prayers, the Bible, ritual or theology. If a Hindu perhaps body yoga or a working knowledge of Sankhya philosophy. As a Kabbalist he has the dynamics of the Tree of Life to learn as well as to read all the relevant books. Hod is in its element. It will absorb theories, mathematics, diagrams, and many other mental exercises. More often than not what amounts to a new language has to be mastered so that conversations with his colleagues or instructor are precisely understood.

When Hod has had its fill of information it usually shows in an overloaded Yesod which thinks and talks about nothing else. At this point the student Kabbalist is usually given yet more Hod work to perform, so that the theoretical side of his studies becomes so saturated that Hod swings from the form pillar to the sefirah of Nezah, and the person is pushed into activity, by his psyche's need to balance. In ordinary circumstances an over-developed Hod is acceptable because the Hod faculty is vital to carry out the skilled tasks of the modern world which needs its talents. The Kabbalist is in a different position. A man's develop-ment can stick in Hod for years while he believes he is practising Kabbalah, when in fact, he is only theorizing in pure form. When a man has more than enough information he is ready to bring the column of force into action. This begins with Nezah.

The Nezah initiation is sometimes quite surprising. It can make one person become incredibly lazy, and turn another into a dynamo of energy. In some people the Nezahian drive can take the form of creativity, in others it has been known to spark off a passionate episode, especially if they have been buried in Hod for years. Occasionally this burst of energy is difficult to handle. This is where the teacher helps the disciple to turn his Tiferet objectively to practical account, because the ego cannot cope, despite all the theory at its command, for the old habits of Yesod rise up to deal with the situation. These, however, are totally useless because the forces involved are unfamiliar. Often as the ego begins to behave like the frightened servant it is, the self moves in to take command. From this time on a full change begins. Gradually or suddenly as the case needs, the self which has the capacity and the authority, draws on the resources of the psyche's pillars, sefirot and triads. From the Solomon's Seat of Tiferet, clear thought, pure emotion and right action are dispensed, and if the ego can learn [even in a disastrous situation] to submit and trust, the basis of a new Yesod can be laid. Such a Foundation centred on Tiferet is really firm and the man can withstand anything, even death.

This crucial initiation is characteristic of Kabbalah, because the whole of the person is involved—people who do not wish to change should stay away from the tradition. One cannot play at Kabbalah. If no serious inner conversion occurs then there is no connection with Kabbalah or any esoteric teaching.

Initiation is not confined to the psychological world. External circumstance often reflects the impending alteration: not only do marriages break up and jobs disappear, but whole ways of life can alter on real contact with the influence of any living tradition. This is because the acceptable lies that a man or woman lives by in the world of natural people are no longer tenable in the supernatural world. In order to grow, the soul must break out of the imprisoning structure of animal and vegetable existence. Changes can sometimes occur, despite the ego's clinging to familiar securities and relationships, for the Self, if it cannot effect the change directly, will, through the side paths avoiding Yesod, influence the person to terminate an old way of life. Sometimes people, on impulse, without knowing why, suddenly leave secure positions, break social conventions, say things they cannot go back on, and begin relationships that will wreck stable situations. After a time, when the confusion begins to clear new inner and outer experiences start to happen. Abruptly or gradually a person finds he is strangely free to be himself. Often out of the blue extraordinary opportunities occur. In one actual example a man was offered a job he had always dreamed about but could never get. Because of his new state someone had seen he could now do it. In another case, a woman after a bad marriage met her match in a new companion. Both these Tiferet initiations were concerned directly with growth and truth. Because both people were courageous, a quality of Tiferet, and were centred exactly between the upper and lower faces of their Tree, Heaven and Earth could aid them. Nothing in Creation works separately When a man is true to himself, his needs are supplied, because the self of the person is the Self of All and can call on the resources of the total Universe. Most people consider that only they are involved in an event, that only they are performing the action. But the Universe is all of one piece and one consciousness. How else could it be? The self knows what is needed and gives not what is desired by the ego, but what is required for that person's development. For someone it may be pain, for another pleasure. Each is a key to open the door to that individual's self-consciousness. In Kabbalah all life is an initiation. There is always profit to be made, but of heavenly treasure. When the self initiation is accomplished the Tiferet of Yezirah is, and wears the Crown of, the asiyyatic Keter. Such a person is no longer just a Natural man.

34. *Individual*

A disciple has to follow and obey, but there comes a time when a man must be himself. This does not mean being without discipline nor does it imply wilfulness. Quite the contrary. In the initial stages of a man's development he is required to study the tradition and practice it, that is, Hod and Nezah. As ego stands at Yesod so it submits for a time to the teacher, rabbi or sheik who represents Tiferet. As such, the teacher instructs the disciple, indicating correctives either on the pillar of form or force. After the disciple has remade his foundation and has a basis to stand firmly on (Christ called it building a house on rock) he can begin to contact his Tiferet directly and often. This may be accomplished by physical exercises, or by meditation, both of which use the reverberation of Hod and the repetition of Nezah in word or action to raise the level of consciousness into Tiferet. A third method is that of contemplation, which in Kabbalah means the application of knowledge to draw the consciousness up from Yesod. Using the Tree of Life as a mandala, or considering the Name of God are examples. There are many variations on these three approaches but all are designed to take the aspirant up the middle column of the Tree.

The constant centring on Tiferet over a period of time strengthens the phenomenon of the Watcher, that curious impartial observer inherent in all of us. With diligent practice the Self can be evoked at will and the man consciously place himself in Solomon's Seat at the nucleus of the Tree. Such a willed act brings about many changes in the psyche. The most dramatic of all is that the whole of the lower natural face becomes more vital and alert, while the field defined as the Individual Unconscious, slowly begins to transform into consciousness. This is the start of a major reversal process whereby the yesodic rulership of natural man is superseded by Tiferet Governance of the supernatural man. The preliminary sign is the increasingly alert state of the Hod, Nezah, Tiferet triad of the Nefesh. This is the beginning of the resurrection spoken of in the New Testament. In the Kabbalah it is called Teshubah or repentance, which means, to be converted or to return to God.

The Hebrew letters allocated to the paths of the Nefesh triad spell NAL, a root word meaning 'to lock in position'. In the context of an evolving man it describes how he is fixing the theories and practices he has learnt firmly into his psyche, and is relating them to his Tiferet. This means that his self is directly engaged in the process of growth and feeds into and off consciously acquired experience. This is quite different from the ordinary intake of experience in natural man which simply disappears across the Hod–Nezah threshold into the subliminal zone to be filed in the Unconscious. In the awakening man's case the exterior and interior events are carefully observed and related to the theory and practice of the tradition being followed. By this method causes and effects are identified in the light of objective knowledge. Being under discipline, constant checks by an experienced mentor prevent the dangers that arise from time to time. An historic example of this was for a man to be put through a water endurance test so that he overcame any fear of that element. While in danger of his life at some points, he was always watched over by an elder. A similar initiation occurs in our own time when a student psychotherapist is put through analysis by a senior in order to face his own difficulties before dealing with others.

All these tasks, trials and initiations are aimed at strengthening a man's ability to find himself and maintain an equilibrium in spite of the inner or outer changes that are always occurring. It is a continuous Hod study and Nezah practice so that the disciple's field of self-consciousness is ever extending, inwardly and outwardly. The end of this stage is when the whole lower part of the Unconscious can be converted into consciousness at will.

Tiferet is the Individual essence of a man. It is that which is peculiarly his and no other's. A man may change his shape, his habits, even his personality, but never his Tiferet. This is the core of his psychologic anatomy and the Crown of his asiyyatic body. This nub of his being is recognized everywhere and at any time. For example, one meets an old school friend. Perhaps he is haggard and worn, and maybe even broken as a man, but his essential nature is still there, still showing through the battered body and the tattered personality. An exceptional case maybe, but it illustrates that only death can remove that part of a man. True, psychological sleep can bury it and an overdeveloped persona mask it over, but it is still there. There is, however, one rare exception already mentioned in a previous chapter and that is Crime in the widest sense. Here a man psychologically dies before his body so that he is only the shell of a person. This phenomenon is not limited to the prison or madhouse. Such people can be found in high office. More than one man in politics, in business, science and the Arts has been no more than an empty animal automaton.

In the Kabbalist, or indeed any aspirant, the aim is to gain permanent and conscious affiliation with Tiferet, because it is the key to the rest of the Tree and the gate to his journey back to his source. In Christian Kabbalah Tiferet is the Christ centre, which is why Christ said: 'I am the Way.' Personally I have enormous respect for Christ (he was a great Jew), but as the commandments say, 'no other gods before Me'. Therefore as a Jewish Kabbalist I hold to the premise that while he may well have been God incarnate, so are the rest of us by virtue of our likeness to the Creator. The chief difference between us and Joshua ben Joseph (Jesus) is that he was a fully realized man, and because of this he must be acknowledged as the Son of God, which is an ancient Biblical title for this level of attainment. However, there have been others who have reached this peak of human flowering, and tradition has it that there has to be one fully developed man on the face of the planet at every period, including today, to maintain the living chain of evolving men between Earth and Heaven.

The above gives some hint at the dimension of Tiferet. For people like ourselves, trying to shift from the dominance of the ego into the objective view of the self, the centring in Tiferet is important. It is important because it shows us what we are and what we can do. The well-worn esoteric saying 'know thy self' is the key to the combination lock to our being. How can it be opened? Again every tradition has its ways.

In Kabbalah the yeziratic Tiferet is the self. Moreover, this same sefirah is the Keter of Asiyyah. It is also the Malkhut of Beriah, so that concentrated into this one sefirah are three Worlds, but individualized into the self. This same self is the spark of the Divine incarnated in Natural and Supernatural man. It therefore follows that if we begin to know ourselves we can know and be known by God. 'The Holy One Blessed be He.'

While realizing the magnitude of this point it is not enough. The disciple must continually practice his discipline and wait patiently. If he lets it drop the cleared path between Yesod and Tiferet is soon overgrown like an unused track in the jungle. Diligently he has to keep up his daily exercise be it action, meditation or contemplation.

Various traditions use sub-systems to aid the disciple. These may include mathematics, grammar, symbolism, cosmology and many other subjects. The Kabbalah is no exception, containing within its scope a whole range of studies from numerology to the nature of angels and demons. Contrary to orthodox Jewish belief Kabbalah also uses astrology. Evidence is found in the zodiacs on the floors of synagogues in Israel, the considerable use of its symbols in the Sefer Yezirah, the Kabbalistic Classic, and even in the Sephardi Yom Kippoor Service where the poem-prayer Keter Malkhut of Ibn Gebirol draws freely on Astrology.

Interpretation, however, must be made in the light of a total system such as the Kabbalah, for without a spiritual frame of reference astrology is merely the study of effects. Its use is that it demonstrates a psychological solar system. And if we believe all is one, that the Universe is of a single whole, it follows there can be no separation between the macrocosm and the microcosm, that is, in the heavens and man, because they are made in the same likeness.

For natural man living in ego, the sun of Tiferet has little meaning. He lives in fact most of the time off his yesodic moon. What does this mean? In terms of Kabbalah he is subject to the cycles of Asiyyah, that is, mass organic movements and elemental rhythms. This does not mean that the supernatural man is not also subject to them, but that he is not dominated by them. The natural man has no choice because his ego is totally unaware of anything but itself. He thinks he is master of his fate, when in fact he is subject to every external condition and internal pressure. Only individuals can stand out against Asiyyah. In time of war, the result of cosmic tension, natural men die by the million, often for the most stupid yesodic reasons. A soldier may rationalize his ideals or self-interest, but the ego must justify itself in the face of social climate generated by celestial tides. And so Yesod sends a man, often against the warning of Tiferet, to his death for something that has no real significance. Natural men, however individualistic they dream they are, are conformists under the laws of Nature. It could not be otherwise or the rhythms and structure of organic life would collapse. Only individuals can rise above natural tides. This requires a totally different standpoint. It needs a shift of consciousness away from the lunar ego up into the sun position.

When a man begins to live off his sun, he begins to follow his individuality, his Fate. This marks him out from natural men who live under the rulership of mass movements and conditions. Such a man lives his life according to his own will. This may be good or evil. At the crucial stage before he submits his will to something greater he has choice. Here is where man is different from the animals and the angels. He has choice. His also is the greatest temptation to make himself a god. By attaining Tiferet a man can look down on and govern natural men. Fortunately an evil decision usually brings his downfall, because by cutting himself off from the upper Tree he is still in fact a natural man and therefore still subject to the rule of the Unconscious. In time Tiferet reveals the truth in the decaying inner quality of his life. If he continues to deny his greater responsibilities as an individual he severs his connection with the upper sefirot of Judgement, Mercy, Knowledge, Understanding and Wisdom. None of these can any men live without for long. The natural man receives their benefit unconsciously, but the half evolved man who is above the law of the Earth and not yet under the laws of Heaven places himself, by wilful choice, in a very precarious position. If he tries to be a law unto himself, he is isolated and eventually, having neither support from above or below, he falls, destroyed from above and below.

An individual who lives his life according to Tiferet will project his true nature and attract the kind of life he needs. Thus a creative man will surround himself with his creations, while someone who has an administrative talent will seek the environment where he can express it. If we look at the life of any great man, we will see this law in his work, his home, his friends and indeed on everything he does. There is a distinct individual flavour in his life. This is the quality of fate. Contrary to popular believe fate is not fixed. It is merely a tendency that an individual follows. No astrologer can predict the fate of an evolving man, because he can alter his psychological solar system to meet his own aims. True a man living off his sun at least does have a fate, but unless he develops a conscious soul he will merely be a more particular and powerful character than his natural fellows. Moreover, although he lives in touch with Tiferet, he is still under the domain of Nature and needs external circumstance to assert himself. The supernatural man does not need this. 'Gold and mud are the same to the sage', the ancient Chinese said. The supernatural man is self-sufficient. He is indifferent to outward good or bad fortune. Fate is superseded by acting correctly within a given moment. This is the objective of all who seek to rise above the lower face of the Tree. In Buddhism it is called Right Action. In Kabbalah, Righteousness. This is the Jewish holy man, the Zadek, the mythical and real Just man. Such a person is concerned with proper conduct, that is with the cultivation of Gevurah or Judgement and Hesed or Mercy, the two emotional sefirot which, with Tiferet, compose the Neshamah triad of the soul.

35. The Neshamah

In the supernatural man the sun of the self rules the moon of the ego. As consciousness becomes more established in the self, so the ego begins to serve as a talented and dutiful intelligence which interacts between the inner and outer worlds. Further in, beyond the natural domain of the lower face of the psychological Tree hovers the triad of the Neshamah, the soul proper. It is defined by the paths between Gevurah, Hesed and Tiferet, the Hebrew letters of which compose the word 'Zache', which means 'to purify'.

It is said that man has three souls, the animal Nefesh, the Neshamah and the Ruah. As previously said, I belong to that Kabbalistic school which uses the Biblical definition of Neshamah, which means a 'living soul' as against Ruah which implies 'Wind' or 'Spirit', that is the Great beriatic Triad of Binah, Hokhmah, Tiferet. Tradition has it that the Nefesh belongs to the body, the soul to Paradise and the Spirit to Heaven. This sets out very precisely the Neshamah's situation between the upper and lower faces.

In the natural man the Neshamah is in a state of sleep, rather like a new-born child in that it only wakes at crucial turning points in a life. The idea is developed further by Kabbalistic tradition, which says that each soul is sent down into Asiyyah to learn the lessons of that World. Observations of most of humanity indicate a very childlike level.

Indeed the motivations behind much private and public activity suggests that many people, in spite of a sophisticated veneer of personality, are extremely infantile. The history of mankind is a fair proof of this, with the bulk of its energy being principally involved in violence, avarice and wilfulness, all the attributes found in children. Where there have been achievements, invention, thought and creation, there has usually been massive resistance from the ignorant, particularly the learned ignorant, who like children are basically conservative and do not want their toys changed or their security threatened. If we take an honest look at ourselves, we will see this is equally true of us as private persons. To alter our way of life, of looking at the universe, is a distinct threat. We say we are open, interested in new ideas, but when it comes to it, we block, duck and even try to discredit or destroy any encroachment on our psychological stability. Observe how we cling to a concept even though we know it to be faulty. 'Better the devil one knows', says the ego. Many people prefer a whole lifetime of lies rather than face a truth. Much drama and literature is a study of this very problem. Hamlet's 'To be, or not to be' is an example. How does this awful situation arise? Why do men, indeed sometimes whole peoples, obliterate the truth, as the Germans ignored the concentration camps? It is because, as often repeated but never really believed, natural man is in a state of sleep. This is not entirely his fault.

The reason natural men slumber is that the planet needs large numbers of reliable organisms within the earth's ecological scheme who will serve the planet's needs. Thus, for example, the mass migrations that periodically spread round the globe are part not of man's will, but the planet's desire to fill the empty spaces of her surface with more sensitive creatures than animals and plants. Men with the wills of individuals are useless to Nature. Such people are not organic automata and cannot be moved back and forth in human waves. An individual has his own aims and while acknowledging that he must serve the Universe he may not wish to be just a cellular body. He possesses consciousness and this can free him from the tooth and claw of the natural world. Why then do not all men take advantage of this escape offer that requires no more than individual effort? The reason is in the hard fact that most people do not wish to stir from their security, however meagre.

Kabbalah says, like many other great traditions, that the soul is recycled through a physical body at least three, if not more times. The purpose is twofold. Firstly, to give the soul experience under the intense pressure of the asiyyatic World and secondly, to raise the lower levels of Creation up towards Heaven. That the soul is involved in a cosmic purpose does not dawn on most people, because their identification with ego limits their view to the body and lower psyche. This occurs because, Kabbalah says, the soul, on being incarnated, forgets its previous state in the blurring density of an asiyyatic body of flesh and blood. Some people do in fact recall something, but of what they are not sure. Occasionally an actual place is remembered, and sometimes people whom they are sure they know from another time. Others remember only the feeling they were somewhere else before they were born and that it was quite unlike anything they have met on earth. Quite often they look forward to death, so that they can return to where they come from, before they were born. All these observations concur with Kabbalistic teaching on life before and after death, and it is interesting to note that the same conclusions have been arrived at all over the world.

According to Kabbalah the soul is sent down into the world often against its will, because it is quite happy at its own original level. For reasons best known to the Almighty we all come here to learn certain lessons and are therefore directed into particular lives. This is accomplished by being born to certain parent above whom our souls (the Zohar says) hover when they make love. If conception is willed, we descend and become attached though not firmly, to the fertilized cell. During gestation, the connection becomes stronger as the growing body begins to fill out our yeziratic mould as a babe. At the moment of emergence from the womb, the soul can, and occasionally does, back away from the shock of asiyyatic life, and as the Hebrew prayer book says, 'A soul can pass by the world without entering it.' More often than not, the Nefesh, which by this time has a distinct interest in maintaining the body, forces the sleepy soul into life and the shock usually wakes the soul up, so that for a brief moment it is fully awake.

In most people the awareness of the Neshamah fades, as they

become more deeply involved with life, into a vague memory, at most a presence occasionally felt. It is commonly called the Unconscious or subconscious and this is quite correct, although not in the way that conventional psychologists think. This is because the Neshamah may well be carrying the residue of the last life. As the synthesis of a man's experience, the Neshamah triad is the individualized part of his psychological Tree, and that identity which survives the lower psychological face, which collapses when the asiyyatic body has died. As such, the Neshamah carries the sins of the father, or the generator of the next life, since that person has by his own choice preferred to be born again, rather than take the next step up and out of the Wheel of Life. It is very important to perceive that the course of this, and our next life, is determined by ourselves in the attitudes we adopt at each moment. In Hindu terms we create our own Karma.

For the natural man repetition is inevitable. He will live the same kind of life over and over again because that is what he wants. He will put up with sorrow, fear, even death because he feels safe in the sameness of it all. Much of the East has remained in a state of stagnation because of the recognition of repeated lives. In such a situation no one except himself can gain his release. It is every man for himself, but not in the way of the natural man. What is the way out of this *impasse*? It is the cultivation of the Neshamah, the growth and purification of the heart, which is created by the emotional sefirot of Hesed and Gevurah linked to the self-consciousness of Tiferet.

Before serious work on the Neshamah can begin several steps have to be taken. Esoteric tradition states that there is a preliminary path up to the Way proper. This involves first the recognition of something more than the needs of the vegetable, the desires of the animal and the vanity of the ego. Here is the position of our 'outsider'. There follows from this a search for something else, beyond the natural world. This of course leads, often while the outsider is going through his social and personal upheaval, to an interest in the supernatural which is often the reason he loses his natural man friends. Such excursions into the unseen are usually disappointing because there is no substance in the other world phenomena that makes any real sense. If the person does not quit the search, he may pass into the organized occult scene where he will meet people who are either genuine, fake or misguided. Here he will encounter magic but this will only take him so far (to Yezirah and no further to be precise). He may also come across many societies, organizations and groups who claim to be the sole possessors of the truth, and he might well be taken in for a number of years until he realizes that his own nature is the method by which he may reach what he is seeking for. At this point he usually leaves the circle he has been studying with and enters a crisis point in his spiritual life. During this crucial period the Neshamah is awake and often in the midst, sometimes, of psychological desolation a new direction appears out of nowhere and it becomes apparent that a certain path and no other has to be followed. Up to that point he has imitated the ways of people who themselves did not know. Quite suddenly he knows what he must do. He begins to live his fate, his life obviously having its own Individual flavour. He still generates and attracts the same circumstance, but his attitude is different. His observations are made from quite another level. He now accepts the full responsibility for his attitudes and actions. This is the beginning of the conscious work of the Neshamah.

How has this come about? It has happened because at some point—and he may even remember when he made the decision— a commitment was made to follow his own path. This momentous choice comes from very deep in the psyche but it is conscious, because at that moment the man is centred in Tiferet and is perhaps, for just that instant, fully self-conscious. This means that for a brief second all the paths leading into Tiferet are alert and everything connected with his life is under review. From the Seat of Solomon he sees what lay behind and what lies before him. In the NOW of that realization he crosses through the Gate of the Temple into the inner courtyard. From there on, there is no going back. 'The Way has been entered upon'. He is no longer the same man. To use another New Testament quotation, 'He has put away childish things.'

From here on things become quite different. While such a man still lives out his true nature's fate, he is in fact no longer subject to it. He uses it as a vehicle for study, sees every trial as a test for his Neshamah's education. Each success and failure is observed with detached interest. This does not mean he loses his zest for life, quite the contrary—everything becomes richer, more full of significance. Nothing is wasted, no small incident, inner or outer, is disregarded for he knows that the total situation is designed for his benefit as he views his life from this seat.

The operation of Gevurah and Hesed is now openly involved in the man as slowly his Individual Unconsciousness is converted into consciousness. This process is carried out by constantly centring on, and in, the self by the techniques of action, devotion and contemplation. About this time, that is, after a short while of working on his own, it is quite common for him to come in contact with a real tradition. This connection is usually made, as previously said, through what appears to be a chance meeting, but on reflection, at this level of operation in the Universe there is no such thing. More often than not, the contact is made with a link that is directly related to the person's own roots, so that when he enters into its orbit its language, symbols and approach is extraordinarily familiar with him. It has often been described as 'Coming home' and certainly no matter which real tradition a man's roots are in, the effect is the same.

Once the connection is made, the work really begins. The man is totally committed. While he conducts his public and private life outwardly in much the same way, his whole outlook is utterly changed. Everything is devoted to the same end and though it may appear an extreme view, in actuality his attitude to life becomes balanced and serene. This state has been described by every tradition and there are many accounts of the phenomenon down the ages. One observes it in Catholic nuns, Buddhist monks and Hasidic rabbis, but it is also seen in many people fully engaged in ordinary life, but not of it, who are committed to some form of self development. Kabbalistically the prerequisite to such a condition is the conscious operation of Tiferet with Gevurah making its contribution through the pillar of Form in discipline and discrimination, while Hesed applies the expanding principle of Love on the Force column. Together they consciously support and check each other in a constant dialogue which is reconciled in the self. In more mundane terms, the inner and outer aspects of the man's emotional life are merged in consciousness so that there is no dichotomy. No event internal or external is unconnected.

While for obvious reasons the attention cannot be centred all the time at Tiferet, the emotional sefirot deal with every happening in the light of the growing and maturing Neshamah. In the natural man the Individual Unconscious absorbs the experience, but it has no direct use for it and so it is merely filed for use at some point which may never occur. In evolving man, such new material is always referred to the problem of development in relation to the total circumstance of the man, and may be used in instant feedback should it be required. Such a continuous processing between Gevurah and Hesed generates great energy and control, and when meeting such a person under spiritual discipline one is often aware of a power and restraint not found in ordinary men. This power of course is not to be abused and any man who docs, for some are tempted, usually loses what it took years to gain. There is plenty of evidence for this. The highly gifted occultist Aleister Crowley was a case in point, and so was the amazing Cagliastro, the magician who died miserably in a papal prison.

With the evolution of the Neshamah the extension of consciousness deepens. Centred on the self, consciousness reaches not only downward and outward to the meeting place between the psyche and the outside world in the ego, but upward and inward to encompass the invisible sefirah of Daat. From this connection comes an imparting of knowledge from the beriatic World and beyond. This is again verified by common experience in that it is possible for a man to know things that he has never been told. The required information or observation just appears out of nowhere. It manifests in Yesod, but its origin is much higher up the axis of consciousness, than even Tiferet. Knowledge is quite different from Wisdom or Understanding. It is to 'know', and it carries a conviction that can only be borne by the person knowing.

Such comments are of course likely to be considered arrogant, but many great teachers and thousands of other people have said that they *know*, and that is that. Some have even died because of this knowledge, so convincing is its inner authority. One does not question the voice of the Holy Spirit, because in both Jewish and Christian terminology, that is what Daat is.

Taking the Christian line further, as Daat is the descent of the Holy Spirit or Ghost so the growth of the Neshamah is the 'Second birth', after that of the flesh. John the Baptist baptized in water but here it occurs with Spirit. Baptism is from the Greek root 'to wash, to purify', which is the Hebrew equivalent of the word composed by the path letters making up the Neshamah triad. The evolution of the Neshamah is the purification of the soul so that it may arise and return up the Tree to its place of Emanation. From this it will be seen that the descent of Daat is a vital part of the progression in the soul's journey home.

From the point of view of the Kabbalist, and this can be in the Christian or Jewish versions, because it is fairly self-evident that Christ and certainly St. Paul were connected with the same inner teaching source that the development of the Individual Consciousness is a preparatory stage for the direct engagement with the upper face of the psychological Tree. So far three major steps have been taken: the first separates the natural man's world from the supernatural world, the second searches for a way into the inner aspect of oneself, and third is the commitment to a distinct way of working on the soul. This last step is most important, because no stage can be missed. One cannot enter in the Way except by the legitimate door. Drugs may give one a glimpse over the wall into Eden, but one soon slips back exhausted and sometimes broken by the fall from so great a height. So while drugs give a fast trip there and back, there is nothing permanent in their investment except depletion, and for some, the hell or Kellippotic realm of a lost chance.

If a man has attained a degree of Individual Consciousness he knows a great deal about himself and all the people, events and things connected with him. His position on the Tree at Tiferet gives him the extraordinary insight of Gevurah and the capacity

for love of Hesed. Combined, these make the quality of 'Charity'.[1]
Below in the awakening consciousness triad of Nefesh, is the
attribute of 'Hope', while above, penetrating down into Tiferet
from the supernal sefirot is the Ruah triad of 'Faith'.[1] These three
attributes make a whole man, but as St. Paul says, if one has no
'Charity' then all one's gifts are as nothing. In the light of what we
have observed about the development of the Neshamah, the significance of this emotional bridge between the upper and lower
faces of the Tree of the psyche can be seen. If one can view
Individual Consciousness as Paradise, it will be understood why
that well-known Kabbalist Joshua ben Miriam of Bethlehem
said, 'No man may enter the Kingdom of Heaven unless he be
born again.'

1. See Plate XIX.

The Spirit

36. Cosmic Consciousness

Above the intermediary triad of the Neshamah hovers the Great Triangle of the Ruah, the lower part of the upper face. This is composed of Hokhmah, Binah and Tiferet and contains the consciousness of the Universe. The letters of its paths make the Hebrew word 'Yatev' which means 'to improve' or 'goodness'. Quite different in scale from the Neshamah, this triad has nothing personal about it. It is cosmic.

The Universe, according to the Tree, is a finely integrated whole. This comes about because of an over-all scheme which takes into account both great and small, and relates them into an interacting total. This is possible because the whole complex is in fact one, and because Creation is designed on a set of laws which operate consistently throughout. It is true that there are different levels, but these are organized so that they contain, or are contained by each other, the largest—Adam Kadman—being enclosed and permeated by the Creator.

Creation begins when the three supernal sefirot come into a creative relationship and the Lightning Flash crosses the Daat point. At this crucial moment, and it is continuous, there emerges that which we will call the manifest Universe. At this stage the laws are basic and simple, but as they descend they double at each step, so that by the time they reach the bottom of the four Trees, all the laws of the Worlds and levels above, accumulate into thousands in the asiyyatic Malkhut. Modern science has observed this phenomenon in the electromagnetic spectrum and the periodic table of elements where the mass or energy density and vitality increases or decreases up and down the scale. Scientists also acknowledge different levels of work, be it mechanical, biological, chemical or atomic. Moreover, they accept, although not in Kabbalistic terms, that all these activities can go on in the same place at the same time, with a constant exchange and inter-penetration of different worlds. Our study of the body illustrated this. Energy and matter obey specific laws whether they are in cellular, molecular or atomic states. These laws are cosmic, that is, applicable anywhere in the Universe.

Nor is this confined to celestial mechanics. The fact that organic life can exist elsewhere than on our planet is not beyond belief today. Astronomers reckon by the law of averages that there are several thousand chances amongst the millions of stars of the Milky Way, not to mention the myriads of other galaxies in the vast space about us. But take it further, cosmic law also implies, and the universality of the Tree certainly indicates, that man on the planet Earth is by no means a unique being. Adam is, after all, all men and it follows that terrestrial man may only be one group of a greater Humanity spread throughout the Universe.

It is said that man is roughly half-way between Heaven and Earth. It is also said, by tradition, that he can live in several different worlds at once. Scientifically he exists in at least three. However, while he can operate the mineral, utilize the vegetable and control the animal both internally and externally, he can still remain earthbound—that is, imprisoned in the lower face. For-tunately his potential does not stop there. By virtue of his con-struction he has been given gratis, an asiyyatic and a yeziratic body. The former is perfected for him by Nature, who has a vested interest in it, but the latter is only half developed; the rest he has to refine himself. While it is true to say that the upper part of his psychological Tree is in full working order, we have seen that he has to grow into it by stages of conscious evolution. This requires much individual effort which takes him beyond the lower face of the Tree of the psyche. Having reached and main-tained the self-conscious stage of the Neshama, such a person then begins to make contact with the Ruah Triad, that is, the cosmic view of the Universe.

For natural man cosmic consciousness has little meaning and yet he does have an inherent appreciation of its presence. This is largely due to the Collective Unconscious at work within him, so that he at least recognizes certain basic human laws even though he may not be able to live up to them. Throughout history those who have been concerned with cosmic law, have presented codifications of the basic rules for the natural man to abide by. Their chief concern has been to protect the natural man from himself, so that in his sleepy ignorance he does not break the rules of his own nature, and have to pay a high price, to buy back his birthright, to be free from the Wheel of Life, or Galgulim in Kabbalistic terms.

If one examines the Ten Commandments of Judaism or the Eightfold Path of Buddhism, as two such examples of a code of laws, one sees that they are principles designed with Right Conduct or Righteousness in mind. They both state, or imply, that for a man to break these laws means to incur misery, while to keep them brings him closer to happiness and even beyond. One might ask what is the difference between these laws and those of any tribe or national constitution. The answer is that social laws are based on local custom while our two examples are grounded in universal rules. One might say that customary law depends on time and place, and cosmic laws do not. Thus in one country it is considered legal to kill in a blood feud, while in another it is a crime. The injunction 'Love thy neighbour' involves an entirely different order of Law, which is timeless. Such laws are universal in their application. As will be appreciated, these laws do not belong to the natural world where survival of the fittest is the rule. They are not found in the mundane government of business or professional societies which only have regulations to preserve the common good. They are spiritual, as against temporal, and to practice them is to be involved in cosmic purpose.

If we take our two codes of the Ten Commandments and the Eightfold path we may get some notion of the scale they work upon. The first thing to strike one is their simplicity. The directions are plain and basic. 'Thou shalt not steal, or bear false witness; right speech and right action' are examples of each tradition. These are disarmingly to the point, unlike the numerous and qualifying regulations in most legal codes. Their simplicity is because they come from a world where the laws are few, but where fundamentals are to be found. One might say they operate at the level of Principles, that is of Beriah or Creation. For man, such a level is Objectivity.

Here are the principles that determine the nature of human existence. Here everything that has, is and can happen are set out. These are the cosmic laws governing all men. Such codes, handed down from the holy mountains of Sinai, or Enlightenment, are fashioned to help man to avoid disaster and improve his possibilities. If we consider the objectives of Buddha it is apparent that he wished to help people release themselves by rising above the law of cause and effect or ordinary existence. This requires a perception of life on a cosmic scale, far beyond the range of the Neshamah level which is concerned with matters appertaining to its own development. The scope of such a view is vast, involving all human time and experience. Indeed the laws governing this level have an eternal quality and this is where the connection with the Ruah triad can be seen.

The Ruah triad is headed by Wisdom and Understanding. This supernal combination, together with the invisible sefirah of Knowledge give a cosmic weight to the paths that focus in on Tiferet. If we look at the great Father and the great Mother complement alone, we can see how they are mighty factors of influence. Situated between Azilut and Beriah they are the bastions at the heads of the male and female columns of the manifest Universe. As such they play a direct role between the Creator and his Creation. From the view of any man attaining this level of spirituality it means he is as close as he can get to God without seeing His face.

The account of Moses's experience on the mountain, high above the Children of Israel, gives both literally and allegorically, a good idea of the relationship between natural man and a person who has entered the Ruah triad. In Exodus XIX the Lord descended upon Mount Sinai in a thick cloud (wind or breath). From its top he called Moses up instructing him that none of the Israelites should come near, and that a barrier should be set up for fear the Lord should break out against them. In modern hippy slang, 'their minds would get blown'. This, in the light of contemporary drug experience, is a very precise description of the full power of the upper Tree, blasting the unprepared structure of the lower face. Even a man with a well-developed Neshamah must be cautious with such a cosmic experience. Not even the priests, Exodus goes on, 'may force their way up to the Lord'. At this point the narrative speaks of the giving of the Ten Commandments.

Even as we read them now, we sense the awe of the occasion and it is not just the frightening picture of a great mountain enveloped with cloud, thunder and lightning. It is something much deeper than the yeziratic image. We perceive, even as we stand today at Sinai's foot with the Children of Israel in the lower face, the fear and trembling in the presence of God. It is not without reason that the path from Tiferet up through Daat to Keter is called 'Awe'.

The Ten Commandments are supernal by nature. They express archetypal law. So fundamental are they, that vast numbers of mankind have accepted them as a basis for their civilizations. This is remarkable, when it is remembered that the Israelites were an insignificant people, at the time of their giving. Here is the power of the Ruah triad and its ability to impart great force and form to a minute religion, amid hostile giants who have sought constantly to destroy the Hebrews down the ages. Perhaps more important than the preservation of a tradition, is the miracle that the Spirit descended to the perception of ordinary men. Indeed such was the side effect of the experience, that when Moses came down the mountain, the people were frightened by the shining of his face. This was no doubt because Moses had seen for a brief moment in Asilut, the World of Emanations as the Lord allowed him to see his back, for no mortal man may see God's face and live (Exodus XXXIII).

As the individual and cosmic experience of Moses's is part of Western man's archetypal heritage, so likewise is that of Buddha for the East. In the moment of cosmic realization Buddha saw the illusion of the Wheel of Life, the nature of the human self and of pure Enlightenment. On this Ruah triad view he based his teaching, each statement an objective fact about man's relationship to the Universe, and how he might be free from the cycling of the natural world. Mohammed too had a cosmic experience. When in a cave on the slopes of a mountain he became aware of a great light bursting in upon his consciousness before the Angel Gabriel appeared, then accompanied him, up through all the levels of Heaven where he saw many wondrous things. It is interesting to note here that Gabriel in the Kabbalistic tradition is the Archangel of the Yesod of the beriatic Tree, that is, the same place occupied by Daat in the yeziratic Ruah triad we are now examining. This says that one must have a firm Foundation in Beriah's lower face before one can ascend. This can only be achieved by yeziratic knowledge, or an image of the next world, that is above.

Such examples of cosmic consciousness are obviously rare, or are they? Even a cursory search reveals quite a few people who have had Ruah experiences. Jocab Boehme, a seventeenth-century shoemaker-philosopher is one: the Spanish mystics, St. John of the Cross, and St. Teresa are others. Among the poets are Wordsworth and Tennyson—Plato certainly had such experience, as did Pascal, Dante, Kabir, Donne and many others, whose writings only hint at the after-image of an entry into the Ruah triad. It is interesting to note that mystical experiences are often unintelligible in a natural man's terms—that is why we hear so little about them and why, when described, they are often seen as the observations of deranged minds, by those centred in the ordinary ego-body mind of the lower face.

How then does a man come into the presence of the Spirit? It appears that there are two ways, one by Grace which is given from above, and the other by conscious preparation, through which a place is made ready for the Ruah to descend as often as needed. Let us then examine the step beyond the Neshamah stage, that of moving out of self-consciousness up the central axis and into the unseen sefirot of Knowledge.

As always the action must begin at the beginning. In most spiritual disciplines it starts with the body in the World of Asiyyah, because if it does not, a man is likely to come adrift in more ways than one. Mohammed said, 'Put your trust in God but do not forget to tie up your camel.' In Kabballah this is to become aware of the asiyyatic Tree both internal and external. Once the position of Malkhut has been established, that is, only when one is aware of the body, can the attention move up the central axis to Yesod. From ego, through some technique such as meditation, the level of consciousness can be raised up to Tiferet which is the door into the upper worlds. The prerequisite is the need to know the truth. A natural man is content with the world, in spite of its difficulties, but someone seeking to know, keeps hammering on the door of Tiferet asking for it to be opened. If he succeeds, and he has to knock at least three times, he passes on into the school of the Neshamah.

Here he begins to attract to himself the kind of life his nature needs to fulfil itself. Unlike natural men who are subject to general law, he finds a special place in the world to match his gifts, while others are pushed by Nature into the nearest niche, which may be a factory bench, an executive desk. It does not matter who fills the post as long as the planet's requirements are met. In the case of the man working on his soul, he is taken care of by the two guardian angels of Judgement and Mercy. They protect and guide him, so that he knows when and where to move and what to avoid. There are many instances of this when people come unscathed through disasters, plagues and wars. Common experience shows that when one is alert the psyche informs the ego and the body exactly what to do. Many people left Germany long before the Nazis came to power. They were forewarned by their Neshamas just as were certain people who cancelled their berths on the doomed *Titanic*.

The development of the Neshamah is a preparation for cosmic experience. It is accomplished by extending the consciousness in Tiferet which is the key to all human spiritual experience. Situated where it is, this sefirah is simultaneously the mingling place of the body, the soul and the Spirit. In every great tradition this place is of vital significance. It is the individualized Self, the human container of the Divine Spark and by its position on the Tree one can see why. According to the Hindus it is called the Atman, the presence of the Godhead in man. The Christians regard it as the

Christ centre, that is God Incarnate, while the Kabbalists call it the place of Adornment in that it is a beautiful appearance behind which lies No-thing. The Buddhists have a similar view in the self and non self of the Universal aspect. As will be seen Tiferet is a paradox. It is a man's true Nature, with all his particular characteristics, as required to fit into the cosmic scheme, and it is also a Divine door which gives him access to the Absolute.

In his state as a natural man he cannot directly know God. But with the cultivation of a soul he begins to see, as St. Paul says, 'through a glass darkly'. With the process of purification in the Neshamah under way, the glass begins to clear, until the man can perceive the world of Spirit, that is, the Ruah triad. This has come about because he has been able to face his self. Moving out of the animal triad of Hope and into the Neshamah triad of Charity or Love, he then begins to know what the Ruah triad of Faith means. From the slowly enlightening position of Tiferet he begins to see things as they really are, that is the objective laws that govern Creation. Such a person enters into a dialogue with the Spirit and this is beautifully set out in the Hindu classic work, the Gita, in the conversation between the warrior Arjuna and Krishna the incarnation of God. Here we have the Individual self being instructed by the Spirit, who teaches him objective law concerning the nature of the World and the paths of men. Krishna explains in detail what is the true situation in the Universe and its purpose and then reveals to Arjuna by direct cognition the knowledge that no man can learn or be taught. On the Tree it is the attainment by Arjuna of Daat. Here in the sefirah of Knowledge he 'knows', because he 'is'. For an instant Arjuna is beyond even eternity, perceiving with Cosmic Consciousness the beginning and End of Existence. The same state is contained in Christ's comment, 'I am Alpha and Omega.' Here is a man as fully conscious as he can be without losing his human frame. To go further is to be completely unified with God and as such there is no need to live.

Any man who has experienced this state can never possibly be the same again. He has seen too much, and can no longer view, the Universe in the same way. This is verified in many people's lives in that they seem to have undergone some form of transformation. Ezekiel is the classic example: so is St. Francis. The Merkabah period in Jewish mysticism and the Greek orthodox philokalia hint at such experiences, such moments, or strange writings such as the Book of Enoch or observations of the upper world in the Zohar. Blaise Pascal, the French mathematician and philosopher, had sewn into his doublet a parchment on which was written the strangest of word sequences. In this he records the hour, day and year and then the word 'fire' followed by an ecstatic series of statements linked with biblical names and quotations. None of it makes sense to the logical mind of Yesod and yet the power of whatever prompted him to write this strange document is self-evident.

The transformation, or conversion, of a person by such an experience may be temporary or permanent, because while one man might seek it, another has it thrust upon him. It is said that epilepsy is sometimes called the Divine disease because of the opening of the gates of Heaven occasionally occurs during an attack; but the epileptic has not got the ability to cope, so his Yesod blacks out. Is this an exception? Observation indicates that nothing happens on this level in the Universe without a purpose. For the man who has it thrust upon him without apparent preparation it may be the result of work in a previous life. Nevertheless, it is his choice to use or forget.

The man who seeks and has the experience, can go on and fill out the upper face. This is his next step in becoming a supernatural man. As he becomes more and more receptive, to this level, his state eventually becomes as permanent as is possible for a human being. In the lives of the world's great teachers the quality of cosmic scale is very evident. Prophecy came to them as a matter of course. They could not only call upon Wisdom and Understanding, but Knowledge. This gave them insights into the history of whole peoples. They knew by observing the past and present what the inevitable future would be. Christ saw the destruction of Jerusalem as if it were tomorrow. He could discern causes and predict their effects on a cosmic scale, as a skilled doctor can prognosticate the path of a disease, because he understood objective laws. He, like Moses before him, knew what destiny was on the individual and national level. Without doubt, being in the same line he saw by his own acts the destiny of Western Civilization and Islam, both of which sprang from the seed bed of Judaism.

Destiny, or the fulfilment of a cosmic task, is the hallmark of this level. It is of a cosmic conscious order. A man may fulfil a lesser destiny by inventing some machine or even by ruling a nation, but this is partly fate in that he was born in that time and place and someone had to do the job. The Wright brothers only brought to a conclusion the work of many others on the flying machine and if Hitler had not become the Fuehrer, the German nation in its psychological state between the two world wars would have found someone else upon whom to project the archetype of leader. Conscious destiny is quite a different matter.

If we take perhaps the most famous example of destiny we know in the West, that of Christ, we might catch a flavour of the Ruah law. It is said that great teachers—that is those who have reached Cosmic Consciousness—have the choice to go on and attain complete union with God, or to return to the world in order to help men on. Buddha took the latter choice and so it would seem did Joshua ben Miriam, known as Jesus, son of Mary. According to cosmic tradition, he returned to inhabit a natural body in Roman occupied Palestine in order, as he said, not to change the law but to give it a new impetus. At this time the West and much of the Middle East was in a decadent state, and Israel was the only nation with any influential esoteric tradition. There were others, but none so organized and possessing the ability to affect the Roman Empire. The Jews could, because they were spread throughout the then known world. Had they kept the Covenant to be a nation of priests, Christ's descent would have been unnecessary.

As a result of this neglect, corruption had set in and the central place, that is Palestine, and particularly the Temple at Jerusalem, had, as Rabbi Jesus pointed out, become a market place. This was a crucial time for the world. If the one religion that had its focus an unmanifest God was about to become as worldly as the rest of the decadent religions of the day, the future for Western man was bleak. Christ came to restate the precepts of Judaism and live his life as a 'Zadek', a Just man. He performed all the duties of a good Jew. Never once did he quarrel with the basic tenets, although he constantly drew attention to the tendency of the establishment to practice only the letter of the Torah.

From the point of view of our study his life was one of destiny. He was chosen, or he chose to live it out, knowing the full consequences of his actions, even his own physical death. This he could do because he knew the laws of Beriah and could use them to perform miracles, if need be. He did not, however, call down the angels because he had to demonstrate as a man to natural men, the conduct necessary to obtain life eternal, that is to reach Azilut. This possibility was for everyone and he showed how to go about it. His death and resurrection were also part of a plan to prove that death was not the end of existence. In order to carry this operation through he had about him men, who either understood the scheme or could be relied on to unconsciously fulfil their roles in the drama to be played out. He chose twelve men. All, except one, are traditionally accepted as good, with Jehuda, or Judas in latin, as the villain.

When the story is examined as a piece of destiny, it is not what it appears. Everyone of the disciples was chosen and trained by Christ himself and yet when it came to the test, only one man performed his task properly. Peter denied his teacher and the others ran away. (John was not directly involved.) Only Judas went right through the ordeal with Christ. The Christian propaganda surrounding Judas is misleading. He was not a mean, but responsible and intelligent, man and some say one of the closest disciples of Christ. He knew what his rabbi had to do and that someone had to help him fulfil it. None of the other disciples were capable as their behaviour during the crisis indicated. Judas may well have chosen, in collusion with Christ, to carry out the task of betrayal. This required either the worst kind of motivations, and thirty pieces of silver does not suggest this—or a profound appreciation of what was involved, so that a prophecy might be fulfilled. This was indeed for Judas a great sacrifice because, to the world he would become the arch villain, loathed over the centuries as the betrayer of betrayers. Christ knew Judas' role. He clearly indicated it to John when he told Judas to complete the assignment at the last supper. He also said 'that no man can have greater love than to lay down his life for his friend'. How do we know he was not referring to Judas, the one man who knew what was really involved? It is suggested that Judas saw on the Ruah level of consciousness. At this cosmic scale his own reputation and life did not matter. His sacrifice was, perhaps, just as great as Christ's and this would be quite feasible, if one remembers that positive and negative poles must match in order for events to occur. A lesser man could never have done this. The time was too critical and dangerous for a natural man to fulfil it. Only someone who grasped the long-term implication could have voluntarily carried out the role.

We have seen now how great the scale of the Ruah triad is and how it is concerned with universals. A man on this level not only knows all the laws, but can make them work for him. He is allowed to perform miracles. Out of Beriah, the World of Creation, he can produce loaves and fishes, strike a rock and bring forth water, provided it is for a cosmic purpose, otherwise it is not permitted. Indeed this point is very important, for while such a man has the knowledge, he may not use it, except in service to the Absolute. If he performs it of his own will he is a magician, which is quite different from being an instrument serving as a connection into Asiyyah. As such he may well retard his spiritual progress, as Moses did when he became annoyed with the Israelites at Kadesh (Numbers 20). Because of the transgression, of claiming as his own the miracle of bringing forth water from the rock, he was not allowed to enter the land flowing with milk and honey, but only to see it from afar. This indicates that while a man may reach the great height of the Ruah triad, he is by no means free of the duties of Righteousness. In order to attain entrance to the World of Azilut he must be a perfect man, a fully realized Adam.

37. Realized Adam

The supernal triangle at the top of the Tree of the psyche is formed by Wisdom and Understanding with the Crown of Keter at the highest point of human consciousness. The Hebrew letters ascribed to the supernal triad's paths make up the word GAB pronounced 'gav' which means 'a well'. In the Middle East a well was a place of sustenance, indeed of life-and-death significance.

Azilut is the realm of Emanations. It is omnipotent, present everywhere at all times. It is divine in quality.

All that can be said of a man who attains the consciousness of Azilut is that he is in union with the Divine Consciousness of that which is Above and Below, to the East, West, North and South. His awareness is as full as is possible for a human being while still incarnate in the body. In such a state he is complete, perfect, a fully realized man.

How is this seen in terms of the Tree of Life? As a man still on earth, still in the flesh, his lower face is fully operative. Christ and Buddha walked, sat, ate and did all those things normal to the asiyyatic body. How else could natural men accept them in their midst? They also possessed an ego and its lower-face psychology. This was cultivated in the early years of their lives, each receiving his education according to the conventional customs of their place and time. On reaching maturity, that is the zenith of the body's powers at the Tiferet point, both began to develop their Neshamah, for no stage of human experience may be left out. Each was trained in the tradition of their culture. Buddha in the forests and Christ, we are led to believe, perhaps by the Essenes. Of Christ's training we know little or nothing, but he was certainly steeped in Kabbalah, the inner teaching of Judaism. At a certain point both Christ, and Buddha, broke with the conventional or outer aspect of their religions, and set out to re-establish the inner connection by individually ascending up the central axis of consciousness of the Tree of man. Both operated from Tiferet, both rose up through the Ruah triad to Daat which descended to meet them granting them direct knowledge of the Absolute. Both were drawn up by the Spirit into the divine presence of the Azilutic triad so that they attained union with the All and Nothing, within the void of the hollow crown of Keter. Both descended from the transcendental experience to return with Knowledge, 'to be', in the Individuality of the self of Tiferet, the non-self of the Absolute. Both demonstrated in their lower faces and asiyyatic bodies how to live and die, how to die and live. This was their ministry.

From the point of view of our study we have seen the evolution of mankind manifest in two well-recorded lives of men who attained perfection. This does not, however, mean they were the only ones.

From our knowledge of the Tree, when applied to the body and psyche, we can see that the same laws apply at each level although they are expressed in terms of a particular world. In the case of the supernatural man, that is the person who lives as consciously in the upper face of the psyche as we do in the lower, the situation is both strange and familiar.

The upper face of Yezirah is the lower face of Beriah, just as the lower face of Yezirah is the upper face of Asiyyah. From applying the principle of 'As above, so Below' we can learn something of the nature of the supernatural man.

The upper face of the Tree of the human psyche contains Wisdom, Understanding and Knowledge, Beauty and the Crown. All these have a direct path connection through Keter to the world beyond. In the case of the Great Tree of Adam Kadmon they connect with Unmanifest Existence. In our extended four Trees the upper-face Yeziratic sefirot are superimposed on the beriatic lower face of Beauty, Eternity, Reverberation, Foundation and Kingdom, so that there is a complete complementary match, the only difference being that the same functions operate

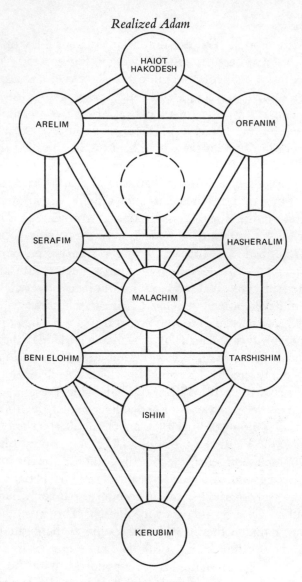

TEN CLASSES OF YEZIRATIC ANGELS

Angelogy is a complex subject. There are often several names to each sefirah, which is why the Western esoteric tradition has a slightly different set. From the view of this book the angels represent the sefirotic principles in Yezirah. Their negative aspect is represented by demons, that is, a Tree out of control. The psychological parallel is demonstrated in madness.

in different worlds. This scheme gives us some idea of how a supernatural man sees the rest of Creation. For him, his Tiferet is the Malkhut or elemental sefirah of the World of Creation.

While to us natural men, such a highly conscious self is at least cosmic, it is in fact less than half-way up the complete Jacob's Ladder of the four interleaved Trees that compose Adam Kadmon. From this we can see why Christ might be called the 'Son of God', as would any man attaining this level deserve to be called. As has been said, more than several men have, during the history of mankind, reached this point and they are known in the Kabbalistic tradition as 'Messiahs' or the 'Annointed'. This title applies to anyone reaching the Malkhut of the beriatic World and could be ascribed to Zoroaster, Hermes–Trismegestus, Enoch and many lesser known and unknown human beings who have returned to help save mankind from its ignorance at certain crucial periods of development. As Christ himself said, he was the Way, and Buddha remarked, 'Do not look at my finger when I point at the moon.' Neither and none of these men were God, although by their attainment to the Keter of Yezirah they became 'Like unto God'—the meaning of the name Michael the Archangel ascribed to Keter's co-sefirah, the Tiferet of the beriatic Tree.

If we consider the Wisdom and Understanding of the supernatural man we can see how they match the Eternity and Reverberation of the World of Creation. Thus the yeziratic Binah is a receptive response to creative communications. It is the information collecting and distributing principle of the beriatic realm. As such the supernatural man can recognize and communicate at least within the asiyyatic triad of Beriah. This gives him the equivalent range in the World of Creation as the natural man's scope in the psychological world. The same is true of Yeziratic Wisdom with its simultaneous correspondence with the beriatic sefirah of Eternity. While such a level of operation is profound to us, with the quality of the Divine in relation to our position in the scale of things, for the supernatural man the beriatic Nezah is the equivalent of our instinctive reactions, except that in Beriah it is the inherent, eternally repeating truths of Creation. Traditionally known as 'Wheels' the yeziratic image for Wisdom gives some insight into the power of this dual Hokhmah–Nezah sefirah. In Beriah the sefirah is ruled by the archangel Haniel which means the 'Grace of God'.

At this point it is a good time to speak of angels and archangels. According to the Kabbalah the yeziratic World is governed by angels. We have not used angels in this book because of the many mis-associations and distorted views of them in our culture. But for the record, an angel might be described as a cosmic intelligence or principle responsible for certain functions and duties in the yeziratic World. The same is true of archangels, but these operate in Beriah. The word 'angel' means 'Swift one' or 'Messenger'. They are also called spirits, gods, sons of God, servants, watchers, hosts and armies in the Bible, and these names give some notion of their work. Moreover, it is said that they can only perform one kind of task. No angel can do the errand of another, although he may carry out several that are within his brief.

The various Cherubim, Aralim, Seraphim and Chashmolim are the Hebrew titles to define the sefirotic function they perform in Yezirah, and by knowing these names one may recognize which sefirah is operating in a situation. Needless to say, over the centuries many sub-differentiations have been made, so that the study of angelology has blurred in its hierarchical arrangement. At one time, however, the use of a particular angelic name was a precise definition of a yeziratic function. The loss of this knowledge is the reason for much confusion in Kabbalistic study, especially amongst the learned who only see the Universe through Hod.

The nearest we can come to an angel is the direct cognition of the workings of our own psyche. An angel governs each sefirah and while we may call the various functions by psychological, even clinical names, we are in fact dealing with the angelic world. The whole of the yeziratic Tree is composed of angelic principles, and these are common to all men, so that they may call on their angels to assist and guide them. The most obvious example are the angels of Gevurah and Hesed. Without these guardians of discrimination and love we would be in great trouble. To illustrate the point, but in the negative, in a Kellippotic or disordered situation, these sefirot, when unbalanced and without the control of the central column of consciousness, become demonic and thus we have the reverse side in the traditional study of demonology with its various names and terms for the disordered sefirot in Yezirah and the archdemons of a Kellippotic world of Creation. Such a study reveals how the absence of consciousness can lead to individual and cosmic cataclysm, and as we observe in the history of the human race the demons of psychology can, and do periodically, rule the world.

In terms of individual experience many people have sensed watchers over their lives. This is not the same as the Watcher in the self, of Tiferet. These observers are less obtrusive and work through the psyche of individuals and groups. The meeting of a number of people usually produces a spirit, and this description is quite accurate, in that one or more of the sefirot in everyone present connects and evokes the angel or angels to preside over the convocation. In a football crowd, the angels of the lower face of the yeziratic Tree are very evident, as are the angels of Gevurah and Hesed in a prayer meeting. Occasionally, if the balance and quality is right, the archangels Raphael and Haniel, the spirits of Wisdom and Understanding, descend upon a group of people met to make contact with the Spirit of Knowledge. In this case the Holy Spirit called Gabriel at this level may come down the Tree and contact the Tiferet of everyone present in themselves. If someone in the room is far away in day dreams, his ego–Yesod does not, nor can it, notice the appearance of what Kabbalists call the Shekinah or the Divine Presence.

As said, directly and intimately connected with the upper part of the Tree of the psyche is the lower face of the archangelic world. These beings are of a higher order than angels, but by no means superior. Their task is to watch over, and administer to the creative functions of the Universe, and their contact with man is through the interleaved lower and upper faces of Yezirah and Beriah. In Kabbalah Yezirah is known as the Merkabah or Chariot and Beriah as the Throne of God.

Taking the Malkhut of Beriah first we have seen that it is equivalent to the self of a man. As such the archangel Sandalphon watches over the Keter of the physical body and the Tiferet of a psychologically unawakened natural man. When the man begins to evolve, Sandalphon guards him as his Neshamah grows, keeping the conscious element always in the right place, because the man has not yet the will to remain awake enough in himself. As the Neshamah becomes stronger there begins to be formed a crystallizing image of knowledge about the beriatic World, that is, the realm of pure spirit. This is the dual function of the Daat of Yezirah and its other role as the Ycsod of Beriah. Slowly a Foundation is formed in the lower face of the beriatic Tree, so that the man not only knows but can perceive an image of the beriatic World. This is the Chariot and Throne that Ezekiel saw.

Here begins the creation of a supernatural man. With the fusing of Yesod and Daat comes the development of consciousness in the Ruah triad. When the crystallization is complete, that is when it is stable within the man, it is no longer a passing flash or a gift from above, but a permanent foundation. Such an evolved man perceives at will the cosmic level of consciousness. In Ezekiel and the Revelations of St. John the visions are the yesodic image of Beriah. In this state, revelations abound in the form of strange journeys through the palaces of the heavens, the receiving of prophecies, the seeing of apocalyptic events and the perceiving of wondrous beings, places and things. In early Kabbalah such experiences belonged to what is known as 'The Work of the Chariot'. Indeed the practitioners of this exercise were called 'Those who descend to the Chariot', which can be taken to mean, to penetrate deep enough into the inner psyche to contact the lower face of Beriah. For a man who has developed as far as Cosmic Consciousness the upper face of his yeziratic Tree becomes the lower face's psychological equivalent of Beriah. Such an advanced mind thinks in complete abstracts and operates off inspiration. These are the qualities of the two vertical triads of Keter, Binah and Tiferet and Keter, Hokhmah, Tiferet. Moreover, there are now paths connecting the Hod and Nezah of the beriatic World, so that with a working yesodic Foundation in Creation, he becomes ready for the next step of evolution beyond the level of supernatural man.

The archangels accredited to this lower face of Beriah are

n.b. Spiritualization of matter — penetration downwards into matter as well as ascent upwards — cf/con Christian 'evil' matter, Satan etc. Separatio of e.g. dualism; interleaving of kabbala; balan of yin-yang, cause + effect of karmaic law.

The Spirit
Tiferet of Azilut

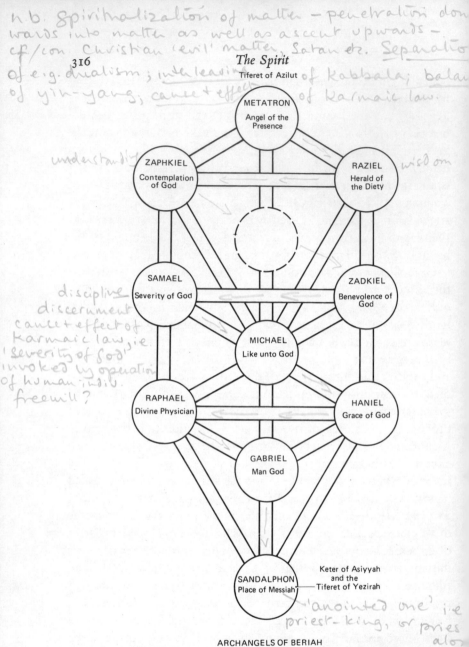

understanding

wisdom

discipline discernment cause + effect of karmaic law, ie. 'Severity of God' invoked by operation of human indiv. freewill?

METATRON
Angel of the
Presence

ZAPHKIEL
Contemplation
of God

RAZIEL
Herald of
the Diety

SAMAEL
Severity of God

ZADKIEL
Benevolence of
God

MICHAEL
Like unto God

RAPHAEL
Divine Physician

HANIEL
Grace of God

GABRIEL
Man God

SANDALPHON
Place of Messiah

Keter of Asiyyah
and the
Tiferet of Yezirah

'anointed one' ie priest-king, or priest alo...

ARCHANGELS OF BERIAH

This is the World of the Spirits who govern Creation. The lower part is called, after
Ezekiel's vision, the Chariot and the upper part the Throne. Sandalphon corresponds
not only to the self of a man but to the level of a manifest Messiah. Gabriel is yeziratic
knowledge of the Spirit, while Michael as the Keter of the psyche is also the Malkhut
of Azilut, that is the Footstool to Divinity. The Daat of Beriah is EL HAI-LIVING
GOD, one of the names of the Divinity. Metatron is chief Archangel, being, tradition
says, the man Enoch transformed into fire.

Sandalphon for Malkhut and as said, Haniel for Nezah, Raphael for Hod, and Gabriel and Michael for the beriatic Yesod and Tiferet respectively. Raphael the archangel of beriatic Reverberation corresponds to Olympian Mercury, the god equivalent in Yezirah. As will now be appreciated all the old classical gods belong to the World of Formations and correspond to the externalized archetypes of the psychological world. If one examines these evocative forms they give a very good idea of the angels and the likeness is not as remote or pagan as orthodox Judaism thinks, for many of the angels are of Babylonian origin, having been picked up during the exile there.

Gabriel means 'Man of God'. As will be seen by the position of the sefirah in the Tree of the human psyche, the name is not without reason. Gabriel is said to stand in the presence of God, and by its position on the central axis of consciousness this makes much sense. As the Yesod of the beriatic World it is the parallel of the ego consciousness of Beriah. This suggests that there is an identity, and a knowledge possible for a beriatic body, and many traditions speak of man as possessing or building himself one or a series of vehicles or bodies so that he can survive physical death. Here are the myths of immortality and ultimate reunion with man's Maker. The presence of four interleaved Trees stretching from Earth to Heaven concerns this idea, although it appears that a man may cease to be in contact with ordinary mortals once he passes beyond a certain point. This is also traditionally borne out. The parable of Lao Tse crossing the mountain passes on the back of a bullock, never to return, is one example. So is the strange end of Enoch in Genesis V where he is described as walking with God until he was seen no more because 'he was not; for God took him.' Enoch means 'initiated'. Tradition says that Enoch rose up through the four Worlds to become the archangel Metatron.

The sefirah occupied by Gabriel is a crucial one. It is the last stage before a man reaches the Keter of his human possibilities. At this point he is still a man, a 'hero of God' is another title. Beyond lies the threshold between Raphael in Hod and Haniel in Nezah. To pass he must rise up the Zadek path of beriatic Honesty, from the beriatic Yesod to the beriatic Tiferet. Yet as the person moves up out of, no doubt, the shadow side of his penultimate ego, all personality must go. All remnants of being a separate entity must be dissolved before he can fully merge with the Keter of Yezirah to become the Tiferet of Beriah. Here, as a fully realized man, he comes under the direct archangelic influence of Michael, that is in English, 'Like unto God.'

From this point on such levels of experience can have little real meaning for us still earth-bound, and for the most part, lower-face yeziratic-orientated people. However, we can speculate as Kabbalists have traditionally done, about Beriah which is the Throne upon which sits the appearance of a man.

Michael is the Tiferet of the beriatic World; as such he is the essential focus of that realm. Traditionally the patron archangel of the Jews he is also depicted as contending with the dragon of Satan in a heavenly or cosmic war between the hosts of order and disorder. As the central pivot of the beriatic world he is the obvious guardian of Heaven, as the self of the Yeziratic Tiferet is the watcher over a man. In him also is invested Divine protection and sovereign power. These are no ambiguous titles but precise descriptions of Michael's position as the Malkhut or Sovereign power of the Divine Tree of Azilut, whose bottom sefirah he is simultaneously, as well as being, the Tiferet of Beriah and Keter of Yezirah. In this position Michael is in contact with three worlds. He rests at the Foot of the Throne that rides in the Chariot of Ezekiel's vision. This describes the difference between the yeziratic lower face and the Azilutic upper face of Beriah.

Just above Michael on the two side pillars and in the equivalent of the Neshamah triad are the beriatic Gevurah and Hesed. These are presided over by the archangels Samael or the Severity of God and Zadkiel, that is the Righteousness or Benevolence of God. These two archangels keep equilibrium, because if beriatic Mercy was not checked by beriatic Judgement Creation would explode, and if Judgement were not mellowed by Mercy the Creation would implode. The result of any imbalance would be either too much rigour or excess power. Michael reconciles the two sefirot under the conscious direction of the Will descending into Heaven from Above. The fact that the Throne of Heaven is not the highest level is quite startling at first, but to quote the opening of Genesis, 'In the beginning God created Heaven and Earth', that is, the Bible opens not with Azilut but Beriah, the World of pure Spirit. Genesis goes on to say 'And the Earth was without form and void', that is, Yezirah, the World of Formations, had yet to be brought into existence.

According to some Kabbalists, Samael is sometimes called Khamael or the Burner of God. This role, like Samael, who is also seen as the archangel of Death, is one of eliminating the imperfections in Creation. Likewise, the task of the archangel is to act as a resistant to the energy coming across from the archangel of Zadkiel whose cosmic task is to act as Hesed in the beriatic Lightning Flash of Creation. Zadkiel's name also means the 'Nobleness of God'. Together, this pair of archangels, with Michael, make the self-consciousness of the beriatic World. As such they have a remote but definite contact with man through the connecting paths down each side pillar and through those flowing into the Keter of Yezirah.

Like the two Trees beneath, the beriatic Tree has its paths and triads. These operate in exactly the same way as below, but in Creation. What this means in beriatic terms one can only guess. All that can be said, is that the principles involved are present and continuous throughout the whole Universe, the six days of creation always beginning and ending at the Sabbath, that is Keter and Malkhut. The archangels are responsible for this order of creative work, each beriatic sefirah carrying out its functional duty under the Will descending from the azilutic World.

Theoretically each of the sefirot is a complete Tree. It therefore follows that angels and archangels are complete Trees. This, however, does not appear to be strictly true, because while they have the attributes of the side pillars, they have no central column. By tradition angelic beings are made of fire and water, the symbols for the active and passive functions, but no air, the element of equilibrium between heaven and earth, according to the Sefer Yezirah. In our terms, angels and archangels have no axis of consciousness. Therefore, although highly evolved, they have no will of their own. This is the reason why, it is said, angels and archangels are jealous of men, because in spite of our initial lowly situation we have will and choice. We can change our status and rise up the column of consciousness through Paradise, Heaven and into the Presence of our Maker. Angelic beings cannot move. They are fixed in their perfection, operating the lower worlds without choice or chance of evolving. This places man in a very privileged and responsible position. His role appears to be a growing point. If it were not so, then the Universe would be like a machine with no awareness but God's to appreciate its beauty and cunning. Human beings are the nerve endings of consciousness at the Earthly end of Existence. We can know that we know, and know that we are known by the Knower. Here is man's uniqueness.

The upper face of the beriatic Tree is the lower face of the World of Emanations, and Azilut, when set out on its Tree comprises the Divine names of God and His attributes. In Ezekiel's vision (2:28) Azilut is 'in the appearance of a man seated upon the likeness of the Throne'. This man, with fire and brightness all about him, is Adam Kadmon, also called the Glory of the Lord.

Beginning with the Tiferet of Beriah, that is the archangel Michael, the corresponding Malkhut of Azilut is ADONAI MELEK, in English the LORD KING. This same sefirah is also the Keter of man's Tree of the psyche and is his direct connection with the Divine World of Adam Kadmon. In Judaism it is one of the speakable titles of God. ADONAI or Lord is said instead of the actual written name of God in the reading aloud of the scrolls of the Torah on the Sabbath. For many centuries the speaking of God's proper Name YHVH has been forbidden, except at a certain time of the year.

Malkhut, it will be remembered, means 'Kingdom' and figures prominently in Christ's great prayer. As the Azilutic Malkhut it can be seen why it is called the Footstool of the Throne, for it is the nearest Divine sefirah to the lower Worlds; Adam Kadmon's toes indeed touching earthbound man at his highest point of realization. The significance for us is immense because the sefirah is our conscious link with God, it being also the Keter of the yeziratic Tree of the psyche. It is known also by the title of Body of God.

Above in the Binah and Hokhmah sefirot of Beriah are the archangels Zaphkiel and Raziel. Zaphkiel as Understanding, contemplates God, while Raziel is the Flash of Wisdom, that is 'The One of God sent forth' who heralds the Deity. Tradition says that Raziel befriended Adam when he was ejected from Eden giving him the gift of a book containing wisdom for his use. This book was given, via Noah to Abraham, then Jacob to Levi, whose descendant Moses passed it on to the seventy elders of Israel until it came in to the hands of Solomon the Wise, who learned from it the secrets of the Universe. As the Hokhmah of Creation Raziel fills this role perfectly.

Zaphkiel, the archangel of Binah, is also called 'the Beholder of God'. As the sefirah of Understanding at the head of the passive column, this archangel is the beriatic receptive and formulating principle of the Universe. Here is the Great Cosmic Mother, the watcher over all that is below, the observer of the worlds with a restraining influence. Zaphkiel has been called the Eye of God, as the Divine World's Hod this title is indeed applicable.

In Azilut Zaphkiel corresponds with ELOHIM ZEVAOT, 'the God of Hosts' while Raziel, the Hokhmah of Beriah and the Nezah of Azilut is called YAHVEH ZEVAOT, 'Existence of Hosts'. Both these God names describe the complex attributes of the Divine active and passive functions in lower Azilut. Of their meaning we can know little or nothing, as they belong, even though to the lesser face of the Glory, to a world far beyond a natural man's ken. For a fully realized man it is a different situation, he has contact with the Divine Hod and Nezah through his attainment of the Keter of Yezirah. As part of the Body of God he can participate not only in the Tiferet of Creation, but as an element in the Kingdom of Azilut. This means he is under the direct influence of the archangels of Wisdom and Understanding, and the two sefirot of Divine Hosts. Such a situation places a man in a special place as regards mankind.

As has been said earlier, one such man is always present on the earth at any time, and it can be seen why this must be if humanity is to have a human point of contact with the Divinity. The long awaited Messiah may in fact always be here, Christ being perhaps one well-known example of a whole line of fully realized men who have been present on the earth since mankind was placed here. For Christians the Messiah resides in the past and for the Jews somewhere in the future. The truth probably is that he is always here but no one knows him or would even recognize him even if they met the Incarnation. The problem is the state of mankind, not the date of the Coming. That will occur on the same principle as the Master appearing when the disciple is ready. It is a question of recognition of what is already present in every man.

According to some Kabbalists the Daat of the Tree of Life is called the Abyss. This is because in one sense there is nothing there, and it is the point in the ascent of human consciousness when the individual Self vanishes before union with Keter. At the beriatic level it is referred to in the Biblical Creation account as the 'Deep'. It is that pause between the supernal triad and the rest of the Tree in the Lightning Flash sequence. It is called Knowledge because it is the synthesis of both Wisdom and Understanding and the Will coming down from Keter. It is the knowing just before total union spoken of in Mysticism.

While for the beriatic World the sefirah is Creative Knowledge, for Azilut it is the Foundation of God's attributes. As such it has the title SHADDAI' EL HAI, that is, ALMIGHTY LIVING GOD. Here in Adam Kadmon's consciousness, the Divine makes His own Image. As the simultaneous Daat of Creation, one can see how the Image of man was made in the likeness of God. The process then continued down through the Worlds of Formation and making until we come to the asiyyatic Adam, as we know him.

The Tiferet of Azilut is called YAHVEH ELOHIM. This sefirah is the Source of Creation, being the simultaneous Keter of Beriah. As the Crown of Creation it is associated with the ascended and transfigured Enoch who became the archangel Metatron, called the Angel of the Presence. Some Kabbalists also address Metatron as the Lesser YHVH. The reason is that this sefirah is the beriatic Crown through which comes the Will of the

Absolute as it descends from the first Keter of All. As the Tiferet of Azilut it is the Divine Beauty of the Glory of the Lord. Focus of paths and triads coming from both the beriatic and azilutic Worlds, the Divine equivalent of the self is manifest as the highest individualized consciousness possible. Metatron is sometimes called YAHEL, which means 'In going out and coming back I am God'. Through this ultimate individual agency the Will of the Absolute can be communicated, and for this reason YAHEL is said to have a particular interest in mankind. His is the power to send down the Presence to aid those who want to draw near to the Divine. In this role Metatron transmits Kabbalah down through all the Worlds via the central axis of consciousness, so that all who wish to receive Kabbalah, can 'welcome' it—another translation of the word Kabbalah.

Above the Tiferet of Azilut, on the left and right columns are the upper attributes or functions of the Divine. At Gevurah is YAH or GOD. This is one traditional name. At Hesed EL—that is GOD THE HIGH. These form the intermediary balances to the great Father and Mother at the head of the active and passive pillars and also combine to make the Tiferet name YAHEL. The Great Parent sefirot are known by the titles of ELOHIM at Binah and YAHVEH at Hokhmah. Both these God Names are part of the three Great Heads of the supernal Azilut trinity. They are untranslatable into English.

At the very top of the Tree resides the FIRST CROWN, which is known in Kabbalah as EHYEH the Name of God that contains all that is, was and will be.

Reversing the process, we descend from the penultimate down Jacob's Ladder of the Manifest Universe.

The Daat of Azilut is the Knowledge of God. The Tiferet of Azilut, the Beauty of God and the Source of Creation, the Keter of Beriah. The Yesod of Azilut is the Image of God and the Knowledge of Creation. The Malkhut of Azilut is the Body of God, the Beauty of Creation and the Source of Formation, it being the Keter of Yezirah. The Yesod of Beriah is the Image of Creation, the Knowledge of Formation, and Knowledge for the psyche of man. The Malkhut of Beriah is the Body of Creation,

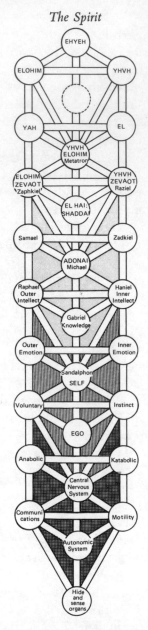

JACOB'S LADDER

the Beauty of Formation and the Source of Action; it is also the self of the psyche. Descending further, the Foundation of Yezirah is the Image of Formation, the Knowledge of Action and the ego of the psyche. The Malkhut of Yezirah is the body of Formation and the Beauty of Action; that is, the asiyyatic Tiferet. Yesod in Asiyyah is the Image of Action, the Foundation of the body. While in the last sefirah is the elemental body of Earthly existence.

Between Heaven and Earth stretches Adam. With a Kingdom and Crown established in every World the perfection of All is realized and resolved into the One of His own likeness.

In this Unity

He is EHYEH ASHER EHYEH

I AM THAT I AM.

Glossary of Terms

ASSIYAH	The World of making, of elements and action.
AZILUT	The World of Emanations. The Divine realm of Adam Kadmon. The Glory.
BERIAH	The World of Creations, of pure Spirit and archangels.
BINAH	Sefirah of Understanding. Head of passive column. Great Mother.
DAAT	Unmanifest sefirah of Knowledge on central column.
EGO	Yesod of Yezirah. Ordinary consciousness.
GEVURAH	Sefirah of Judgement on the passive column.
GREAT ASIYYATIC TRIAD	Triad formed by Malkhut–Hod–Nezah with Yesod on any Tree.
GUT BODY TYPE	Yesod–Hod–Nezah triad of asiyyatic Tree.
HESED	Sefirah of Mercy on active column.
HOKHMAH	Sefirah of Wisdom at head of Active pillar. Great Father.
INTELLECTUAL BODY TYPE	Malkhut–Hod–Hesod triad of asiyyatic Tree.

INTUITIVE EGO TYPE	Yesod–Hod–Tiferet triad of yeziratic Tree.
INSTINCTIVE BODY TYPE	Malkhut–Nezah–Yesod triad of asiyyatic Tree.
KELLIPPOT	World of Shells, demons and disorder.
KETER	The Crown. Sefirah at head of central pillar of Equilibrium.
LOGIC EGO TYPE	Yesod–Hod–Malkhut triad of Yezirah.
LOWER FACE	Figure described on any Tree by Malkhut–Hod–Tiferet–Nezah and Yesod.
MALKHUT	The Kingdom. Lowest Sefirah on Tree.
NATURAL MAN	Animal-vegetable part of man.
NEFESH	Animal or vital soul.
NESHAMAH	Human soul.
NEZAH	Eternity. Sefirah at base of active pillar.
RESPONSIVE EGO TYPE	Yesod–Nezah–Tiferet triad of yeziratic Tree.
RUAH	Spirit.
SELF	Tiferet of Yezirah. Watchman, guide, guardian angel of psyche.
SEFIROT	Containers, numbers, lights of the Attributes of God on the Tree Singular: sefirah.
SENSUAL EGO TYPE	Malkhut–Nezah–Yesod triad of yeziratic Tree.
SHEKINAH	The Presence of God. The Bride in exile located in Malkhut.
TIFERET	Central sefirah called Beauty. Meeting place of upper and lower faces.

TO GO ROUND IN A CIRCLE	Triad, Hod–Nezah–Yesod on any Tree.
TO LOCK IN POSITION	Triad, Hod–Nezah–Tiferet on any Tree. Subliminal in natural man.
UPPER FACE	Figure described on Tree by Tiferet – Binah – Keter – Hokhmah and Daat.
YESOD	Foundation. Sefirah in middle of lower face. Ego-mind in psyche.
YEZIRAH	World of Formations. Psychological realm in man. World of Angels.
ZADEK	The just and righteous man associated with Yesod and Tiferet path.

Index